TExES Mathematics 4-8
114-115 Teacher Certification Exam

By: Sharon Wynne, M.S.
Southern Connecticut State University

XAMonline, INC.
Boston

To obtain permission(s) to use the material from this work for any purpose including workshops or seminars, please submit a written request to:

XAMonline, Inc.
25 First St. Suite 106
Cambridge, MA 02141
Toll Free 1-800-509-4128
Email: info@xamonline.com
Web www.xamonline.com
Fax: 1-781-662-9268

Library of Congress Cataloging-in-Publication Data

Wynne, Sharon A.
    Mathematics 4-8 114-115: Teacher Certification / Sharon A. Wynne. -3rd ed.
    ISBN 978-1-60787-111-8
    1. Mathematics 4-8 114-115.   2. Study Guides.   3. TExES
    4. Teachers' Certification & Licensure.   5. Careers

Disclaimer:
The opinions expressed in this publication are the sole works of XAMonline and were created independently from the National Education Association, Educational Testing Service, or any State Department of Education, National Evaluation Systems or other testing affiliates.

Between the time of publication and printing, state specific standards as well as testing formats and website information may change that is not included in part or in whole within this product. Sample test questions are developed by XAMonline and reflect similar content as on real tests; however, they are not former tests. XAMonline assembles content that aligns with state standards but makes no claims nor guarantees teacher candidates a passing score. Numerical scores are determined by testing companies such as NES or ETS and then are compared with individual state standards. A passing score varies from state to state.

Printed in the United States of America   œ-1

TExES: Mathematics 4-8 114-115
ISBN: 978-1-60787-111-8

About the Subject Assessments

TEXES™: Subject Assessment in the Mathematics 4-8 examination

Purpose: The assessments are designed to test the knowledge and competencies of prospective secondary level teachers. The question bank from which the assessment is drawn is undergoing constant revision. As a result, your test may include questions that will not count towards your score.

Test Version: There are two versions of subject assessment for Mathematics in Texas. The Mathematics 4-8 (115) exam emphasizes comprehension in Number Concepts; Patterns and Algebra; Geometry and Measurement; Probability and Statistics; Mathematical Processes and Statistics; Mathematical Learning, Instruction, and Assessment .The Mathematics 8-12 (135) exam emphasizes comprehension in Number Concepts; Patterns and Algebra; Geometry and Measurement; Probability and Statistics; Mathematical Processes and Statistics; Mathematical Learning, Instruction, and Assessment. The Mathematics 8-12 study guide is based on a typical knowledge level of persons who have completed a *bachelor's degree program* in Mathematics.

Time Allowance: You will have 5 hours to finish the exam. There are approximately 90 multiple-choice questions in the exam.

Weighting: Approximately 16% of the tests material consists of Number Concepts; 21% consists of Patterns Algebra; 21% consists of Geometry and Measurement; 16% consists of Probability and Statistics; 10% consists of Mathematical Processes and Perspectives; 16% consists of Mathematical Learning, Instruction, and Assessment.

Additional Information about the TEXES Assessments: The TEXES series subject assessments are developed by *National Evaluation Systems.* They provide additional information on the TEXES series assessments, including registration, preparation and testing procedures and study materials such topical guides that have about 72 pages of information including approximately 37 additional sample questions.

TABLE OF CONTENTS

Great Study and Testing Tips!

What to study in order to prepare for the subject assessments is the focus of this study guide but equally important is *how* you study.

You can increase your chances of truly mastering the information by taking some simple, but effective, steps.

Study Tips:

1. <u>Some foods aid the learning process</u>. Foods such as milk, nuts, seeds, rice, and oats help your study efforts by releasing natural memory enhancers called CCKs (*cholecystokinin*) composed of *tryptophan*, *choline*, and *phenylalanine*. All of these chemicals enhance the neurotransmitters associated with memory. Before studying, try a light, protein-rich meal of eggs, turkey, and fish. All of these foods release the memory enhancing chemicals. The better the connections, the more you comprehend.

Likewise, before you take a test, stick to a light snack of energy boosting and relaxing foods. A glass of milk, a piece of fruit, or some peanuts all release various memory-boosting chemicals and help you to relax and focus on the subject at hand.

2. <u>Learn to take great notes</u>. A by-product of our modern culture is that we have grown accustomed to getting our information in short doses (i.e. TV news sound bites or *USA Today* style newspaper articles.)

Consequently, we have subconsciously trained ourselves to assimilate information better in <u>neat little packages</u>. If your notes are scrawled all over the paper, it fragments the flow of the information. Strive for clarity. Newspapers use a standard format to achieve clarity. Your notes can be much clearer through use of proper formatting. A very effective format is called the *"Cornell Method."*

Take a sheet of loose-leaf lined notebook paper and draw a line all the way down the paper about 1-2" from the left-hand edge.

Draw another line across the width of the paper about 1-2" up from the bottom. Repeat this process on the reverse side of the page.

Look at the highly effective result. You have ample room for notes, a left hand margin for special emphasis items or inserting supplementary data from the textbook, a large area at the bottom for a brief summary, and a little rectangular space for just about anything you want.

3. Get the concept than the details. Too often, we focus on the details and do not gather an understanding of the concept. However, if you simply memorize only dates, places, or names, you may well miss the whole point of the subject.

A key way to understand things is to put them in your own words. If you are working from a textbook, automatically summarize each paragraph in your mind. If you are outlining text, do not simply copy the author's words.

Rephrase them in your own words. You remember your own thoughts and words much better than someone else's and subconsciously tend to associate the important details with the core concepts.

4. Ask Why? Pull apart written material paragraph by paragraph and do not forget the captions under the illustrations.

Example: If the heading is "Stream Erosion", flip it around to read "Why do streams erode?" Then answer the questions.

If you train your mind to think in a series of questions and answers, not only will you learn more, but it also helps to lessen the test anxiety because you are used to answering questions.

5. Read for reinforcement and future needs. Even if you only have ten minutes, put your notes or a book in your hand. Your mind is similar to a computer; you have to input data in order to have it processed. *By reading, you are creating the neural connections for future retrieval.* The more times you read something, the more you reinforce the learning of ideas.

Even if you do not fully understand something on the first pass, *your mind stores much of the material for later recall.*

6. Relax to learn, so go into exile. Our bodies respond to an inner clock called biorhythms. Burning the midnight oil works well for some people but not everyone.

If possible, set aside a particular place to study that is free of distractions. Shut off the television, cell phone, and pager and exile your friends and family during your study period.

If you really are bothered by silence, try background music. Light classical music at a low volume has been shown over other types to aid in concentration. Music without lyrics that evokes pleasant emotions is highly suggested. Try just about anything by Mozart. It relaxes you.

7. <u>Use arrows not highlighters</u>. At best, it is difficult to read a page full of yellow, pink, blue, and green streaks. Try staring at a neon sign for a while and you will soon see that the horde of colors obscures the message.

A quick note, a brief dash of color, an underline, or an arrow pointing to a particular passage is much clearer than a horde of highlighted words.

8. <u>Budget your study time</u>. Although you should not ignore any of the material, *allocate your available study time in the same ratio that topics may appear on the test.*

Testing Tips:

1. <u>Get smart; play dumb</u>. Don't read anything into the question. Do not assume that the test writer is looking for something else than what is asked. Stick to the question as written and do not read extra things into it.

2. <u>Read the question and all the choices *twice* before answering the question</u>. You may miss something by not carefully reading, and then re-reading, both the question and the answers.

If you really do not have a clue as to the right answer, leave it blank on the first time through. Go on to the other questions, as they may provide a clue as to how to answer the skipped questions.

If later on, you still cannot answer the skipped ones . . . *Guess.* The only penalty for guessing is that you *might* get it wrong. Only one thing is certain; if you don't put anything down, you will get it wrong!

3. <u>Turn the question into a statement</u>. Look at the way the questions are worded. The syntax of the question usually provides a clue. Does it seem more familiar as a statement rather than as a question? Does it sound strange?

By turning a question into a statement, you may be able to spot if an answer sounds right, and it may also trigger memories of material you have read.

4. <u>Look for hidden clues</u>. It is actually very difficult to compose multiple-foil (choice) questions without giving away part of the answer in the options presented.

In most multiple-choice questions you can often readily eliminate one or two of the potential answers. This leaves you with only two real possibilities and automatically your odds go to fifty-fifty for very little work.

5. <u>Trust your instincts</u>. For every fact that you have read, you subconsciously retain something of that knowledge. On questions that you are not certain about, go with your basic instincts. **Your first impression on how to answer a question is usually correct.**

6. <u>Mark your answers directly on the test booklet</u>. Do not bother trying to fill in the optical scan sheet on the first pass through the test.

Just be very careful not to mis-mark your answers when you eventually transcribe them to the scan sheet.

7. <u>Watch the clock</u>! You have a set amount of time to answer the questions. Do not get bogged down trying to answer a single question at the expense of ten questions you can more readily answer.

DOMAIN I. NUMBER CONCEPTS

Competency 001   **The teacher understands the structure of number systems, the development of a sense of quantity, and the relationship between quantity and symbolic representations.**

This section reviews number systems, the properties of the real numbers, and the various representations of numbers. The discussion begins with numeration systems and place values, relative magnitude, and representations of rational numbers and then goes on to review the characteristics of the set of real numbers and its subsets as well as problem solutions that lie outside the rational or real number sets.

1A.   **Analyze the structure of numeration systems and the roles of place value and zero in the base ten system**

Place Value

In a number, every digit has a face value and a place value. The face values of the digits in the number 3467 are 3, 4, 6 and 7. The place value of a digit depends on its position in the number.

Whole number place values are where the digits fall to the left of the decimal point. Consider the number 792; reading from left to right, the first digit (7) represents the hundreds place. Thus, there are 7 sets of one hundred in the number 792. The second digit (9) represents the tens place. The last digit (2) represents the ones place.

Decimal place value is where the digits fall to the right of the decimal point. Consider the number 4.873; reading from left to right, the first digit (4) is in the ones place. After the decimal, 8 is in the tenths place and indicates that the number contains 8 tenths. The digit 7 is in the hundredths' place and tells us the number contains 7 hundredths. The same pattern applies to the rest of the number, with each successive digit to the right of the decimal point decreasing progressively in powers of ten.

<u>Example:</u> 12345.6789 occupies the following powers of ten positions:

10^4	10^3	10^2	10^1	10^0		10^{-1}	10^{-2}	10^{-3}	10^{-4}
1	2	3	4	5	.	6	7	8	9

The number zero in the base ten system, as it stands independently, indicates the lack of a value in a particular place. Zero is shown alone only in the ones place (10^0 place). On the left side of the decimal point, zeroes appear only to the right of some non-zero value; on the right side of the decimal point, zeroes usually appear to the left of some non-zero value. (The exception in this latter case is when there is a need to express the accuracy of a particular value. In such a case, it is not uncommon to see expressions such as 1.000, which usually indicates that the number is accurate to a value of 0.001.)

Number Bases

A numeration system is a set of numbers represented by a set of symbols (numbers, letters, or pictographs). Numbers can be represented using different bases. Instead of the standard base 10 or decimal representation, a system may use any base set from 2 (binary) on up. The position of a number in a particular representation defines its exact value. Thus, the numeral 1 has a value of ten when represented in base 10 as "10." In base 2, the numeral 1 has a value of two when represented as "10." Early systems, such as the Babylonian system, used position in relation to other numerals or column position for this purpose because the system lacked a zero to represent an empty position.

A base of 2 uses only the numerals 0 and 1.

Decimal Binary Conversion		
Decimal	Binary	Place Value
1	1	2^0
2	10	2^1
4	100	2^2
8	1000	2^3

Thus, 9 in Base 10 becomes 1001 in Base 2. Also, 9 + 4 = 13 (Base 10) becomes 1001 + 100 = 1101 (Base 2). Fractions, ratios, and other functions operate in the same way.

Number Systems and Bases

Base	Number System
2	Binary
3	Ternary
4	Quarternary
5	Quinary
6	Senary
8	Octal
16	Hexadecimal

Fundamentally, computers use a binary system, because the transistors and logic circuitry that composes these machines uses two basic states (which can be interpreted as 0 and 1, off and on, false and true, or a similar representation). Particular computers may be implemented such that they perform arithmetic on groups of bits (eight bits, for instance, which is called a byte), but the fundamental operation of the machine is still binary.

1B.   Understand the relative magnitude of whole numbers, integers, rational numbers, and real numbers

To compare relative magnitudes of numbers, it is typically necessary that both be in the same general form. (It may be simple to compare numbers such as 0.5 and $\frac{1}{2}$, but it is generally much simpler to compare numbers of the same form—fractions with fractions, decimals with decimals, and so on.) A solid understanding of place value makes comparison of the relative magnitudes of numbers very simple. For instance, to compare decimals, simply look at the most significant (leftmost) place value of each of the two numbers: whichever number has a value in a more significant place (or, second, which has a larger value in a particular place) is the larger of the two numbers. Thus, it is not necessary to compare all the digits of 492.239 and 29.328— 492.239 is greater by virtue of its having a non-zero value in the hundreds place, whereas 29.328 does not (and it has no non-zero values in any place greater than tens).

If a numerical comparison is needed, two numbers can be compared according to **orders of magnitude**. Using the previous example, 492.239 has its largest non-zero value in the hundreds (10^2) place, and 29.328 has its largest non-zero value in the tens (10^1) place. Thus, 492.239 is one order of magnitude ($\frac{10^2}{10^1} = 10$) larger than 29.328.

Comparison of whole numbers, integers, rational numbers, and real numbers all generally follows the above pattern. Conversion of these numbers to decimal form (even if the number is an integer) is usually the easiest way to compare the magnitudes.

1C. **Demonstrate an understanding of a variety of models for representing numbers (e.g., fraction strips, diagrams, patterns, shaded regions, number lines)**

Numbers need not be represented exclusively as standard Arabic numerals. The following are examples of different ways in which numbers are represented.

The use of shaded regions is a legitimate way to represent a number (whether a whole number or a fraction). The shaded region below represents 47 out of 100 total area units, which also equals 0.47, $\frac{47}{100}$, or 47%.

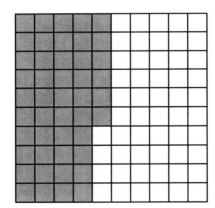

Fraction strips are another method of representing numbers, as shown below. Each strip could, for instance, represent unity. The number of equal subdivisions is the denominator of the fraction; the number of subdivisions that are shaded (for example) could represent the numerator.

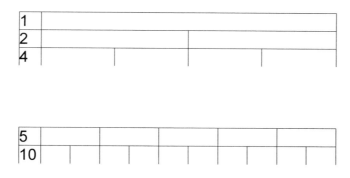

Number lines are also a common method for representing numbers. An example of a number line is shown below.

Diagrams are yet another method. One particular diagram involves a particular number of objects of the same type to represent that number. Below, the number four is represented using four boxes.

1D. Demonstrate an understanding of equivalency among different representations of rational numbers

A firm grasp of equivalency among the different representations of real numbers can be a tremendous help both in problem solving and in more theoretical applications of mathematics. The skill section below treats the different representations of rational numbers and their relationships (including interconversion procedures). By reviewing that skill section, the reader should be convinced that the representations of a particular number using a decimal, percent, fraction, scientific notation, or other format are all equal.

1E. **Select appropriate representations of real numbers (e.g., fractions, decimals, percents, roots, exponents, scientific notation) for particular situations**

Real numbers can be represented in a variety of formats. Some of these formats are more amenable to certain problems than others, and it is important to be able to select the proper representation of a real number for a given situation.

For instance, if exact calculations are required, **decimal representations** (or, similarly, **percent representations**—which are simply the decimal representation multiplied by 100) of irrational numbers are not appropriate. The use of a decimal necessarily requires use of a finite representation; thus, the decimal form of an irrational number must be rounded to some digit, leading to inaccuracies in calculations. Thus, irrational numbers such as the number π and square roots of certain integers should often be left in their symbolic or square root forms. If inexact calculations are acceptable, then a decimal or approximate fractional representation may be suitable.

If the decimal is repeating (such as 0.1111111...), a **fractional representation** may be the best approach. A fraction can be manipulated easily, and it is sometimes more conducive to exact calculations than are repeating decimals (or even long non-repeating decimals in some cases).

In other instances, an **exponential form** is useful. Exponentials (or their inverses, **logarithms**) may be a preferred representation of real numbers in various cases. In addition to considering whether exact or inexact calculations are needed for a particular problem, the simplicity of the calculation is also important when selecting an appropriate representation of a number. For hand/mental calculations, simplicity may be paramount, for instance.

Scientific notation is a convenient method for writing very large and very small numbers. It employs two factors: the first factor is a number between −10 and 10, and the second factor is a power of 10. This notation is a shorthand way to express large numbers (like the weight in kilograms of 100 freight cars) or small numbers (like the weight in grams of an atom).

For example, 356.73 can be written in various forms.

$$356.73 = 3567.3 \times 10^{-1} \qquad (1)$$
$$= 356.73 \times 10^{-0} \qquad (2)$$
$$= 35.673 \times 10^{1} \qquad (3)$$
$$= 3.5673 \times 10^{2} \qquad (4)$$
$$= 0.35673 \times 10^{3} \qquad (5)$$

Only (4) is written in proper scientific notation format.

Example: Write 46,368,000 in scientific notation.

1. Introduce a decimal point. 46,368,000 = 46,368,000.0

2. Move the decimal place to **left** until only one nonzero digit is in front of it, in this case between the 4 and 6.

3. Count the number of digits the decimal point moved, in this case seven. This is the nth the power of 10 and is **positive** because the decimal point moved **left**.

Therefore, 46,368,000 = 4.6368×10^{7}.

Example: Write 0.00397 in scientific notation.

1) Decimal point is already in place.

2) Move the decimal point to the **right** until there is only one nonzero digit in front of it, in this case between the 3 and 9.

3) Count the number of digits the decimal point moved, in this case three. This is the nth the power of ten and is **negative** because the decimal point moved **right**.

Therefore, 0.00397 = 3.97×10^{-3}.

Thus, there are a number of possible representations for a given real number depending on the problem or situation under consideration. The following examples illustrate some problems where certain representations of given real numbers are better than others.

Example: A particular material has a mass of 0.01 grams in one liter. What is the material's density in grams per milliliter?

A cursory examination of this problem shows that it will be necessary to divide a small number (0.01 grams) by a large number (1000 milliliters = 1 liter) to get the density. Thus, scientific notation is a helpful representation of the numbers in the problem. The density d is then the following:

$$d = \frac{1 \times 10^{-2}\,g}{1 \times 10^{3}\,mL} = 1 \times 10^{-5}\,\frac{g}{mL}$$

The calculation and the result in this case are simplified considerably through the use of scientific notation. The solution is in a much neater form than 0.00001.

Example: Express the repeating decimal $0.\overline{254}$ as a number in closed form.

This problem calls for selecting an appropriate closed-form representation in the real number system for a repeating decimal. First, note that because the decimal repeats, the three repeating digits can be isolated as follows. Let d be equal to the repeating decimal $0.\overline{254}$.

$$1000d = 254.\overline{254} = 254 + d$$
$$999d = 254$$
$$d = \frac{254}{999}$$

Thus, this repeating decimal can be expressed in closed form using a fractional representation.

1F. **Understand the characteristics of the set of whole numbers, integers, rational numbers, real numbers, and complex numbers (e.g., commutativity, order, closure, identity elements, inverse elements, density)**

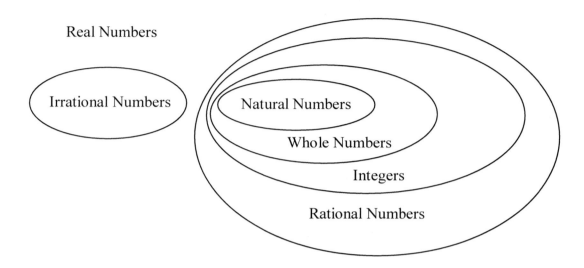

Real numbers are denoted by $\mathbb{R}$ and are numbers that can be shown by an infinite decimal representation such as 3.286275347.... Real numbers include rational numbers, such as 242 and −23/129, and irrational numbers, such as $\sqrt{2}$ and π, and they can be represented as points along an infinite number line. Real numbers are also known as "the unique complete Archimedean *ordered field*." Real numbers are to be distinguished from imaginary numbers, which involve a factor of $\sqrt{-1}$.

Real numbers are classified as follows:

A. **Natural numbers, denoted by** $\mathbb{N}$: the counting numbers, 1, 2, 3,…

B. **Whole numbers**: the counting numbers along with zero, 0, 1, 2, 3,…

C. **Integers, denoted by** $\mathbb{Z}$: the counting numbers, their negatives, and zero, …,−2, −1, 0, 1, 2,…

D. **Rationals, denoted by** $\mathbb{Q}$: all of the fractions that can be formed using whole numbers. Zero cannot be the denominator. In decimal form, these numbers will either be terminating or repeating decimals. Simplify square roots to determine if the number can be written as a fraction.

E. **Irrationals**: Real numbers that cannot be written as a fraction. The decimal forms of these numbers are neither terminating nor repeating. Examples include π, e and $\sqrt{2}$.

$$z_1 z_2 = (a_1 a_2 - b_1 b_2) + (a_1 b_2 + a_2 b_1)i$$

$$\frac{z_1}{z_2} = \frac{z_1}{z_2} \frac{z_2^*}{z_2^*} = \frac{a_1 a_2 + b_1 b_2}{a_2^2 + b_2^2} + \frac{a_2 b_1 - a_1 b_2}{a_2^2 + b_2^2}i$$

Fields, Rings, and Groups

A useful property that can describe arbitrary sets of numbers (including fields, rings, and groups) is **closure**. A set is closed under an operation if the operation performed on any given elements of the set always yields a result that is likewise an element of the set. For instance, the set of real numbers is closed under multiplication, because for any two real numbers a and b, the product ab is also a real number.

Another property that can be used to classify sets (of whatever kind) of numbers is **density**. A set of numbers is dense whenever there are an infinite number of members of the set between any two members. (This concept can also be stated as follows: there is a number between any two numbers in the set. Logically, this implies that there are an infinite number or numbers between any two numbers in the set.) The set of real numbers, for instance, is dense, since there is always a number between any two real numbers a and b, as shown below, where $a < b$.

$$a < \frac{a+b}{2} < b$$

The integers are not dense: given any two consecutive integers, there are no numbers between them. The proof shown above for real numbers, however, also applies to rational numbers (if a and b are rational, so is $\frac{a+b}{2}$). Irrational numbers are also dense. Whole and natural numbers (like the integers) are not.

Any set that includes at least two nonzero elements that satisfies the field axioms for addition and multiplication is a **field**. The real numbers, R, as well as the complex numbers, C, are each a field, with the real numbers being a subset of the complex numbers. The field axioms are summarized below.

Addition:

Commutativity	$a + b = b + a$
Associativity	$a + (b + c) = (a + b) + c$
Identity	$a + 0 = a$
Inverse	$a + (-a) = 0$

Multiplication:

Commutativity	$ab = ba$
Associativity	$a(bc) = (ab)c$
Identity	$a \cdot 1 = a$
Inverse	$a \cdot \dfrac{1}{a} = 1 \qquad (a \neq 0)$

Addition and multiplication:

Distributivity	$a(b + c) = (b + c)a = ab + ac$

Note that both the real numbers and the complex numbers satisfy the axioms summarized above.

A **ring** is an integral domain with two binary operations (addition and multiplication) where, for every non-zero element a and b in the domain, the product ab is non-zero. A field is a ring where multiplication is commutative, or $a \cdot b = b \cdot a$, and all non-zero elements have a multiplicative inverse. The set Z (integers) is a ring that is not a field in that it does not have the multiplicative inverse; therefore, integers are not a field. A polynomial ring is also not a field, as it also has no multiplicative inverse. Furthermore, matrix rings do not constitute fields because matrix multiplication is not generally commutative.

Note: Multiplication is implied when there is no symbol between two variables. Thus, $a \times b$ can be written ab. Multiplication can also be indicated by a raised dot ($\cdot$).

A **group** is a set of numbers that obeys certain axioms with respect to a particular binary operation (such as addition). For a set G to be a group, G must be closed under the defined operation, the operation must obey associativity, G must contain an identity element, and each element in G must have an inverse element also in G. These rules are summarized below for elements a, b, and c in G for the binary operation $*$.

Closure	$a * b \in G$
Associativity	$a * (b * c) = (a * b) * c$
Identity	$I \in G$ such that $I * a = a * I = a$
Inverse	$a_{inv} \in G$ such that $a_{inv} * a = a * a_{inv} = I$

In the inverse rule, I is the same as the identity element. An example of a group is the set of integers under addition. For any two integers a and b, the sum $a + b$ is also an integer—thus, the set of integers is closed under addition. Also, associativity applies, since $a + (b + c) = (a + b) + c$ for any integers a, b, and c. The identity element 0 (zero) is also in the set of integers and $0 + a = a + 0 = a$ for all a. Furthermore, the inverse element $-a$ for element a leads to $a + (-a) = 0$. Thus, the set of integers also obeys the identity and inverse axioms, meaning that the integers are a group under the binary operation of addition.

Real numbers are an ordered field and can be ordered. As such, an ordered field F must contain a subset P (such as the positive numbers) such that if a and b are elements of P, then both $a + b$ and ab are also elements of P. (In other words, the set P is closed under addition and multiplication.) Furthermore, it must be the case that for any element c contained in F, exactly one of the following conditions is true: c is an element of P, $-c$ is an element of P or $c = 0$.

Likewise, **the rational numbers also constitute an ordered field**. The set P can be defined as the positive rational numbers. For each a and b that are elements of the set $\square$ (the rational numbers), $a + b$ is also an element of P, as is ab. (The sum $a + b$ and the product ab are both rational if a and b are rational.) Since P is closed under addition and multiplication, $\square$ constitutes an ordered field.

For information regarding complex numbers, see **Competency 002**.

1G. **Demonstrate an understanding of how some situations that have no solution in one number system (e.g., whole numbers, integers, rational numbers) have solutions in another number system (e.g., real numbers, complex numbers)**

The set of real numbers is composed entirely of the union of two mutually exclusive sets: the set of rational numbers and the set of irrational numbers. In many cases, the solutions to certain problems may not be found among the rational numbers, yet the solutions are indeed real numbers. Consider the following examples.

<u>Example:</u> Find the hypotenuse of a right triangle with legs of length 2 and 3.

The diagram below illustrates the problem.

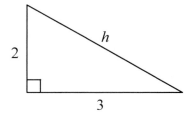

The length h of the hypotenuse can be found using the Pythagorean theorem as follows.

$$h^2 = 2^2 + 3^2 = 4 + 9 = 13$$
$$h = \sqrt{13}$$

The result, $\sqrt{13}$, is not a rational number. Thus, in this case, although the length h is obviously in the set of real numbers, it is not in the set of rational numbers. Logically, the result must be an irrational number then, as calculated above.

<u>Example:</u> Calculate the volume of a circular cylinder with a diameter of 4 centimeters and a height of 10 centimeters.

The volume of a circular cylinder is $\pi r^2 h$. In this case, the radius r is 2cm and the height h is 10cm. The volume is then the following.

$$V = \pi r^2 h = \pi (2)^2 (10) = 40\pi$$

Since π is an irrational number, the product 40π is likewise irrational. Here, again, although the volume of the cylinder is not an integer or otherwise a rational number, it is a real number (and hence irrational).

Numerous problems do not have solutions that are contained in the set of real numbers. In such cases, complex solutions may be required. Consider the following canonical example.

$$x^2 + 1 = 0$$

This equation cannot be solved for x in the real domain.

$$x^2 = -1$$
$$x = \pm\sqrt{-1}$$

Since there is no real number whose square is −1, there is no real solution for x. The imaginary number i is a solution, however; thus, this equation can be solved in the complex domain.

$$x = \pm i$$

More generally, the Fundamental Theorem of Algebra states that any polynomial of degree n must have n solutions (or roots), which may include real, complex, or non-distinct roots (or some combination thereof).

Other operations can likewise lead to imaginary results. Consider, for instance, the natural logarithm of a negative numbers.

$$\ln(-1) = ?$$

In the real domain, this expression is undefined, because there is no real exponent of e that results in a negative number. If Euler's formula is applied, however, a solution from the set of complex numbers becomes apparent.

$$\ln(-1) = \ln(\cos\pi + i\sin\pi) = \ln(e^{i\pi})$$
$$\ln(-1) = i\pi\ln(e) = i\pi$$

Thus, the expression has an equivalent numerical expression from the set of complex numbers. (For precision, it is noteworthy that the general result is $in\pi$, where n is an integer.)

Example: Find all the roots of the polynomial $x^3 - x^2 + 3x - 3$.

This problem can be tackled in any of several ways. First, note that the Fundamental Theorem of Algebra requires that the polynomial must have three solutions. In this case, the polynomial can be factored. By inspection, it appears that $x = 1$ might be a solution:

$$(1)^3 - (1)^2 + 3(1) - 3 = 1 - 1 + 3 - 3 = 0$$

Thus, $(x - 1)$ must be a factor in the expression. The remaining factor must be a polynomial of degree two.

$$x^3 - x^2 + 3x - 3 = (x - 1)(ax^2 + bx + c)$$

Obviously, a must be equal to 1. Likewise, c must be equal to 3. Then

$$(x - 1)(x^2 + bx + 3) = x^3 - x^2 + bx^2 - bx + 3x - 3$$
$$x^3 - x^2 + 3x - 3 = x^3 - (1 - b)x^2 - (b - 3)x - 3$$

Thus, $b = 0$.

$$x^3 - x^2 + 3x - 3 = (x - 1)(x^2 + 3)$$

Factoring once more yields
$$0 = (x - 1)(x + i\sqrt{3})(x - i\sqrt{3})$$

The roots are then 1, $i\sqrt{3}$, and $-i\sqrt{3}$.

Competency 002   The teacher understands number operations and computational algorithms

This competency reviews complex numbers in terms of both their associated operations and their algebraic structure. The discussion then goes on to cover various aspects of the four basic operations on real numbers, including justification of algorithms for performing these operations, concrete and visual representations of the connections between operations and algorithms, and extension of operations beyond the real numbers.

2A.   Work proficiently with real and complex numbers and their operations

The set of complex numbers is denoted by $\Box$. The set $\Box$ is defined as $\{a + bi : a, b \in \Box\}$ ($\in$ means "element of"). In other words, complex numbers are an extension of real numbers made by attaching an imaginary number i, which satisfies the equality $i^2 = -1$. Complex numbers are of the form $a + bi$, where a and b are *real* numbers and $i = \sqrt{-1}$. Thus, a is the real part of the number and b is the imaginary part of the number. When i appears in a fraction, the fraction is usually simplified so that i is not in the denominator. The set of complex numbers includes the set of real numbers, where any real number n can be written in its equivalent complex form as $n + 0i$. In other words, it can be said that $\Box \subseteq \Box$ (or $\Box$ is a subset of $\Box$).

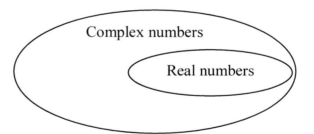

The number $3i$ has a real part 0 and imaginary part 3; the number 4 has a real part 4 and an imaginary part 0. As another way of writing complex numbers, we can express them as **ordered pairs**:

Complex number	Ordered pair
$3 + 2i$	$(3, 2)$
$\sqrt{3} + \sqrt{3}i$	$\left(\sqrt{3}, \sqrt{3}\right)$
$7i$	$(0, 7)$
$\dfrac{6 + 2i}{7}$	$\left(\dfrac{6}{7}, \dfrac{2}{7}\right)$

The basic operations for complex numbers can be summarized as follows, where $z_1 = a_1 + b_1 i$ and $z_2 = a_2 + b_2 i$. Note that the operations are performed in the standard manner, where i is treated as a standard radical value. The result of each operation is written in the standard form for complex numbers. Also note that the **complex conjugate** of a complex number $z = a + bi$ is denoted as $z^* = a - bi$.

$$z_1 + z_2 = \left(a_1 + a_2\right) + \left(b_1 + b_2\right)i$$

$$z_1 - z_2 = \left(a_1 - a_2\right) + \left(b_1 - b_2\right)i$$

$$z_1 z_2 = \left(a_1 a_2 - b_1 b_2\right) + \left(a_1 b_2 + a_2 b_1\right)i$$

$$\frac{z_1}{z_2} = \frac{z_1}{z_2}\frac{z_2^*}{z_2^*} = \frac{a_1 a_2 + b_1 b_2}{a_2^2 + b_2^2} + \frac{a_2 b_1 - a_1 b_2}{a_2^2 + b_2^2}i$$

Note that because the division operation above is defined, the **multiplicative inverse** of any complex number $z \neq 0$ is also defined (where z_1 is 1 and z_2 is z) in the set of complex numbers.

In addition to these operations, the **absolute value of a complex number** $z = a + bi$ (written $|z|$ or $|a + bi|$) is also defined. (The absolute value may also be termed the "magnitude" or the "modulus" of the number.)

$$|z| = \sqrt{zz^*} = \sqrt{a^2 + b^2}$$

The set of complex numbers forms a field, and thus, it obeys all the field axioms discussed in **Competency 001**. Nevertheless, **the complex numbers are not an ordered field**. Consider the number $i = \sqrt{-1}$ contained in the set $\square$ of complex numbers. Assume that $\square$ has a subset P (positive numbers) that is closed under both addition and multiplication. Assume that $i > 0$. A difficulty arises in that $i^2 = -1 < 0$, so i cannot be included in the set P. Likewise, assume $i < 0$. The problem once again arises that $i^4 = 1 > 0$, so i cannot be included in P. It is clearly the case that $i \neq 0$, so there is no place for i in an ordered field. Thus, the complex numbers cannot be ordered.

Because the complex numbers include the real numbers, they also include all the subsets of the real numbers (such as integers, rational numbers, and irrational numbers). Likewise, complex numbers can be organized into sets that contain, for instance, numbers with irrational imaginary parts, integer real parts, or other specific properties (or combinations thereof).

2B. **Analyze and describe relationships between number properties, operations, and algorithms for the four basic operations involving integers, rational numbers, and real numbers**

The relationships between number properties, operations, and algorithms for various subsets of the real numbers are described in **Skill 2D**. These relationships are best illustrated in the context of the justifications of the algorithms associated with the four basic operations performed on subsets of real numbers.

2C. **Use a variety of concrete and visual representations to demonstrate the connections between operations and algorithms**

Concrete and visual representations can help demonstrate the logic behind operational algorithms. Blocks or other objects modeled on the base ten system are useful concrete tools. Base ten blocks represent ones, tens and hundreds. Modeling the partial sums algorithm with base ten blocks, for instance, helps clarify the thought process. Consider the sum of 242 and 193: represent 242 with two one hundred blocks, four ten blocks and 2 one blocks. Represent 193 with one one hundred block, nine ten blocks and three one blocks. In the partial sums algorithm, manipulate each place value separately and add the results. Thus, we group the hundred blocks, ten blocks, and one blocks and derive a total for each place value. We combine the place values to complete the sum.

An example of a visual representation of an operational algorithm is the modeling of a two-term multiplication as the area of a rectangle. For example, consider the product of 24 and 39: we can represent the product in geometric form. Note that the four sections of the rectangle equate to the four products of the partial products method.

	30	9
20	A = 600	A = 120
4	A = 120	A = 36

Thus, the final product is the sum of the areas or 600 + 180 + 120 + 36 = 936.

The main algorithm of rational number division is multiplication by the reciprocal. Thus,

$$\frac{\frac{1}{3}}{\frac{1}{4}} = \left(\frac{1}{3}\right)\left(\frac{4}{1}\right) = \frac{4}{3}$$

The definition of multiplication and division as inverse operations justifies the use of reciprocal multiplication.

2D. **Justify procedures used in algorithms for the four basic operations with integers, rational numbers, and real numbers, and analyze error patterns that may occur in their application**

Algorithms are methods or strategies for solving problems. There are several different algorithms for solving addition, subtraction, multiplication, and division problems involving integers, rational numbers, and real numbers. In general, algorithms make use of number properties to simplify mathematical operations.

Teachers must justify the procedures used in operational algorithms to ensure student understanding. The following are examples of operational algorithms, their justifications, and common errors in implementation.

Integer algorithms—Addition

Three common algorithms for addition of integers are the partial sums method, column addition method, and fast method. All of the integer addition algorithms rely on the commutative and associative properties of addition, allowing regrouping and reordering of numbers.

The **partial sums method** is a two-stage process. First, add the columns from left to right. To complete the operation, add the column values.

$$
\begin{array}{r}
125 \\
+ \ 89 \\
+ \ 376 \\
\hline
400 \\
+ \ 170 \\
+ \ \ 20 \\
\hline
590
\end{array}
$$

Step 1 – column addition

Step 2 – final sum

The associative property of addition shows why this method works. We can rewrite the above problem as follows:

$(100 + 20 + 5) + (80 + 9) + (300 + 70 + 6)$

Using the associative property to group the terms,

$$(100 + 300) + (20 + 80 + 70) + (5 + 9 + 6) = 400 + 170 + 20$$
$$= 590$$

Note the final form is the same as the second step of the partial sums algorithm. When evaluating addition by partial sums, teachers should look for errors in assigning place values of the partial sums; for example, in the problem above, a student might record the sum of eight and two in the tens column as 10 instead of 100.

The **column addition method** is also a two-stage process. First, add the digits in each column. To complete the operation, perform the place carries from right to left.

```
     1 |  2|  5
  +  |  8|  9          Stage 1 – column addition
  + 3|  7|  6
     4| 17| 20
     4| 19|  0    ◄────── First carry
     5|  9|  0 = 590  ◄────── Second carry = final answer
```

The **fast method** of addition is the traditional method of right to left addition. This method involves adding the columns from left to right and performing carries mentally or writing them down.

```
      12  ◄──── Carries
      125
   +   89
   +  376
      590
```

Integer algorithms—Subtraction

Three common algorithms of integer subtraction are left to right subtraction, partial differences, and the same change rule. Like the addition algorithms, the subtraction algorithms rely on the commutative and associative properties of addition (because subtraction is addition of a negative number).

In **left to right subtraction**, decompose the second number into smaller values and perform the individual subtractions. For example, to solve 335 – 78, break 78 down into 70 + 8.

$$
\begin{array}{r}
335 \\
-\ \ 70 \\
\hline
265 \\
-\ \ \ \ 8 \\
\hline
257
\end{array}
$$

The **partial differences method** is a two-stage process. First, operate on each column individually, being careful to record the sign of each result. Then, sum the results to yield the final answer.

$$
\begin{array}{r}
335 \\
-\ \ 78 \\
\hline
+300 \\
-\ 40 \\
-\ \ \ 3 \\
\hline
257
\end{array}
$$

The **same change rule** takes advantage of the knowledge that subtraction is easier if the smaller number ends in zero. Thus, change each number by the same amount to produce a smaller number ending in zero.

$$
\begin{array}{rcr}
335 & \rightarrow & 337 \\
-\ \ 78 & \rightarrow & -\ \ 80 \\
\hline
257 & & 257
\end{array}
$$

The same change rule of substitution takes advantage of the property of addition of zero. The addition of zero does not change the value of a quantity.

$$
289 - 97 = (289 + 3) - (97 + 3) = (289 - 97) + (3 - 3)
$$
$$
= 289 - 97 + 0
$$
$$
289 - 97 = 292 - 100
$$

Note the use of the distributive property of multiplication over addition, the associative property of addition, and the property of addition of zero in proving the accuracy of the same change algorithm. A common mistake when using the same change rule is adding from one number and subtracting from the other. This is an error in reasoning resulting from misapplication of the distributive property (e.g., failing to distribute –1).

Integer algorithms—Multiplication

Two common multiplication algorithms are the partial products method and the short method. These algorithms rely on the associative and commutative properties of multiplication and the distribution of multiplication over addition.

In the **partial products method**, decompose each term into base-ten forms and multiply each pair of terms.

$$
\begin{array}{r}
84 \\
\times\ 26 \\
\end{array}
$$

80 x 20 ➤	1600
80 x 6 ➤	480
20 x 4 ➤	80
6 x 4 ➤	24
	2184

We can justify this algorithm by using the "FOIL" method of binomial multiplication and the distributive property of multiplication over addition.

$$(80 + 4)(20 + 6) = (80)(20) + (4)(20) + (6)(80) + (6)(4)$$

Common errors in partial product multiplication result from mistakes in binomial multiplication and mistakes in pairing terms of the partial products (e.g., multiplying incorrect terms).

The **short method** is the traditional multiplication algorithm. In the short method, only decompose the second term.

$$
\begin{array}{r}
84 \\
\times\ 26 \\
\end{array}
$$

84 x 20 ➤	1680
84 x 6 ➤	504
	2184

Integer algorithms—Division

A common division algorithm is the **partial quotients method**. In this method, we make note of two simple products and estimate our way toward a final answer. For example, to find the quotient of 1440 divided by 18, first make note that 5 x 18 = 90 and 2 x 18 = 32.

```
18)   1440 |
    −  900 | 50
       540 |
    −  360 | 20
       180 |
    −   90 | 5
        90 |
    −   90 | 5
         0   80  ──→  final quotient = 80 with no remainder
```

We can justify the partial quotients algorithm for division by using the distributive property of multiplication over division. Because multiplication is the reverse of division, we check the result by multiplying the divisor by the partial sums, as shown below.

$$18 (50 + 20 + 5 + 5) = (18)(50) + (18)(20) + (18)(5) + (18)(5)$$
$$= 1440$$

Common errors in division often result from mistakes in translating words to symbols: for example, misinterpreting 10 divided by 5 as 5/10. In addition, errors in subtraction and addition can produce incorrect results.

Rational and Real Number Algorithms

Operations involving rational numbers represented as fractions require unique algorithms.

Rational number addition relies on the distributive property of multiplication over addition and the understanding that multiplication by any number by one yields the same number. Consider the addition of 1/4 to 1/3 by means of common denominator.

$$\frac{1}{4} + \frac{1}{3} = \frac{3}{3}\left(\frac{1}{4}\right) + \frac{4}{4}\left(\frac{1}{3}\right) = \left(\frac{3}{12}\right) + \left(\frac{4}{12}\right) = \frac{7}{12}$$

Recognize that $\frac{3}{3}$ and $\frac{4}{4}$ both equal unity.

A common error in rational number addition is the failure to find a common denominator and the addition of both numerators and denominators.

When completing operations involving real numbers in decimal form, we use algorithms similar to those used with integers. We use the associative, commutative and distributive properties of numbers to generate algorithms.

2E. **Relate operations and algorithms involving numbers to algebraic procedures (e.g., adding fractions to adding rational expressions, division of integers to division of polynomials)**

Many **algebraic procedures** are similar to and rely upon number operations and algorithms. Two examples of this similarity are the addition of rational expressions and division of polynomials.

Addition of rational expressions is similar to fraction addition. The basic algorithm of addition for both fractions and rational expressions is the common denominator method. Consider an example of the addition of numerical fractions.

$$\frac{3}{5}+\frac{2}{3}=\frac{3(3)}{3(5)}+\frac{5(2)}{5(3)}=\frac{9}{15}+\frac{10}{15}=\frac{19}{15}$$

To complete the sum, it is necessary to first find the least common denominator. Now, consider an example of rational expression addition.

$$\frac{(x+5)}{(x+1)}+\frac{2x}{(x+3)}=\frac{(x+3)(x+5)}{(x+3)(x+1)}+\frac{(x+1)2x}{(x+1)(x+3)}$$

$$=\frac{x^2+8x+15}{(x+3)(x+1)}+\frac{2x^2+2x}{(x+3)(x+1)}=\frac{3x^2+10x+15}{(x+3)(x+1)}$$

Note the similarity to fractional addition. The basic algorithm—finding a common denominator and adding numerators—is the same.

Division of polynomials follows the same algorithm as numerical long division. Consider an example of numerical long division.

$$6\overline{)4321}$$ quotient 720

$$\frac{42}{12}$$
$$\frac{12}{1}$$

$720\frac{1}{6}$ = final quotient

Compare the process of numerical long division to polynomial division.

$$x+1\overline{)x^2-8x-9}$$ quotient $x-9$

$$\frac{-x^2-x+0}{-9x-9}$$
$$\frac{+9x+9}{0}$$

$\longrightarrow$ $x-9$ = final quotient

Note that the step-by-step process is identical in both cases.

2F.   **Extend and generalize the operations on rationals and integers to include exponents, their properties, and their applications to the real numbers**

Other examples of number operations are those involving **exponents**. If a and b are real numbers and m and n are rational numbers, then

1. $a^m \times a^n = a^{(m+n)}$

2. $\dfrac{a^m}{a^n} = a^{(m-n)}$

3. $(a^m)^n = a^{(mn)}$

4. $(ab)^m = a^m b^m$

5. $a^{-n} = \dfrac{1}{a^n} = (1/a)^n$

6. $a^0 = 1$ for $a \neq 0$

7. $a^{m/n} = \left(a^{1/n}\right)^m = \left(a^m\right)^{1/n}$

8. $\sqrt[n]{a^m} = a^{m/n}$

Note: Radicals ($\sqrt{\ }$) are inverse operators of exponents and are represented in the form $\sqrt[n]{a^x}$, where

      n is called the index or root (assumed to be 2 if omitted)
      a^x is called to radicand
      x is the exponent or power of 'a'

In the notation above, we are finding the nth root of a^x. In other words, we want to find the number that, when multiplied by itself n times, yields a^x. An example is shown below for the number 16.

$$\sqrt{16} = \sqrt[2]{16}$$
$$\sqrt{16} = \pm 4$$

Both the positive and negative values of 4 are solutions because the square of +4 and the square of –4 are both 16. The number +4 is called the principal square root of 16, because the principal square root is the only one that makes sense in some cases (for example, in measurements).

We can only add or subtract radicals that have the same index and the same radicand. The following examples illustrate legitimate results of addition and subtraction operations.

$$2\sqrt{5} + 3\sqrt{5} = 5\sqrt{5}$$
$$5\sqrt[3]{2} - 3\sqrt[3]{2} = 2\sqrt[3]{2}$$

If the radicand is raised to a power that is equal to the index, then the root operation will cancel out the power operation.

Example: Perform the indicated operations.

a) $\sqrt[3]{2}^3$

The power and the index are equal to each other. Thus,

$$\sqrt[3]{2}^3 = 2$$

b) $2\sqrt{32}$

Rewrite the number 32 as follows:

$$32 = 2 \times 16 = 2 \times 4 \times 4 = 2 \times 4^2$$

Thus,

$$2\sqrt{32} = 2\sqrt{2 \times 4^2} = 2 \times 4\sqrt[2]{2} \text{ or } 8\sqrt{2}$$

If the radicand is raised to a power different from the index, convert the radical to its exponential form and apply laws of exponents.

Competency 003 **The teacher understands ideas of number theory and uses numbers to model and solve problems within and outside of mathematics**

This competency deals with the application of number theory and the set of real numbers to solving problems in a variety of contexts. In addition to application of number theory, this section reviews the use of real numbers for quantifying various phenomena, the use of mental math and computational estimation techniques, and application of real numbers to problems of various types.

3A. **Demonstrate an understanding of ideas from number theory (e.g., prime factorization, greatest common divisor) as they apply to whole numbers, integers, and rational numbers, and uses these ideas in problem situations**

Divisibility Rules

a. A number is **divisible by 2** if that number is an even number (which means the last digit is 0, 2, 4, 6 or 8).

Consider a number *abcd* defined by the digits *a*, *b*, *c* and *d* (for instance, 1,234). Rewrite the number as follows.

$$10abc + d = abcd$$

Note that $10abc$ is divisible by 2. Thus, the number *abcd* is only divisible by 2 if *d* is divisible by two; in other words, *abcd* is divisible by two only if it is an even number. For example, the last digit of 1,354 is 4, so it is divisible by 2. On the other hand, the last digit of 240,685 is 5, so it is not divisible by 2.

b. A number is **divisible by 3** if the sum of its digits is evenly divisible by 3.

Consider a number *abcd* defined by the digits *a*, *b*, *c* and *d*. The number can be written as

$$abcd = 1000a + 100b + 10c + d$$

The number can also be rewritten as

$$abcd = (999 + 1)a + (99 + 1)b + (9 + 1)c + d$$
$$abcd = 999a + 99b + 9c + (a + b + c + d)$$

Note that the first three terms in the above expression are all divisible by 3. Thus, the number is evenly divisible by 3 only if $a + b + c + d$ is divisible by 3. The same logic applies regardless of the size of the number. This proves the rules for divisibility by 3.

The sum of the digits of 964 is 9+6+4 = 19. Since 19 is not divisible by 3, neither is 964. The digits of 86,514 are 8+6+5+1+4 = 24. Since 24 is divisible by 3, 86,514 is also divisible by 3.

c. A number is **divisible by 4** if the number in its last 2 digits is evenly divisible by 4.

Let a number $abcd$ be defined by the digits a, b, c and d.

$$ab(100) + cd = abcd$$

Since 100 is divisible by 4, $100ab$ is also divisible by 4. Thus, $abcd$ is divisible by 4 only if cd is divisible by 4.

$$25ab + \frac{cd}{4} = \frac{abcd}{4}$$

The number 113,336 ends with the number 36 for the last 2 digits. Since 36 is divisible by 4, 113,336 is also divisible by 4. The number 135,627 ends with the number 27 for the last 2 digits. Since 27 is not evenly divisible by 4, 135,627 is also not divisible by 4.

d. A number is **divisible by 5** if the number ends in either a 5 or a 0.

Use the same number $abcd$.

$$100ab + cd = abcd$$

The first term is evenly divisible by 5, but the second term is only evenly divisible by 5 if it is 0, 5, 10, 15,…,95. In other words, $abcd$ is divisibly by 5 only if it ends in a 0 or 5. For instance, 225 ends with a 5, so it is divisible by 5. The number 470 is also divisible by 5 because its last digit is a 0. The number 2,358 is not divisible by 5 because its last digit is an 8.

e. A number is **divisible by 6** if the number is even and the sum of its digits is evenly divisible by 3 or 6.

Let a number *efgh* be defined by the digits *e*, *f*, *g* and *h*. If *efgh* is even, then it is divisible by 2. Write *abcd* as follows.

$$\frac{efgh}{2} = abcd = 999a + 99b + 9c + (a + b + c + d)$$

$$efgh = 2abcd = 2(999)a + 2(99)b + 2(9)c + 2(a + b + c + d)$$

Then divide *efgh* by 6.

$$\frac{efgh}{6} = \frac{2(999)}{6}a + \frac{2(99)}{6}b + \frac{2(9)}{6}c + \frac{2}{6}(a + b + c + d)$$

$$\frac{efgh}{6} = 333a + 33b + 3c + \frac{2}{6}(a + b + c + d)$$

Notice that *efgh* is divisible by 6 only if the sum of the digits is divisible by 3 or by 6. The number *efgh* must also be even, since 2 is a factor of 6. For instance, 4,950 is an even number and its digits add to 18 (4 + 9 + 5 + 0 = 18). Since the number is even and the sum of its digits is 18 (which is divisible by 3 and 6), then 4,950 is divisible by 6. On the other hand, 326 is an even number, but its digits add up to 11. Since 11 is not divisible by 3 or 6, then 326 is not divisible by 6.

f. A number is **divisible by 8** if the number in its last 3 digits is evenly divisible by 8.

The logic for the proof of this case follows that of numbers divisible by 2 and 4. The number 113,336 ends with the 3-digit number 336 in the last 3 columns. Since 336 is divisible by 8, then 113,336 is also divisible by 8. The number 465,627 ends with the number 627 in the last 3 columns. Since 627 is not evenly divisible by 8, then 465,627 is also not divisible by 8.

g. A number is **divisible by 9** if the sum of its digits is evenly divisible by 9.

The logic for the proof of this case follows that for the case of numbers that are divisible by 3 and 6. The sum of the digits of 874, for example, is 8 + 7 + 4 = 19. Since 19 is not divisible by 9, neither is 874. The sum of the digits of 116,514 is 1 + 1 + 6 + 5 + 1 + 4 = 18. Since 18 is divisible by 9, 116,514 is also divisible by 9.

The Fundamental Theorem of Arithmetic

Every integer greater than 1 can be written uniquely in the form

$$p_1^{e1} \, p_2^{e2} \cdots p_k^{ek},$$

The pi are distinct prime numbers and the ei are positive integers. Any integer $n > 1$ that is divisible by at least one positive integer that is not equal to one or n is called a **composite number**. A natural number n that is only divisible by one and n is called a **prime number**.

GCF is the abbreviation for the **greatest common factor**. The GCF is the largest number that is a factor of all the numbers given in a problem. The GCF can be no larger than the smallest number given in the problem. If no other number is a common factor, then the GCF will be the number 1. To find the GCF, list all possible factors of the smallest number given (include the number itself). Starting with the largest factor (which is the number itself), determine if it is also a factor of all the other given numbers. If so, that is the GCF. If that factor does not work, try the same method on the next smaller factor. Continue until a common factor is found. This is the GCF. Note: There can be other common factors besides the GCF.

Example: Find the GCF of 12, 20, and 36.

The smallest number in the problem is 12. The factors of 12 are 1, 2, 3, 4, 6 and 12. 12 is the largest factor, but it does not divide evenly into 20. Neither does 6, but 4 will divide into both 20 and 36 evenly. Therefore, 4 is the GCF.

Example: Find the GCF of 14 and 15.

Factors of 14 are 1, 2, 7 and 14. 14 is the largest factor, but it does not divide evenly into 15. Neither does 7 or 2. Therefore, the only factor common to both 14 and 15 is the number 1, which is the GCF.

The **Euclidean Algorithm** is a formal method for determining the **greatest common devisor** (GCD) (another name for GCF) of two positive integers. The algorithm can be formulated in a recursive manner that simply involves repetition of a few steps until a terminating point is reached. The algorithm can be summarized as follows, where a and b are the two integers for which determination of the GCD is to be undertaken. (Assign a and b such that $a > b$.)

    1. If $b = 0$, a is the GCD.
    2. Calculate $c = a$ mod b.
    3. If $c = 0$, b is the GCD.
    4. Go back to step 2, replacing a with b and b with c.

Note that the "**mod**" operator in this case is simply a remainder operator. Thus, a mod b is the remainder of division of a by b.

Example: Find the GCD of 299 and 351.

To find the GCD, first let $a = 351$ and $b = 299$. Begin the algorithm as follows.

    1. $b \neq 0$.
    2. $c = 351$ mod $299 = 52$
    3. $c \neq 0$

Perform the next iteration, starting with step 2.

    2. $c = 299$ mod $52 = 39$
    3. $c \neq 0$

Continue to iterate recursively until a solution is found.

    2. $c = 52$ mod $39 = 13$
    3. $c \neq 0$

    2. $c = 39$ mod $13 = 0$
    3. $c = 0$: GCD = 13

Thus, the GCD of 299 and 351 is thus 13.
LCM is the abbreviation for **least common multiple**. The least common multiple of a group of numbers is the smallest number that all of the given numbers will divide into. The least common multiple will always be the largest of the given numbers or a multiple of the largest number.

<u>Example:</u> Find the LCM of 20, 30 and 40.

The largest number given is 40, but 30 will not divide evenly into 40. The next multiple of 40 is 80 (2 × 40), but 30 will not divide evenly into 80 either. The next multiple of 40 is 120. 120 is divisible by both 20 and 30, so 120 is the LCM (least common multiple).

<u>Example:</u> Find the LCM of 96, 16 and 24.

The largest number is 96. 96 is divisible by both 16 and 24, so 96 is the LCM.

The fundamental theorem of arithmetic can be used to show that **every fraction is equivalent to a unique fraction where the numerator and denominator are relatively prime.**

Given a fraction $\dfrac{a}{b}$, the integers a and b can both be written uniquely as a product of prime factors.

$$\frac{a}{b} = \frac{p_1^{x_1} p_2^{x_2} p_3^{x_3} \ldots p_n^{x_n}}{q_1^{y_1} q_2^{y_2} q_3^{y_3} \ldots q_m^{y_m}}$$

When all the common factors are cancelled, the resulting numerator a_1 (the product of remaining factors $p_n^{x_n}$) and the resulting denominator b_1 (the product of remaining factors $q_m^{y_m}$) have no common divisor other than 1; i.e., they are **relatively prime**.

Since, according to the Fundamental Theorem of Arithmetic, the initial prime decomposition of the integers a and b is unique, the new reduced fraction $\dfrac{a_1}{b_1}$ is also **unique**. Hence, any fraction is equivalent to a unique fraction where the numerator and denominator are relatively prime.

The proof that the square root of any integer, not a perfect square number, is irrational may also be demonstrated using prime decomposition.

Let n be an integer. Assuming that the square root of n is rational, we can write

$$\sqrt{n} = \frac{a}{b}$$

Since every fraction is equivalent to a unique fraction where the numerator and denominator are relatively prime (shown earlier), we can reduce the fraction $\dfrac{a}{b}$ to the fraction $\dfrac{a_1}{b_1}$ and write

$$\sqrt{n} = \frac{a_1}{b_1};\ n = \frac{a_1^2}{b_1^2}$$

where a_1 and b_1 are relatively prime.

Since a_1 and b_1 are relatively prime, a_1^2 and b_1^2 must also be relatively prime. Also, since n is an integer, $\dfrac{a_1^2}{b_1^2}$ must be an integer.

The only way the above two conditions can be satisfied is if the denominator $b_1^2 = 1$. Thus, $n = a_1^2$

As a result, the square root of an integer can be rational only if the integer is a perfect square. Stated in an alternative manner, the square root of an integer, not a perfect square, is irrational.

3B. **Use integers, rational numbers, and real numbers to describe and quantify phenomena such as money, length, area, volume, and density**

To apply numbers to describe and quantify phenomena in the real world, one must first select an appropriate unit or set of units. For instance, to simply use a bare number such as "3" in reference to a length is unhelpful (except in a relative sense in comparison with other unitless lengths). The number 3 could refer to miles, inches, meters, yards, or any number of other length units. If unitless numbers are used, they must all be expressed relative to an unspecified (but consistently used) standard (that is, they must maintain certain proportionality). The consistent and explicit use of units also prevents confusion by clearly identifying the parameter being measured or associated with the number.

Once an appropriate unit is chosen, the phenomenon of interest can be expressed numerically. The type of number that is most appropriate depends on the phenomenon being measured. For instance, parameters that span a continuous range of values can typically be expressed using rational numbers. (Note that the use of irrational numbers in a measurement assumes that the measurement is infinitely accurate—this is not the case, however. Every measurement has limited accuracy, and thus, irrational numbers generally are inappropriate. In certain cases, however, the use of certain irrational numbers such as π can be helpful in expressing a value. Irrational numbers may also be used in theoretical calculations, where exact values can legitimately be used.)

A parameter may also span only a discrete range of values: for instance, the population of a city. In such cases, integers are the most appropriate number (and, in cases such as population, whole numbers are the most appropriate).

Some examples of parameters that can be quantified using real numbers are money (in dollars, euros, or some other currency), length (using English, metric, or some other system of units), area, volume, and density. These latter three parameters can be expressed respectively in terms of the square of a length unit, the cube of a length unit, and a mass unit divided by the cube of a length unit.

3C. **Apply knowledge of place value and other number properties to develop techniques of mental mathematics and computational estimation**

Mental math and computational estimation techniques are often closely linked. Even modestly lengthy numbers can make mental calculation impossible in any reasonable amount of time. For instance, although relatively simple algorithms exist for multiplying numbers like 24 and 30, multiplication of numbers that involve many more places can be virtually impossible. Thus, good estimation skills are an integral part of much of mental math. Although estimation cannot provide exact answers generally, it can provide a way to check exact answers for reasonableness.

The most common estimation strategies taught in schools involve replacing numbers with ones that are simpler to compute with. These methods include **rounding off**, **front-end digit estimation** and **compensation**. Although rounding off is done to a specific place value (e.g., nearest ten or hundred), front-end estimation involves rounding off or truncating to whatever place value the first digit in a number represents. The following example uses front-end estimation.

Example: Estimate the answer:

$$\frac{58 \times 810}{1989}$$

By letting 58 become 60, 810 become 800, and 1989 become 2000, the following simplified expression can be evaluated (even mentally):

$$\frac{60 \times 800}{2000} = 24$$

Compensation involves replacing different numbers in different ways so that one change can more or less compensate for the other. For example, one might take the addition of 32 and 53 and convert this to the addition of 30 and 55, which are slightly easier to handle mentally. Here, both numbers are replaced in a way that minimizes the change; one number is increased and the other is decreased.

Another estimation strategy is to **estimate a range** for the correct answer. For example, given the addition 458 + 873, note the following inequalities:

$$458 + 873 > 400 + 800 = 1200$$
$$458 + 873 < 500 + 900 = 1400$$

Thus, one can estimate that the sum of 458 and 873 lies in the range of 1200 to 1400.

Converting to an **equivalent fraction, decimal, or percentage** can often be helpful. For example, to calculate 25% of 520, realize that 25% = 1/4 and simply divide 520 by 4 to get 130.

Clustering is a useful strategy when dealing with a set of numbers. Similar numbers can be clubbed together to simplify computation, as with the example addition below.

$$1210 + 655 + 1178 + 683 + 628 + 1223 + 599$$

Rewrite as follows:

$$600 + 600 + 600 + 600 + 1200 + 1200 + 1200.$$

Thus, an estimate of the sum is 6,000. (The exact value is 6176.)

Clubbing together **compatible numbers** is a variant of clustering. Here, instead of similar numbers, numbers that together produce easy-to-compute numbers are clubbed together. For instance, consider the following:

$$5 + 17 + 25 + 23 + 40 = (5+25) + (17+23) + 40$$

Often a problem does not require exact computation. An estimate may sometimes be all that is needed to solve a word problem as in the example below. Therefore, **assessing the needed level of precision** in a particular situation is an important skill.

Example: Janet goes into a store to purchase a CD on sale for $13.95. While shopping, she sees two pairs of shoes, prices $19.95 and $14.50. She only has $50. Can she purchase everything? (Assume there is no sales tax.)

Solve by rounding up to the nearest dollar:

$19.95 → $20.00
$14.50 → $15.00
$13.95 → $14.00
$49.00   Yes, she can purchase the CD and both pairs of shoes.

3D. **Apply knowledge of counting techniques such as permutations and combinations to quantify situations and solve problems**

For a discussion of permutations and combinations, see **Competency 013**.

3E. **Apply properties of the real numbers to solve a variety of theoretical and applied problems**

The set of real numbers is a crucial component of innumerable mathematical problems. Selection of the appropriate subset and representation of the real numbers, as well as accurate calculation in accordance with the characteristics of that subset, are critical to correctly modeling and solving problems. The other skill sections in this competency, as well as numerous other sections throughout the guide, provide example problems that illustrate the proper use of real numbers in modeling and solving problems in a variety of mathematical contexts. The example problems below also illustrates the use of real numbers.

Example: If a, b, and c are positive real numbers, prove that $c(a+b) = (b+a)c$.

Use the properties of the set of real numbers.

$$c(a+b) = c(b+a)$$ Additive commutativity
$$= cb + ca$$ Distributivity
$$= bc + ac$$ Multiplicative commutativity
$$= (b+a)c$$ Distributivity

The following examples illustrate the use of the properties of numbers (such as integers, fractions, decimals, percents, and ratios) in problem solving.

Example: The sum of two consecutive integers is 51, find the integers.

Let the consecutive integers be x and $(x + 1)$. Then,

$$x + (x + 1) = 51$$
$$2x + 1 = 51$$
$$2x = 50$$
$$x = 25$$

Thus, the numbers are 25 and 26.

Example: Find the item with the best unit price: $1.79 for 10 ounces,

$1.89 for 12 ounces, or, $5.49 for 32 ounces.

For each price and weight, find the ratio of these values. The item with the lowest price-to-unit ratio is the best value (i.e., it has the best unit price).

$$\frac{\$1.79}{10oz} = \$0.179 / oz$$

$$\frac{\$1.89}{12oz} = \$0.158 / oz$$

$$\frac{\$5.49}{32oz} = \$0.172 / oz$$

Thus, $1.89 for 12 ounces is the best price.

Example: An item that is on sale costs $18. The sale is 10% off the original price. What was the original price?

Let the original price of the item be x. Write the following equation to solve for x:

$$x - (10\%)x = x - 0.10x = \$18$$
$$0.90x = \$18$$
$$x = \$20$$

Thus, the original price of the item was $20.

Example: Two numbers have a ratio of 3:5. Find the numbers if the difference between their squares is 144.

Let the numbers be x and y. Then

$$\frac{y}{x} = \frac{3}{5} \text{ and } x^2 - y^2 = 144$$

Substituting $y = \frac{3}{5}x$ into the second equation yields

$$x^2 - \frac{9}{25}x^2 = 144$$
$$\frac{16}{25}x^2 = 144$$
$$x^2 = \frac{(144)(25)}{16} = 225$$
$$x = 15$$

Based on this result, y = 9. Thus, the numbers are 9 and 15.

DOMAIN II. PATTERNS AND ALGEBRA

Competency 004   **The teacher understands and uses mathematical reasoning to identify, extend, and analyze patterns and understands the relationships among variable, expressions, equations, inequalities, relations, and functions.**

This competency discusses various types of mathematical patterns and the use of inductive reasoning for understanding, extending and deriving rules for these patterns. This is followed by an explanation of what functions and relations are, different ways in which a function can be represented and the effect of transformations on functions.

4A.   Use inductive reasoning to identify, extend, and create patterns using concrete models, figures, numbers, and algebraic expressions

Inductive reasoning is the process of finding a pattern from a group of examples. Tabular, numeric, graphical, symbolic or even pictorial data sometimes contain inherent patterns and relationships. Identifying these patterns allows one to extend them and make predictions about data outside the given range.

A numerical sequence is a pattern of numbers arranged in a particular order. Inspection of a sequence sometimes reveals a particular rule that is followed in creating it. For instance, 1, 4, 9, 16... is a series that consists of the squares of the natural numbers. Using this rule, the next term in the series 25 can be found by squaring the next natural number 5.

Example: Find the next term in the series 1, 1, 2, 3, 5, 8,.....

Inspecting the terms in the series, one finds that every term in the series is a sum of the previous two terms.

Thus, the next term = 5 + 8 = 13.

This particular sequence is a well-known series named the Fibonacci sequence.

Other patterns can be created using algebraic variables. Patterns may also be pictorial. In each case, one can predict subsequent terms or find a missing term by first discovering the rule that governs the pattern.

<u>Example:</u> Find the next term in the sequence $ax^2y, ax^4y^2, ax^6y^3,....$

Inspecting the pattern we see that this is a geometric sequence with common ratio x^2y.

Thus, the next term = $ax^6y^3 \times x^2y = ax^8y^4$.

<u>Example</u>: Find the next term in the pattern:

Inspecting the pattern one observes that it has alternating squares and circles that include a number of hearts that increases by two for each subsequent term.

Hence, the next term in the pattern will be as follows:

Sometimes a diagram makes it easier to see the next number in a series. Take the following:

1 3 6 10 15

Organizing the diagram gives:

				*	* ** ***		
			*	* ** ***	** *** ****		
		*	* ** ***	** *** ****	*** **** *****		
	*	* **	** ***	*** ****	**** *****		
	*	**	***	****	*****		
Total	1	3	6	10	15		
# Added:	1	2	3	4	5		
	1st term	2nd term	3rd term	4th term	5th term	6th term	nth term

The 6th term will be 1 + 2 + 3 + 4 + 5 + 6 = 21
The 10th term will be 1 + 2 + 3 + 4 + 5 + 6 + 7 + 8 + 9 + 10 = 55
The nth terms will be 1 + 2 + 3 + 4 +..... + n

4B. **Formulate implicit and explicit rules to describe and construct sequences verbally, numerically, graphically, and symbolically**

The examples given in **Skill 4A** are those of sequences defined with the governing rules **implicit**, i.e. the rules have not been stated but can be discovered by studying the patterns. The task in each of the examples is to uncover the **explicit** rule that governs the sequence.

The most common **numerical patterns** based on explicit rules are arithmetic sequences and geometric sequences. In an arithmetic sequence, each term is separated from the next by a fixed number (e.g. 3, 6, 9, 12, 15...). In a geometric sequence, each term in the series is multiplied by a fixed number to get the next term (e.g. 3, 6, 12, 24, 28...)

Arithmetic Sequences
An arithmetic sequence is a set of numbers with a common difference between the terms. Terms and the distance between terms can be calculated using use the following formula:
$a_n = a_1 + (n-1)\,d$ where
a_1 = the first term
a_n = the nth term (general term)
n = the number of the term in the sequence
d = the common difference

The formula essentially expresses the arithmetic sequence as an **algebraic pattern** a_1, a_1+d, a_1+2d, a_1+3d .... and so on where any number can be substituted for a_1 and d to derive different numerical sequences.

<u>Example</u>: Find the 8th term of the arithmetic sequence 5, 8, 11, 14...

$a_n = a_1 + (n-1)d$
$a_1 = 5$ identify the 1st term
$d = 8 - 5 = 3$ find d
$a_8 = 5 + (8-1)3$ substitute
$a_8 = 26$

<u>Example</u>: Given two terms of an arithmetic sequence, find a_1 and d

$a_4 = 21$ $a_6 = 32$
$a_n = a_1 + (n-1)d$ $a_4 = 21$, $n = 4$
$21 = a_1 + (4-1)d$ $a_6 = 32$, $n = 6$
$32 = a_1 + (6-1)d$

$21 = a_1 + 3d$ solve the system of equations
$32 = a_1 + 5d$

  $32 = \ \ a_1 + 5d$
$\underline{-21 = -a_1 - 3d}$ multiply by -1
  $11 = \ \ \ \ \ \ \ \ \ 2d$ add the equations

$5.5 = d$

$21 = a_1 + 3(5.5)$ substitute $d = 5.5$ into either equation
$21 = a_1 + 16.5$
$a_1 = 4.5$

The sequence begins with 4.5 and has a common difference of 5.5 between numbers.

Geometric Sequences
A geometric sequence is a series of numbers in which a common ratio can be multiplied by a term to yield the next term. The common ratio can be calculated using the formula:

$$r = \frac{a_{n+1}}{a_n}$$ where r = common ratio and a_n = the nth term

The ratio is then used in the geometric sequence formula:

$$a_n = a_1 r^{n-1}$$

The formula essentially expresses the geometric sequence as an algebraic pattern $a_1, a_1r, a_1r^2, a_1r^3, a_1r^4$.... and so on where any numbers can be substituted for a1 and r to derive different numerical sequences.

Example: Find the 8th term of the geometric sequence 2, 8, 32, 128...

$r = \dfrac{a_{n+1}}{a_n}$ use common ratio formula to find the ratio

$r = \dfrac{8}{2}$ substitute $a_n = 2$, $a_{n+1} = 8$

$r = 4$

$a_n = a_1 \bullet r^{n-1}$ use $r = 4$ to solve for the 8th term

$a_8 = 2 \bullet 4^{8-1}$

$a_8 = 32,768$

Example: The seventh and fourth terms of a geometric sequence are $\dfrac{1}{64}$ and $\dfrac{1}{8}$ respectively. Find the first term and the common ratio.

$a_7 = \dfrac{1}{64}$ and $a_4 = \dfrac{1}{8}$

Dividing we get $\dfrac{a_7}{a_4} = \dfrac{\frac{1}{64}}{\frac{1}{8}} = \dfrac{1}{8}$

$a_n = a_1 r^{n-1}$

But $\dfrac{a_7}{a_4} = \dfrac{a_1 r^6}{a_1 r^3} = r^3$

Therefore, $r^3 = \dfrac{1}{8}$ and $r = \dfrac{1}{2}$

Now $a_4 = a_1 r^3 = \dfrac{1}{8}$

That is $a_1 \left(\dfrac{1}{8} \right) = \dfrac{1}{8}$

So $a_1 = 1$

First term = 1 and the common ratio is ½.

For pictorial and diagrammatic patterns that follow a certain rule, see **Skill 4A**.

4C. **Make, test, validate, and use conjectures about patterns and relationships in data presented in tables, sequences, or graphs**

In many cases, particularly with statistical data or data obtained experimentally, the patterns within the data may not be as exact as the rule-based patterns described above. One can still use a rule or algebraic relationship to describe the data as long as the deviation from the rule fits predetermined criteria. **Regression analysis** (see **Competency 14**) is used in statistics to fit a set of data to a formula and also to assess how good the fit is. Graphing the data is often a preliminary step in making conjectures about the kind of formula one can use to fit the data.

The extremely simplified example below gives an idea of how data can be described using an algebraic relationship.

Example: Kepler discovered a relationship between the average distance of a planet from the sun and the time it takes the planet to orbit the sun.

The following table shows the data for the six planets closest to the sun:

	Mercury	Venus	Earth	Mars	Jupiter	Saturn
Average distance, x	0.387	0.723	1	1.523	5.203	9.541
x^3	0.058	0.378	1	3.533	140.852	868.524
Time, y	0.241	0.615	1	1.881	11.861	29.457
y^2	0.058	0.378	1	3.538	140.683	867.715

Looking at the data in the table, we can assume that $x^3 = y^2$
We can conjecture the following function for Kepler's relationship:
$$y = \sqrt{x^3}$$

4D. **Give appropriate justification of the manipulation of algebraic expressions**

Since the variables in algebraic expressions represent numbers, algebraic processes follow the same logic used in numerical computations. The following **properties of real numbers** (where a, b, c, d are any real numbers) are useful for manipulation of algebraic expressions.

$a=a$	Reflexive property
$a + b$ is a unique real number	Closure property of addition
ab is a unique real number	Closure property of multiplication
If $a = b$, then $b = a$	Symmetric property
If $a = b$ and $b = c$, then $a = c$	Transitive property
If $a+b=c$ and $b=d$, then $a+d = c$	Substitution property
If $a=b$, then $ac = b - c$	Substitution property
If $a=b$, then $ac = bc$	Multiplication property
If $a=b$ and $c \neq 0$, then $\dfrac{a}{c} = \dfrac{b}{c}$	Division property
$a + b = b + a$	Property of addition
$ab = ba$	Property of multiplication
$a+(b+c) = (a+b)+c$	Associative property of addition
$a(bc) = (ab)c$	Associative property of multiplication
$a+0=0+a=a$	Additive identity; the number 0 is called the additive identity
$a(1)=1(a)=a$	Associative identity; the number 1 is called the multiplicative identity
$a(b+c)=a(b)+a(c)$ and $(b+c)a=b(a)+c(a)$	Distributive Property

Just as for numbers, the **order of operations** must be followed when evaluating algebraic expressions. Remember the mnemonic **PEMDAS** (Please Excuse My Dear Aunt Sally) to follow these steps in order:

1. Simplify inside grouping characters such as parentheses, brackets, radicals, fraction bars, etc.
2. Multiply out expressions with exponents.
3. Do multiplication or division from left to right.

Note: Multiplication and division are equivalent even though multiplication is mentioned before division in the mnemonic PEMDAS.

4. Do addition or subtraction from left to right

Note: Addition and subtraction are equivalent even though addition is mentioned before subtraction in the mnemonic PEMDAS.

<u>Example:</u> Simplify. $3^3 - 5(b + 2)$

$$= 3^3 - 5b - 10$$

$$= 27 - 5b - 10 = 17 - 5b$$

An **algebraic formula** is an equation that describes a relationship among variables. To express one variable in terms of the others in a formula:

1. Combine like terms
2. Isolate the terms that contain the variable you wish to solve for
3. Isolate the variable (removing the coefficients)
4. Substitute the answer into the original equation and verify

<u>Example:</u> Given the equation $2(5x + z) = 30x + 3y + 10$, find the value of x in terms of y and z.

1. Combine like terms
   Expand the equation by removing the parentheses using the distributive property
   $10x + 2z = 30x + 3y + 10$
   $10x - 10x + 2z = 30x - 10x + 3y + 10$ (subtract $10x$ from both sides)
   $2z = 20x + 3y + 10$

2. Isolate the terms that contain the variable x
   $2z - 3y - 10 = 20x + 3y - 3y + 10 - 10$ (subtract $3y$ and 10 from both sides)
   $2z - 3y - 10 = 20x$

3. Isolate the variable (divide both sides by the coefficient)
   $2z - 3y - 10 = 20x$
   $$\frac{2z - 3y - 10}{20} = x$$

Example: Given that the relationship of voltage, V, applied across a material with electrical resistance, R, when a current, I, is flowing through the material is expressed by the formula V = IR. Find the resistance of the material if a current of 10 milliamps flows through it when the applied voltage is 2 volts.

$$V = IR. \text{ Solve for R.}$$
$$IR = V;$$
$$R = V/I$$

Substituting the values of the voltage and current in R = V/I, we get,

$$R = \frac{2}{10^1 \times 10^{-3}}$$
$$R = \frac{2}{10^{-2}}$$
$$R = 2 \times 10^2$$
$$R = 200 \text{ ohms}$$

Example: Given the formula I = PRT, where I is the simple interest on an amount P, the principal, deposited at the rate of R % for T years, find what principal must be deposited to yield an interest of $586.00 over a period of 2 years at the interest of 23.5%.

$$I = PRT$$

Solving for P, $P = \dfrac{I}{RT}$

Substituting I = 586; R = 23.5% = 0.235 and T = 2 in the above formula we get

$$P = \frac{586}{0.235 \times 2} = \frac{586}{0.47} \qquad \text{Substitute.}$$

$$P = \frac{586}{0.47} = 1246.80 = \$1246.80$$

Check; I = PRT; $1246.8 \times 0.235 \times 2 = 586$

4E. **Illustrate the concept of a function using concrete models, tables, graphs, and symbolic and verbal representations**

A relationship between two quantities can be shown using a table, graph, written description or symbolic rule. In the following example, the rule y= 9x describes the relationship between the total amount earned, y, and the total amount of $9 sunglasses sold, x.

A table using this data would appear as:

number of sunglasses sold	1	5	10	
total dollars earned	9	45	90	

Each *(x,y)* relationship between a pair of values is called the coordinate pair and can be plotted on a graph. The coordinate pairs *(1,9), (5,45), (10,90),* and *(15,135),* are plotted on the graph below.

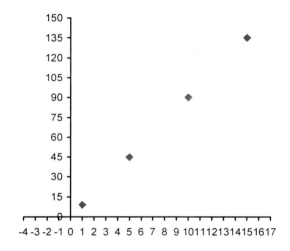

In this case, the graph shows a linear relationship. A linear relationship is one in which two quantities are proportional to each other. Doubling *x* also doubles *y*. On a graph, a straight line depicts a linear relationship.

The function or relationship between two quantities may be analyzed to determine how one quantity depends on the other. Any set of ordered pairs of numbers, however, do not constitute a mathematical function.

A **relation** is any set of ordered pairs. The **domain** of a relation is the set containing all the first coordinates of the ordered pairs, and the **range** of a relation is the set containing all the second coordinates of the ordered pairs. A **function** is a relation in which each value in the domain corresponds to only one value in the range. Thus, although a function is necessarily a relation, not all relations are functions, since a relation is not bound by this rule.

Example: Which set illustrates a function?

A) { (0,1) (0,2) (0,3) (0,4) }
B) { (3,9) (−3,9) (4,16) (− 4,16)}
C) {(1,2) (2,3) (3,4) (1,4) }
{ (2,4) (3,6) (4,8) (4,16) }

Each number in the domain can only be matched with one number in the range. A is not a function because 0 is mapped to 4 different numbers in the range. In C, 1 is mapped to two different numbers. In D, 4 is also mapped to two different numbers. So answer is B.

A relation may also be described algebraically. An equation such as $y = 3x + 5$ describes a relation between the independent variable x and the dependent variable y. Thus, y is written as $f(x)$ "function of x." On a graph, use the **vertical line test** to check whether a relation is a function. If any vertical line intersects the graph of a relation in more than one point, then the relation is not a function.

Example: Determine whether the following graph depicts a function.

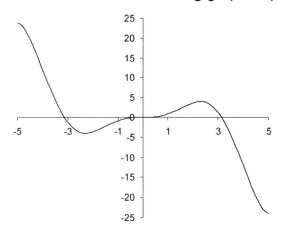

Use the vertical line test on the graph, as shown below. For every location of the vertical line, the plotted curve crosses the line only once. Therefore, the graph depicts a function.

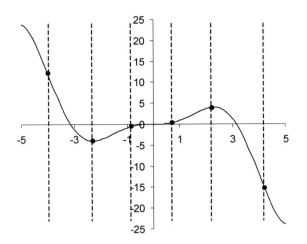

A **mapping** is essentially the same as a relation. Mappings (or maps) can be depicted using diagrams with arrows drawn from each element of the domain to the corresponding element (or elements) of the range. If two arrows originate from any single element in the domain, then the mapping is not a function. Likewise, for a function, if each arrow is drawn to a unique value in the range (that is, there are no cases where more than one arrow is drawn to a given value in the range), then the relation is one-to-one.

Example: Are the mappings shown below true functions?

f   h

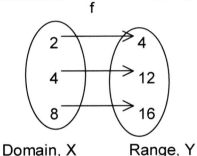   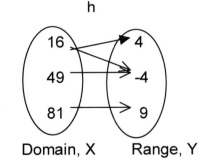

Domain, X   Range, Y   Domain, X   Range, Y

This is a "true" function.   This is not a "true" function.

4F. **Use transformations to illustrate properties of functions and relations and to solve problems**

Different types of **function transformations** affect the graph and characteristics of a function in predictable ways. The basic types of transformation are horizontal and vertical shift, horizontal and vertical scaling, and reflection. As an example of the types of transformations, we will consider transformations of the functions $f(x) = x^2$.

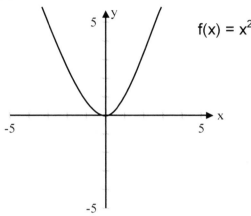

$f(x) = x^2$

Horizontal shifts take the form $g(x) = f(x \pm c)$. For example, we obtain the graph of the function $g(x) = (x + 2)^2$ by shifting the graph of $f(x) = x^2$ two units to the left. The graph of the function $h(x) = (x - 2)^2$ is the graph of $f(x) = x^2$ shifted two units to the right.

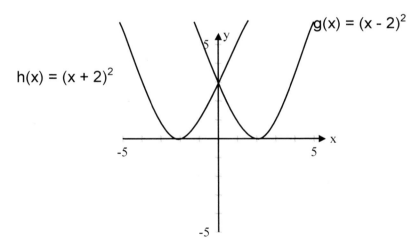

Vertical shifts take the form g(x) = f(x) ± c. For example, we obtain the graph of the function g(x) = (x²) − 2 by shifting the graph of f(x) = x² two units down. The graph of the function h(x) = (x²) + 2 is the graph of f(x) = x² shifted two units up.

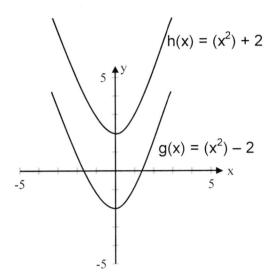

Horizontal scaling takes the form g(x) = f(cx). For example, we obtain the graph of the function g(x) = (2x)² by compressing the graph of f(x) = x² in the x-direction by a factor of two. If c > 1 the graph is compressed in the x-direction, while if 1 > c > 0 the graph is stretched in the x-direction.

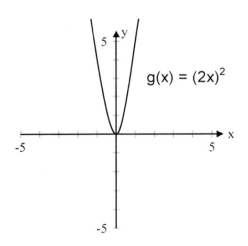

Competency 005   The teacher understands and uses linear functions to model and solve problems.

This competency discusses linear functions in detail. In addition to the various representations of linear functions, the use of linear functions, inequalities and systems to model data and methods used to solve linear inequalities and systems are discussed.

5A.   Demonstrate an understanding of the concept of linear function using concrete models, tables, graphs, and symbolic and verbal representations

A linear function is a function defined by the equation $y = mx + b$. With linear functions, the difference between successive y's for a constant change in x, is constant. It is determined by m, the slope of the line, otherwise known as the rate of change. The slope of a linear function measures rise over run, or how much y changes for every change of 1 in x. The slope is constant everywhere on the line.

<u>Example:</u> Consider the function $y = 2x + 1$. This function can be represented as a table of values as well as a graph as shown below. The relationship could also be written in words by saying "The value of y is equal to two times the value of x, plus one."

x	y
-2	-3
-1	-1
0	1
1	3
2	5

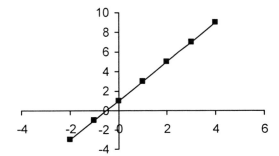

It is clear that all the points lie on a straight line and the difference between successive y's is constant. We, therefore, can determine any value of y by picking an x-coordinate and finding the corresponding point on the line. For example, if we want to know the value of y when x is equal to 4, we find the corresponding point and see that y is equal to 9.

5B. **Demonstrate an understanding of the connections among linear functions, proportions, and direct variation**

Proportion problems involve a relationship between two quantities characterized by a constant ratio. If the ratio of one variable to another is constant, this is known as **direct variation**. If the ratio of one variable to the reciprocal of the other variable is constant, this is known as **inverse variation**. Quantities can also vary with each other in other ways. For instance, the square of one variable and the cube root of another may be related through a constant ratio.

In the case of direct variation, the constant ratio, known as the **constant of proportionality**, corresponds to the slope of a linear function:

$y = kx$ where k is a constant, $k \neq 0$.

k is the slope of the straight line that represents this relationship graphically.

Example: If y varies directly as x and y = –8 when x = 4, find y when x = 11

First find the constant of variation, k.

$$k = \frac{y}{x} = \frac{-8}{4} = -2$$

Thus y = kx = -2x

For x = 11, y = –2(11) = –22

Example: If $30 is paid for 5 hours work, how much would be paid for 19 hours work?

Since pay is varies directly with work:
$30 = c(5 hours) where c is the constant of proportionality.

Solving for *c* which is the hourly pay rate in this case, we find that *c* = \$6/hour.

Thus, pay for 19 hours of work = (\$6/hour) (19 hours) = \$114. This could also be done

as a proportion:
$$\frac{\$30}{5} = \frac{y}{19}$$

$$5y = \$570$$
$$y = \$114$$

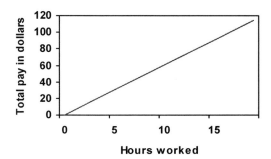

5C.   Determine the linear function that best models a set of data

See **Competency 14** for discussion of regression analysis, a statistical method used to fit a set of data to a particular function.

5D.   Analyze the relationship between a linear equation and its graph

First degree equations have exponents no greater than one and are also known as **linear equations** because their graphs are straight lines.

To graph a first degree equation, find both one point on the line and the slope of the line. The best way to find a point and the slope is to solve the equation for y. A linear equation that has been solved for y is in **slope intercept form, y = mx+b**. The point (0,**b**) is where the line intersects with the y-axis, **b is the y-intercept** and **m is the slope of the line.**

Another way to graph a linear equation is to find any two points on the line and connect them. To find points on the line, substitute any number for x, solve for y, then repeat with another number for x. Often the two easiest points to find are the intercepts. To find the intercepts, substitute 0 for x and solve for y, then substitute 0 for y and solve for x. Note that this method will only work when the slope is a nonzero and defined. It will not work for vertical and horizontal lines as defined below.

Remember that graphs will go up as they go to the right when the slope is positive. Negative slopes make the lines go down as they go to the right.
If the equation solves to **x = any number**, then the graph is a **vertical line**. It only has an x intercept. Its slope is **undefined**.

If the equation solves to **y = any number**, then the graph is a **horizontal line**. It only has an y intercept. Its slope is 0 (zero).

To graph **an inequality**, solve the inequality for y. This gets the inequality in the **slope intercept form**, (for example: $y < mx + b$). The point (0,b) is the y-intercept and m is the line's slope.

- If the inequality solves to **x** >, ≥, < **or** ≤ **any number**, then the graph includes a **vertical line**.

- If the inequality solves to **y** >, ≥, < **or** ≤ **any number**, then the graph includes a **horizontal line**.

When graphing a linear inequality, the line will be dotted if the inequality sign is < or >. If the inequality signs are either ≥ or ≤, the line on the graph will be a solid line. Shade above the line when the inequality sign is ≥ or >. Shade below the line when the inequality sign is < or ≤. Inequalities of the form $x >, x ≤, x <,$ or $x ≥$ number, draw a vertical line (solid or dotted). Shade to the right for > or ≥. Shade to the left for < or ≤. Remember: **Dividing or multiplying by a negative number will reverse the direction of the inequality sign.**

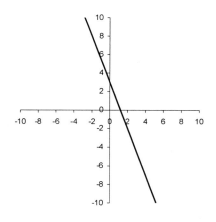

$$5x + 2y = 6$$
$$y = -5/2\,x + 3$$

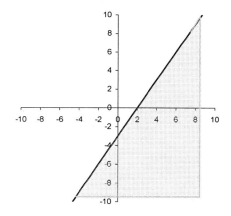

$$3x - 2y \geq 6$$
$$y \leq 3/2\,x - 3$$

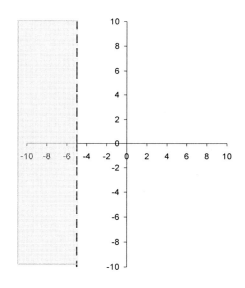

$$3x + 12 < -3$$
$$x < -5$$

Example: Sketch the graph of the line represented by $2x + 3y = 6$.

Let $x = 0 \to 2(0) + 3y = 6$
$\to 3y = 6$
$\to y = 2$
$\to (0,2)$ is the y intercept.

Let $y = 0 \to 2x + 3(0) = 6$
$\to 2x = 6$
$\to x = 3$
$\to (3,0)$ is the x intercept.

Let $x = 1 \to 2(1) + 3y = 6$
$\to 2 + 3y = 6$
$\to 3y = 4$
$\to y = \dfrac{4}{3}$
$\to \left(1, \dfrac{4}{3}\right)$ is the third point.

Plotting the three points on the coordinate system, we get the following:

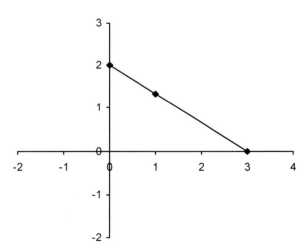

5E. Use linear functions, inequalities, and systems to model problems

Many real world situations involve linear relationships. One example is the relationship between distance and time traveled when a car is moving at a constant speed. The relationship between the price and quantity of a bulk item bought at a store is also linear assuming that the unit price remains constant. These relationships can be expressed using the equation of a straight line and the slope is often used to describe a constant or average rate of change expressed in miles per hour or dollars per year for instance. Where the line intercepts the x- and y- axis indicates a starting point or a point at which values change from positive to negative or negative to positive.

Example: A man drives a car at a speed of 30 mph along a straight road. Express the distance d traveled by the man as a function of the time t assuming the man's initial position is d_0. The equation relating d and t is given by:

$$d = 30t + d_0$$

Notice that this equation is in the familiar slope-intercept form $y = mx + b$. In this case, time t (in hours) is the independent variable, the distance d (in miles) is the dependent variable. The **slope** is the **rate of change** of distance with time, i.e. the speed (in mph). The **y-intercept** or intercept on the distance axis d_0 represents the **initial position** of the car at the start time $t = 0$.

The above equation is plotted below with $d_0 = 15$ miles (the point on the graph where the line crosses the y-axis).

$$d = 30t + 15$$

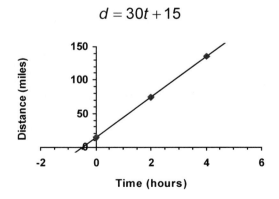

The **x-intercept** or intercept on the time axis represents the time at which the car would have been at $d = 0$ assuming it was traveling with the same speed before $t = 0$. This value can be found by setting d=0 in the equation:

$$0 = 30t + 15$$
$$30t = -15$$
$$t = \frac{-15}{30} = -\frac{1}{2}\text{hr}$$

This simply means that if the car was at $d = 15$ miles when we started measuring the time ($t = 0$), it was at $d = 0$ miles half an hour before that.

Example: A model for the distance traveled by a migrating monarch butterfly looks like $f(t) = 80t$, where t represents time in days.

We interpret this to mean that the average speed of the butterfly is 80 miles per day and distance traveled may be computed by substituting the number of days traveled for t. In a linear function, there is a **constant** rate of change.

Example: The town of Verdant Slopes has been experiencing a boom in population growth. By the year 2000, the population had grown to 45,000, and by 2005, the population had reached 60,000. Using the formula for slope as a model, find the average rate of change in population growth, expressing your answer in people per year. Then using the average rate of change determined, predict the population of Verdant Slopes in the year 2010.

Let t represent the time and p represent population growth. The two observances are represented by (t_1, p_1) and (t_2, p_2)

1st observance = (t_1, p_1) = (2000, 45000)
2nd observance = (t_2, p_2) = (2005, 60000)

Use the formula for slope to find the average rate of change.

$$\text{Rate of change} = \frac{p_2 - p_1}{t_2 - t_1}$$

$$= \frac{60000 - 45000}{2005 - 2000}$$

$$= \frac{15000}{5} = 3000 \text{ people / year}$$

The average rate of change in population growth for Verdant Slopes between the years 2000 and 2005 was 3000 people/year.

The population of Verdant Slopes can be predicted using the following:

3000 people/year x 5 years = 15,000 people
60000 people + 15000 people = 75,000 people

At a continuing average rate of growth of 3000 people/year, the population of Verdant Slopes could be expected to reach 75,000 by the year 2010.

Example: The YMCA wants to sell raffle tickets to raise at least $32,000. If they must pay $7,250 in expenses and prizes out of the money collected from the tickets, how many tickets worth $25 each must they sell?

Since they want to raise at least $32,000, that means they would be happy to get $32,000 or more. This requires an inequality.

Let x = number of tickets sold
Then $25x$ = total money collected for x tickets

Total money minus expenses is greater than $32,000.
$25x - 7250 \geq 32000$

$25x \geq 39250$

$x \geq 1570$

If they sell 1,570 tickets or more, they will raise AT LEAST $32,000.

5F. **Use a variety of representations and methods (e.g., numerical methods, tables, graphs, algebraic techniques) to solve systems of linear equations and inequalities**

Problems with more than one unknown quantity may be modeled and solved using **linear systems of equations and inequalities**. Some examples are given below.

Example: Farmer Greenjeans bought 4 cows and 6 sheep for $1700. Mr. Ziffel bought 3 cows and 12 sheep for $2400. If all the cows were the same price and all the sheep were another price, find the price charged for a cow or for a sheep.

Let x = price of a cow
Let y = price of a sheep

Then Farmer Greenjeans' equation would be: $4x + 6y = 1700$
Mr. Ziffel's equation would be: $3x + 12y = 2400$

To solve by **addition-subtraction**:

Multiply the first equation by $^-2$: $^-2(4x + 6y = 1700)$
Keep the other equation the same : $(3x + 12y = 2400)$
By doing this, the equations can be added to each other to eliminate one variable and solve for the other variable.

$$^-8x - 12y = ^-3400$$
$$\underline{3x + 12y = 2400} \qquad \text{Add these equations.}$$
$$^-5x \qquad = ^-1000$$

$x = 200 \leftarrow$ the price of a cow was $200.
Solving for y, $y = 150 \leftarrow$ the price of a sheep, $150.

(This problem can also be solved by substitution or determinants.)

Example: Mrs. Allison bought 1 pound of potato chips, a 2-pound beef roast, and 3 pounds of apples for a total of $8.19. Mr. Bromberg bought a 3-pound beef roast and 2 pounds of apples for $9.05. Kathleen Kaufman bought 2 pounds of potato chips, a 3-pound beef roast, and 5 pounds of apples for $13.25. Find the per pound price of each item.

To solve by **substitution**:

Let x = price of a pound of potato chips
Let y = price of a pound of roast beef
Let z = price of a pound of apples

Mrs. Allison's equation would be: $1x + 2y + 3z = 8.19$
Mr. Bromberg's equation would be: $3y + 2z = 9.05$
K. Kaufman's equation would be: $2x + 3y + 5z = 13.25$

Take the first equation and solve it for x. (This was chosen because x is the easiest variable to get alone in this set of equations). This equation would become:

$$x = 8.19 - 2y - 3z$$

Substitute this expression into the other equations in place of the letter x:

$$3y + 2z = 9.05 \leftarrow \text{ equation 2}$$
$$2(8.19 - 2y - 3z) + 3y + 5z = 13.25 \leftarrow \text{ equation 3}$$

Simplify the equation by combining like terms:

$$3y + 2z = 9.05 \leftarrow \text{ equation 2}$$
$$-1y - 1z = -3.13 \leftarrow \text{equation 3}$$

Solve equation 3 for either y or z:

* $y = 3.13 - z$ Substitute this into equation 2 for y:

$$3(3.13 - z) + 2z = 9.05 \leftarrow \text{ equation 2}$$
$$-1y - 1z = -3.13 \leftarrow \text{ equation 3}$$

Combine like terms in equation 2:

$$9.39 - 3z + 2z = 9.05$$
$$z = \$0.34 \quad \text{per pound price of apples}$$

Substitute .34 for z in the * equation above to solve for y:
    $y = 3.13 - z$ becomes $y = 3.13 - .34$, so
    $y = \$2.79$ = per pound price of roast beef

Substituting .34 for z and 2.79 for y in one of the original equations, solve for x :

$1x + 2y + 3z = 8.19$
$1x + 2(2.79) + 3(.34) = 8.19$
$x + 5.58 + 1.02 = 8.19$
$x + 6.60 = 8.19$
$x = \$1.59$ per pound of potato chips

$(x, y, z) = (\$1.59, \$2.79, \$0.34)$

Example: Aardvark Taxi charges \$4 initially plus \$1 for every mile traveled. Baboon Taxi charges \$6 initially plus \$.75 for every mile traveled. Determine the mileage at which it becomes cheaper to ride with Baboon Taxi than it is to ride Aardvark Taxi.

Aardvark Taxi's equation: $y = 1x + 4$
Baboon Taxi's equation : $y = .75x + 6$
Use substitution: $.75x + 6 = x + 4$
Multiply both sides by 4: $3x + 24 = 4x + 16$
Solve for x : $8 = x$

This tells you that, at 8 miles, the total charge for the two companies is the same. If you compare the charge for 1 mile, Aardvark charges \$5 and Baboon charges \$6.75. Therefore, Aardvark Taxi is cheaper for distances up to 8 miles, but Baboon is cheaper for distances greater than 8 miles.

This problem can also be solved by graphing the 2 equations.

$y = 1x + 4$ $y = .75x + 6$

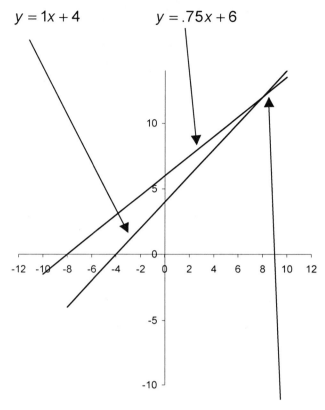

The lines intersect at (8, 12), therefore at 8 miles, both companies charge $12. For distances less than 8 miles, Aardvark Taxi charges less (the graph is below Baboon). For distances greater than 8 miles, Aardvark charges more (the graph is above Baboon).

Linear programming is the optimization of a linear quantity that is subject to constraints expressed as linear equations or inequalities. It is often used in various industries, ecological sciences and governmental organizations to determine or project production costs, the amount of pollutants dispersed into the air, etc. The key to most linear programming problems is to organize the information in the word problem into a chart or graph of some type.

Example: A printing manufacturer makes two types of printers: a Printmaster and a Speedmaster printer. The Printmaster requires 10 cubic feet of space, weighs 5,000 pounds and the Speedmaster takes up 5 cubic feet of space and weighs 600 pounds. The total available space for storage before shipping is 2,000 cubic feet and the weight limit for the space is 300,000 pounds. The profit on the Printmaster is $125,000 and the profit on the Speedmaster is $30,000. How many of each machine should be stored to maximize profitability and what is the maximum possible profit?

First, let x represent the number of Printmaster units sold and let y represent the number of Speedmaster units sold. Then, the equation for the space required to store the units is the following.

$$10x + 5y \leq 2000$$
$$2x + y \leq 400$$

Since the number of units for both models must be no less than zero, also impose the restrictions that $x \geq 0$ and $y \geq 0$. The restriction on the total weight can be expressed as follows.

$$5000x + 600y \leq 300000$$
$$25x + 3y \leq 1500$$

The expression for the profit P from sales of the printer units is the following.

$$P = \$125,000x + \$30,000y$$

The solution to this problem, then, is found by maximizing P subject to the constraints given in the preceding inequalities, along with the constraints that $x \geq 0$ and $y \geq 0$. The equations are grouped below for clarity.

$$x \geq 0$$
$$y \geq 0$$
$$2x + y \leq 400$$
$$25x + 3y \leq 1500$$
$$P = \$125,000x + \$30,000y$$

The two inequalities in two variables are plotted in the graph below. The shaded region represents the set of solutions that obey both inequalities. (Note that the shaded region in fact only includes points where both x and y are whole numbers.)

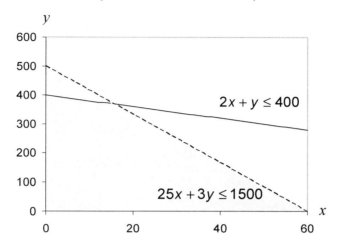

Note that the border of the shaded region that is formed by the two inequalities includes the solutions that constitute the maximum value of y for a given value of x. Note also that x cannot exceed 60 (since it would violate the second inequality). The solution to the problem, then, must lie on the border of the shaded region, since the border spans all the possible solutions that maximize the use of space and weight for a given number x.

To visualize the solution, plot the profit as a function of the solutions to the inequalities that lie along the border of the shaded area.

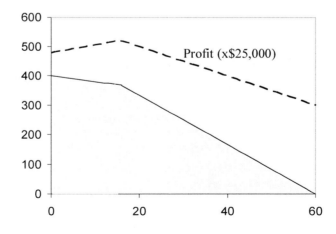

The profit curve shows a maximum at about $x = 16$. Test several values using a table to verify this result.

x	y	P (x$25,000)
15	370	519
16	366	519.2
17	358	514.6

Also double check to be sure that the result obeys the two inequalities.

$$2(16) + (366) = 398 \le 400$$
$$25(16) + 3(366) = 1498 \le 1500$$

Thus, the optimum result is storage of 16 Printmaster and 366 Speedmaster printer units.

Example: Sharon's Bike Shoppe can assemble a 3-speed bike in 30 minutes and a 10-speed bike in 60 minutes. The profit on each bike sold is $60 for a 3 speed or $75 for a 10-speed bike. How many of each type of bike should it assemble during an 8-hour day (480 minutes) to maximize the possible profit? Total daily profit must be at least $300.

Let x be the number of 3-speed bikes and y be the number of 10-speed bikes. Since there are only 480 minutes to use each day, the first inequality is the following.

$$30x + 60y \le 480$$
$$x + 2y \le 16$$

Since the total daily profit must be at least $300, then the second inequality can be written as follows, where P is the profit for the day.

$$P = \$60x + \$75y \ge \$300$$
$$4x + 5y \ge 20$$

To visualize the problem, plot the two inequalities and show the potential solutions as a shaded region.

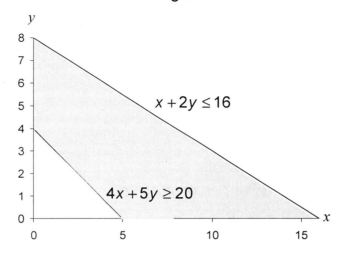

The solution to the problem is the ordered pair of whole numbers in the shaded area that maximizes the daily profit. The profit curve is added as shown below.

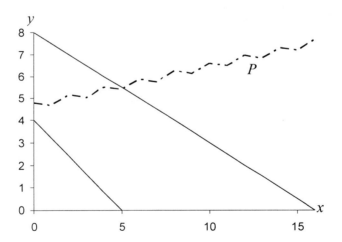

Based on the above plot, it is clear that the profit is maximized for the case where only 3-speed bikes (corresponding to x) are manufactured. Thus, the correct solution can be found by solving the first inequality for $y = 0$.

$$x + 2(0) \leq 16$$
$$x \leq 16$$

The manufacture of 16 3-speed bikes (and no 10-speed bikes) maximizes profit to $960 per day.

5G. Demonstrate an understanding of the characteristics of linear models and the advantages and disadvantages of using a linear model in a given situation

See **Skills 5E** and **5F** for examples of many real-life situations (time and distance, unit price and cost) that can be modeled exactly using linear functions. One must keep in mind, however, that **the domain of the problem is typically much smaller than the domain of the function** used to model it. For a problem where time in hours is the independent variable, for instance, time = -5 hours or time = 10,000 hours is likely to be outside the domain of the problem. The linear function modeling the problem, however, spans all real values of time.

In some cases, a problem may not be exactly linear but close enough for all practical purposes (the rate of population growth) or a non-linear problem may approximate linear behavior over a specific range of a variable. In this case one can use a linear function to model the problem under conditional constraints.

In other cases, a linear model may be a useful starting point for a situation where there is no other available model. The model can then be refined through successive iterations to develop a more accurate one.

Competency 006   The teacher understands and uses nonlinear functions and relations to model and solve problems

This competency discusses nonlinear functions such as quadratic, polynomial, rational, radical and exponential functions. Graphs and properties of different functions and their use in the modeling and solving of various problems are considered.

6A.   **Use a variety of methods to investigate the roots (real and complex), vertex, and symmetry of a quadratic function or relation**

A quadratic equation is expressed in the form $ax^2 + bx + c = 0$, where a, b, and c are real numbers and $a \neq 0$. The degree of a quadratic equation (i.e. the highest exponent of the unknown variable x) is 2. Examples of quadratic equations are $5x^2 + 6x + 7 = 0$, $9x^2 - 4 = 0$, $2x^7 - 3x = 0$.

If $p(x) = 0$ is a quadratic equation, then the zeros of the polynomial $p(x)$ are called the roots or solutions of equation $p(x) = 0$. Finding the roots of a quadratic equation is known as solving for "x".

There are several different methods for solving quadratic equations:

1) Factoring
2) Completing the Square
3) Quadratic Formula
4) Graphing

Factoring is only applicable for quadratic equations where the polynomial can be expressed as a product of linear factors.

If a quadratic polynomial $ax^2 + bx + c = 0$ is expressible as a product of two linear factors, say (px + q) and (rx + s), where p, q, r, s are real numbers, then $ax^2 + bx + c = 0$ may be rewritten as

$$(px + q)(rx + s) = 0$$

This implies that either of the two factors must be equal to zero:
$$(px + q) = 0 \text{ or } (rx + s) = 0$$

Solving these linear equations, we get the possible roots of the given quadratic equation as:

$$x = -\frac{q}{p} \text{ and } x = -\frac{s}{r}$$

<u>Example</u>: Solve the following equation.

$$x^2 + 10x - 24 = 0$$
$$(x + 12)(x - 2) = 0 \qquad \text{Factor.}$$
$$x + 12 = 0 \text{ or } x - 2 = 0 \qquad \text{Set each factor equal to 0.}$$
$$x = -12 \qquad x = 2 \qquad \text{Solve.}$$

Check:

$$x^2 + 10x - 24 = 0$$

$$(-12)^2 + 10(-12) - 24 = 0 \qquad (2)^2 + 10(2) - 24 = 0$$
$$144 - 120 - 24 = 0 \qquad\qquad 4 + 20 - 24 = 0$$
$$0 = 0 \qquad\qquad\qquad\qquad 0 = 0$$

A quadratic equation may be solved by **completing the square**. To complete the square, the coefficient of the x^2 term must be 1.

To solve a quadratic equation using this method:

1. Isolate the x^2 and x terms.
2. Add half of the coefficient of the x term squared to both sides of the equation.
3. Finally take the square root of both sides and solve for x.

<u>Example</u>: Solve the following equation:

$$x^2 - 6x + 8 = 0$$

$$x^2 - 6x = -8 \qquad \text{Move the constant to the right side.}$$

$$x^2 - 6x + 9 = -8 + 9 \qquad \text{Add the square of half the coefficient}$$
$$\qquad\qquad\qquad\qquad\quad \text{of } x \text{ to both sides.}$$

$$(x - 3)^2 = 1 \qquad \text{Write the left side as a perfect square.}$$

$$x - 3 = \pm\sqrt{1} \qquad \text{Take the square root of both sides.}$$

$$x - 3 = 1 \qquad x - 3 = -1 \qquad \text{Solve.}$$

$$x = 4 \qquad\quad x = 2$$

Check:

$$x^2 - 6x + 8 = 0$$

$$4^2 - 6(4) + 8 = 0 \qquad\qquad 2^2 - 6(2) + 8 = 0$$
$$16 - 24 + 8 = 0 \qquad\qquad 4 - 12 + 8 = 0$$
$$0 = 0 \qquad\qquad\qquad\quad 0 = 0$$

To solve a quadratic equation using the **quadratic formula**, be sure that your equation is in the form $ax^2 + bx + c = 0$. Substitute the values of a, b and c into the formula:

$$x = \frac{-b \pm \sqrt{b^2 - 4ac}}{2a}$$

Simplify the result to find the answers.

The **discriminant** is the portion of the quadratic formula which is found under the square root sign; that is b^2 - 4ac. The discriminant can be used to determine the nature of the solution of a quadratic equation.

1)   If $b^2 - 4ac < 0$, there are **no real roots** and **two complex roots** that include the imaginary number I (square root of -1).

2)   If $b^2 - 4ac = 0$, there is only **one real rational root**.
3)   If $b^2 - 4ac > 0$ and also a perfect square, there are **two real rational roots.** (There are no longer any radical signs.)

4)   If $b^2 - 4ac > 0$ and not a perfect square, then there are **two real irrational roots.** (There are still unsimplified radical signs.)

Example: Find the value of the discriminant for the equation $2x^2 - 5x + 6 = 0$. Then determine the number and nature of the solutions of that quadratic equation.
a = 2, b = ⁻5, c = 6 so $b^2 - 4ac = (^-5)^2 - 4(2)(6) = 25 - 48 = {}^-23$.

Since ⁻23 is a negative number, there are **no real roots** and **two complex roots** .

$$x = \frac{5}{4} + \frac{i\sqrt{23}}{4}, \qquad x = \frac{5}{4} - \frac{i\sqrt{23}}{4}$$

Example: Find the value of the discriminant for the equation $3x^2 - 12x + 12 = 0$. Then determine the number and nature of the solutions of the quadratic equation.

$a = 3$, $b = {}^-12$, $c = 12$ so $b^2 - 4ac = ({}^-12)^2 - 4(3)(12) = 144 - 144 = 0$

Since 0 is the value of the discriminant, there is only **1 real rational root** $x = 2$.

Example: Solve the following equation using the quadratic formula:
$$3x^2 = 7 + 2x \rightarrow 3x^2 - 2x - 7 = 0$$

$$a = 3 \quad b = {}^-2 \quad c = {}^-7$$

$$x = \frac{-({}^-2) \pm \sqrt{({}^-2)^2 - 4(3)({}^-7)}}{2(3)}$$

$$x = \frac{2 \pm \sqrt{4 + 84}}{6}$$

$$x = \frac{2 \pm \sqrt{88}}{6}$$

$$x = \frac{2 \pm 2\sqrt{22}}{6}$$

$$x = \frac{1 \pm \sqrt{22}}{3}$$

The general technique for **graphing quadratics** is the same as for graphing linear equations. Graphing a quadratic equation, however, results in a parabola instead of a straight line.

The general form of a quadratic function is $y = ax^2 + bx + c$. Once a function is identified as quadratic, it is helpful to recognize several features that can indicate the form of the graph. The parabola has an axis of symmetry along $x = -\dfrac{b}{2a}$ which is the x-coordinate of the vertex (turning point) of the graph.

This can be understood more clearly if we consider an alternate form of a quadratic equation, the standard form for a parabola
$$y = a(x - h)^2 + k$$
where (h, k) denote the coordinates of the vertex of the parabola.

Transforming the general form $y = ax^2 + bx + c$ into the above form,

$$y = ax^2 + bx + c$$

$$\Rightarrow y = a(x^2 + \frac{b}{a}x) + c$$

$$\Rightarrow y = a(x^2 + 2.\frac{b}{2a}x + (\frac{b}{2a})^2) - \frac{b^2}{4a} + c$$

$$\Rightarrow y = a(x + \frac{b}{2a})^2 - \frac{b^2}{4a} + c$$

Thus the coordinates of the vertex are given by $(-\frac{b}{2a}, -\frac{b^2}{4a} + c)$.

Example: Graph $y = 3x^2 + x - 2$

Expressing this function in standard form we get

$$y = 3(x + \frac{1}{6})^2 - \frac{25}{12}$$

Thus, the graph is a parabola with an axis of symmetry $x = -\frac{1}{6}$

and the vertex is located at the point $(-\frac{1}{6}, -\frac{25}{12})$.

x	$y = 3x^2 + x - 2$
-2	8
-1	0
0	-2
1	2
2	12

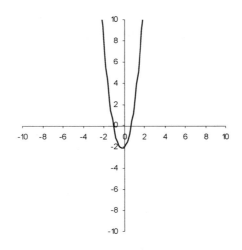

If the quadratic term is positive, then the parabola is concave up; if the quadratic term is negative, then the parabola is concave down. The function $-x^2 - 2x - 3$ is one such example and is shown below.

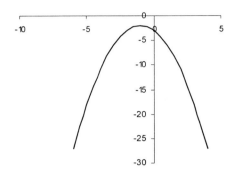

A quadratic function with two real roots (see example problems) will have two crossings of the *x*-axis. A quadratic function with one real root will graph as a parabola that is tangent to the *x*-axis. An example of such a quadratic function is shown in the example below for the function $x^2 + 2x + 1$. The function has a single real root at *x* = −1.

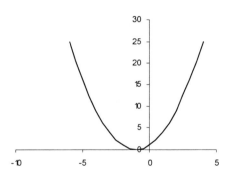

A quadratic function with no real roots will not cross the axis at any point. An example is the function $x^2 + 2x + 2$, which is plotted below.

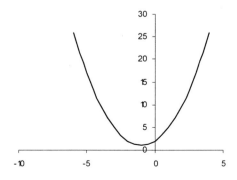

<u>Example</u>: Solve by graphing $x^2 - 8x + 15 = 0$

The roots of the polynomial $x^2 - 8x + 15$ are the x values for which the graph intersects the x-axis.

x	$y = x^2 - 8x + 15$
–2	35
–1	24
0	15
1	8
2	3

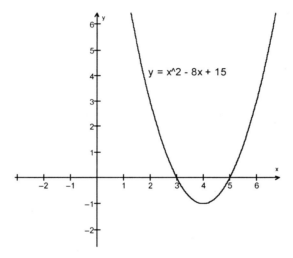

From the above graph, the *x*-intercepts or zeroes are 3 and 5. So the solutions of the given quadratic equation are 3 and 5.

To **graph a quadratic inequality**, graph the quadratic as if it were an equation; however, if the inequality has just a > or < sign, then make the curve dotted. Shade above the curve for > or ≥. Shade below the curve for < or ≤.

<u>Example</u>: $y < -x^2 + x - 2$

The quadratic function $-x^2 + x - 2$ is plotted with a dotted line since the inequality sign is $<$ and not $\leq$. Since y is "less than" this function, the shading is done below the curve.

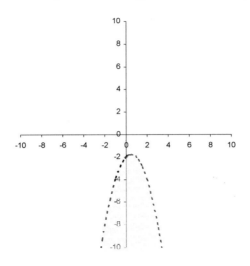

<u>Example</u>: $y \geq x^2 - 2x - 9$

The quadratic function $x^2 - 2x - 9$ is plotted with a solid line since the inequality sign is $\geq$. Since y is "greater than or equal to" this function, the shading is done above the curve.

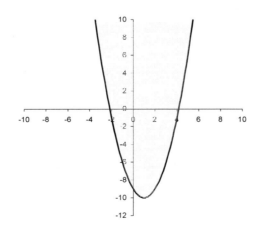

6B. **Demonstrate an understanding of the connections among geometric, graphic, numeric, and symbolic representations of quadratic functions**

See **Skill 6A.**

6C. **Analyze data and represent and solve problems involving exponential growth and decay**

An **exponential function** is defined by the equation $y = ab^x$, where a is the starting value, b is the growth factor, and x is the exponent of the growth factor. For exponential functions, the **ratio** between successive y's or outputs are **constant**. In other words, each y or output, is a constant multiple of the previous y.

If $a > 0$ and b is between 0 and 1 the graph of the exponential function will be decreasing or decaying.

If $a > 0$ and b is greater than 1, the graph will be increasing or growing.

Example: Graph the function $f(x) = 2^x - 4$.

The domain of the function is the set of all real numbers and the range is y > -4. Because the base is greater than 1, the function is increasing. The y-intercept of f(x) is (0,-3). The x-intercept of f(x) is (2,0). The horizontal asymptote of f(x) is y = -4.

Finally, to construct the graph of f(x) we find two additional values for the function. For example, f(-2) = -3.75 and f(3) = 4.

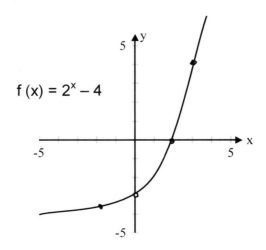

$f(x) = 2^x - 4$

Note that the horizontal asymptote of any exponential function of the form $g(x) = a^x + b$ is $y = b$. Note also that the graph of such exponential functions is the graph of $h(x) = a^x$ shifted b units up or down. Finally, the graph of exponential functions of the form $g(x) = a^{(x + b)}$ is the graph of $h(x) = a^x$ shifted b units left or right.

A quantity which grows by a fixed percent at regular intervals, i.e. in proportion to the existing amount, demonstrates **exponential growth**. If a population has a constant birth rate through the years and is not affected by food or disease, it has exponential growth. The birth rate alone controls how fast the population grows exponentially.

Example: A population of a city is 20,000 and it increases at an annual rate of 20%. What will be the population of the city after 10 years?

The formula for the growth is $y = a(1 + r)^t$
where a is the initial amount, r is the growth rate, and t is the number of time intervals

Here $a = 20000$ $r = 20\% = 0.2$ $t = 10$

Substituting the values,

$$\begin{aligned}
\text{Population Growth} = y &= 20000(1 + 0.2)^{10} \\
&= 20000(1 + 0.2)^{10} \\
&= 20000(1.2)^{10} \\
&= 20000(6.19) \\
&= 123800
\end{aligned}$$

So the population of the city after 10 years is 123,800.

What will be the population of the city after 50 years?

$$\begin{aligned}
\text{In 50 years, population} &= 20000(1 + 0.2)^{50} \\
&= 20000(1 + 0.2)^{50} \\
&= 20000(1.2)^{50} \\
&= 20000(9100.44) \\
&= 182008800
\end{aligned}$$

The population after 50 years will be 182,008,800.

Another example of exponential growth is the growth of money through compound-interest.

<u>Example:</u> How long will it take $2,000 to triple if it is invested at 15% compounded continuously?

Exponential growth formula for continuously compounding interest is

$$A = Pe^{rt}$$

where A is the amount of money in the account, P is Principal amount invested, r stands for rate of interest, t is the period in years, and e is the base of the natural log (an irrational number with value 2.71828…).

Substituting the given values in the formula:

$$A = Pe^{rt}$$
$$6000 = 2000e^{0.15t}$$
$$3 = e^{0.15t}$$

taking natural log of both sides,

$$\ln 3 = \ln e^{0.15t}$$

using the property of logarithm $\ln x^r = r \ln x$,

$$\ln 3 = 0.15t \, (\ln e)$$
$$\ln 3 = 0.15t \, (\text{since } \ln e = 1)$$

using the calculator to find the value of $\ln 3$,

$$1.098 = 0.15t$$
$$t = \frac{1.098}{0.15} = 7.3$$

Therefore, the amount of $2,000 is tripled in 7.3 years.

Exponential decay is decrease by a fixed percent at regular intervals of time. Radioactive decay is an example of this.

<u>Example:</u> If 40 grams of Iodine has reduced to 20 grams in 6 days, what is the rate of decay?

The formula for exponential decay is $Q = ae^{rt}$ where Q is the amount of material at time t, a is the initial amount, r is the decay rate and t is the time period in days.

$Q = ae^{rt}$

$20 = 40e^{r(6)}$ Isolate e

$0.5 = e^{6r}$ Take ln of both sides

$\ln 0.5 = 6r$ Solve for r

$\dfrac{\ln 0.5}{6} = r$

$r = -0.1155$ Note : r is negative because it is decay

rate of decay is $0.1155 = 11.55\%$

Example: A 10-gram sample of Einsteinium-254 decays radioactively with a half-life of about 276 days. What is the remaining mass of Einsteinium-254 after 5 years (assume each year is 365 days).

Use the exponential decay formula derived above, where $m(t)$ is the mass of Einsteinium in the sample at time t.

$$m(t) = Ce^{kt}$$

The initial mass of Einsteinium-254 is 10 grams. Use this to find the value of C.

$$m(0) = 10g = Ce^{k(0)} = C$$

Thus, C is 10 grams. To find k, note that after 276 days, the amount of remaining Einsteinium-254 must be half the initial amount.

$$m(276d) = (10g)e^{k(276d)} = 5g$$
$$e^{k(276d)} = \frac{1}{2}$$

Solve for k. Note that, to make the argument of the exponential dimensionless, the units of k should be inverse days.

$$\ln\left[e^{k(276d)}\right] = \ln\frac{1}{2}$$
$$(276d)k = \ln\frac{1}{2}$$
$$k = \frac{1}{276d}\ln\frac{1}{2}$$
$$k \approx -0.00251\frac{1}{d}$$

The complete expression for *m* is then the following, where *t* is in days.

$$m(t) \approx (10\text{g})e^{-0.00251t}$$

Finally, calculate the amount of Einsteinium remaining after 5 years (1,825 days).

$$m(1825) \approx (10\text{g})e^{-0.00251(1825)}$$
$$m(1825) \approx 0.102\text{g}$$

Thus, after 5 years, only about 0.102 grams of the initial sample remain.

6D. **Demonstrate an understanding of the connections among proportions, inverse variation, and rational functions**

For an introduction to proportion and variation, see **Skill 5B**. Here we will introduce rational functions and then show how inverse variation is expressed in the form of one.

A **rational function** can be written as the ratio of two polynomial expressions. A rational function is given in the form $f(x) = p(x)/q(x)$. In the equation, p (*x*) and q (*x*) both represent polynomial functions where q (*x*) does not equal zero.

Examples of rational functions are:

$$r(x) = \frac{x^2 + 2x + 4}{x - 3} \quad \text{and} \quad r(x) = \frac{x}{x - 3}$$ which is clearly the ratio of 2 polynomials.

The branches of rational functions approach asymptotes. Setting the denominator equal to zero and solving will give the value(s) of the **vertical asymptotes**(s) since the function will be undefined at this point. If the value of f (*x*) approaches *b* as the $|x|$ increases, the equation $y = b$ is a **horizontal asymptote**. To find the horizontal asymptote it is necessary to make a table of values for *x* that are to the right and left of the vertical asymptotes. The pattern for the horizontal asymptotes will become apparent as the $|x|$ increases.

If there is more than one vertical asymptote, remember to choose numbers to the right and left of each one in order to find the horizontal asymptotes and have sufficient points to graph the function.

<u>Example</u>: Graph $f(x) = \dfrac{3x+1}{x-2}$.

$x - 2 = 0$
$x = 2$

1. Set denominator $= 0$ to find the vertical asymptote.

x	$f(x)$
3	10
10	3.875
100	3.07
1000	3.007
1	$^-4$
$^-10$	2.417
$^-100$	2.93
$^-1000$	2.99

2. Make a table choosing numbers to the right and left of the vertical asymptote.

3. The pattern shows that as the $|x|$ increases $f(x)$ approaches the value 3, therefore a horizontal asymptote exists at $y = 3$

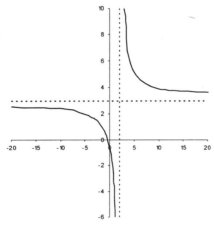

Note that x = 2 are excluded from the domain of the function and y = 3 is excluded from the range.

In some cases, the restriction on a rational function due to the denominator being zero will not be a vertical asymptote but simply a **hole in the graph**. This happens when the value of x that reduces the denominator to zero is also a zero of the numerator.

<u>Example</u>: Plot the function $\dfrac{x-2}{x^2-4}$.

Factoring the denominator, we see that the denominator goes to zero at x = -2 and x = 2.

$$\frac{x-2}{x^2-4} = \frac{x-2}{(x+2)(x-2)}$$

There is a **vertical asymptote at x = -2**. Since the function can be simplified to the form 1/(x+2) by canceling (x-2) from the numerator and denominator, there is no asymptote at x = 2. The point x = 2, however, must be excluded from the function. Hence, there is a **hole in the graph at x = 2**.

Studying the function, we see that for large values of x the function goes to zero. Thus there is a **horizontal asymptote at y = 0**.

X	Y
-6	-1/4
-4	-1/2
-3	-1
-2.5	-2
-1.5	2
-1	1
0	1/2
1	1/3
2	1/4 (location of hole)
3	1/5

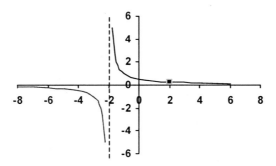

An **inverse variation** can be expressed by the formula

$xy = k$, where k is a constant, $k \neq 0$.

It is clear that $y = \dfrac{k}{x}$ is a rational function with a vertical asymptote at x = 0 and horizontal asymptote at y = 0 as shown in the example below. An inverse variation is typically represented by a rational function with a constant in the numerator and a power of the independent variable in the denominator.

<u>Example</u>: On a 546 mile trip from Miami to Charlotte, one car drove 65 mph while another car drove 70 mph. How does this affect the driving time for the trip?

This is an inverse variation, since increasing your speed should decrease your driving time. Use the equation

$t = \dfrac{d}{r}$ where t=driving time, r = speed and d = distance traveled.

(65 mph) t = 546 miles	and	(70 mph) t = 546 miles
t = 8.4 hours	and	t = 7.8 hours
slower speed, more time		faster speed, less time

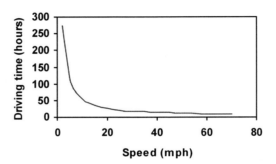

A quantity may also vary with different exponents of another quantity as shown in the examples below.

<u>Example:</u> A varies inversely as the square of R. When A = 2, R = 4. Find A if R = 10.

Since A varies inversely as the square of R,

$$A = \dfrac{k}{R^2} \text{ (equation 1), } k \text{ is a constant.}$$

Use equation 1 to find k when A = 2 and R = 4.

$$2 = \dfrac{k}{4^2} \rightarrow 2 = \dfrac{k}{16} \rightarrow k = 32 .$$

Substituting k = 32 into equation 1 with R =10, we get:
$$A = \dfrac{32}{10^2} \rightarrow A = \dfrac{32}{100} \rightarrow A = 0.32$$

6E. **Understand the effects of transformations such as $f(x \pm c)$ on the graph of a nonlinear function $f(x)$**

See **Skill 4F**.

6F. **Apply properties, graphs, and applications of nonlinear functions to analyze, model, and solve problems**

Quadratic equations and inequalities, described in **Skill 6A**, are the simplest nonlinear relationships that can be used to model real world problems. Several examples follow.

Example: A family is planning to add a new room to their house. They would like the room to have a length that is 10 ft more than the width and a total area of 375 sq. feet. Find the length and width of the room.

Let x be the width of the room.
Length of the room = x+10

Thus, $x(x + 10) = 375$
$x^2 + 10x - 375 = 0$

Factor the quadratic expression to solve the equation:
$x^2 + 25x - 15x - 375 = 0$ Break up the middle
$x(x + 25) - 15(x + 25) = 0$ term using factors of 375
$(x + 25)(x - 15) = 0$
$x = -25$ or $x = 15$

Since the dimension of a room cannot be negative, we choose the positive solution x=15. Thus, the width of the room is 15 ft and the length of the room is 25ft.

Example: The height of a projectile fired upward at a velocity of v meters per second from an original height of h meters is $y = h + vx - 4.9x^2$. If a rocket is fired from an original height of 250 meters with an original velocity of 4800 meters per second, find the approximate time the rocket would drop to sea level (a height of 0).

Substituting the height and velocity into the equation yields: $y = 250 + 4800x - 4.9x^2$. If the height at sea level is zero, then $y = 0$ so $0 = 250 + 4800x - 4.9x^2$. Solving for x could be done by using the quadratic formula.

$$x = \frac{-4800 \pm \sqrt{4800^2 - 4(-4.9)(250)}}{2(-4.9)}$$

$x \approx 979.53$ or $x \approx -0.05$ seconds

Since the time has to be positive, it will be approximately 980 seconds until the rocket reaches sea level.

Example: A family wants to enclose 3 sides of a rectangular garden with 200 feet of fence. A wall borders the fourth side of the garden. In order to have a garden with an area of **at least** 4800 square feet, find the dimensions the garden should be.

Existing Wall

Solution:
Let $x =$ distance
from the wall

x [   ] x

Then 2x feet of fence is used for these 2 sides. The side opposite the existing wall would use the remainder of the 200 feet of fence, that is, $200 - 2x$ feet of fence. Therefore the width (w) of the garden is x feet and the length (l) is $200 - 2x$ feet.

The area is calculated using the formula
$a = lw = x(200-2x) = 200x - 2x^2$, and needs to be greater than or equal to 4800 sq. ft., yielding the inequality $4800 \le 200x - 2x^2$. Subtract 4800 from each side and the inequality becomes

$$200x - 2x^2 \ge 4800$$
$$-2x^2 + 200x - 4800 \ge 0$$
$$2\left(-x^2 + 100x - 2400\right) \ge 0$$

solved for x.

$$-x^2 + 100x - 2400 \ge 0$$
$$(-x + 60)(x - 40) \ge 0$$
$$-x + 60 \ge 0$$
$$-x \ge -60$$
$$x \le 60$$
$$x - 40 \ge 0$$
$$x \ge 40$$

The area will be at least 4800 square feet if the width of the garden is from 40 up to 60 feet. (The length of the rectangle would vary from 120 feet to 80 feet depending on the width of the garden.)

For other kinds of nonlinear models see **Skill 6H**.

6G. **Use a variety of representations and methods (e.g., numerical methods, tables, graphs, algebraic techniques) to solve systems of quadratic equations and inequalities**

The methods used to solve systems of quadratic equations or inequalities are the same as the ones used for linear systems. Algebraic methods first extract single-variable equations from the system and then find the other variables using the solutions of these equations. These methods include addition-subtraction or substitution. Systems of equations may also be solved graphically. Overlapping points or regions of the graph constitute the solution. (See **Skill 5F** for linear examples of systems of equations and **Skill 6A** for solutions of quadratic equations and inequalities.)

<u>Example</u>: Solve the following system of equations algebraically as well as graphically.

$$y = 3x^2$$
$$y = 2x^2 + 1$$

Substituting the first equation in the second we get:

$$3x^2 = 2x^2 + 1$$
$$\Rightarrow x^2 = 1$$
$$\Rightarrow x = \pm 1;\ y = 3x^2 = 3$$

The graph below shows the two parabolas represented by the equations intersecting each other at the solution points (1, 3) and (-1, 3).

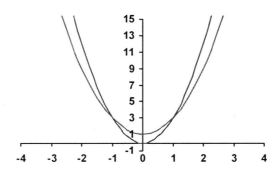

6H. **Understand how to use properties, graphs, and applications of nonlinear relations including polynomial, rational, radical, absolute value, exponential, logarithmic, trigonometric, and piecewise functions and relations to analyze, model, and solve problems**

In **Skill 6F** we modeled and solved problems using quadratic functions. Some situations require higher order polynomials. Other problems may be modeled using rational or radical functions. Some examples are given below.

In cases where a polynomial is highly complicated or involves constants that do not permit methods such as factoring, a numerical approach may be appropriate. Newton's method is one possible approach to solving a polynomial equation numerically. At other times it may require a graphical approach whereby the behavior of the function is examined on a visual plot. When using Newton's method, graphing the function can be helpful for estimating the locations of the real roots (if any).

<u>Example:</u> A cubic container is modified so that its length is increased by 4 inches and its width is shortened by 2 inches. The height of the container remains unchanged. If the volume of the container is 16 cubic inches, what is it height?

Let the side of the original cube be x inches.
The volume of the modified container is given by
$$x(x+4)(x-2) = 16$$

Distributing and rearranging we get
$$x(x^2 + 2x - 8) = 16$$
$$\Rightarrow x^3 + 2x^2 - 8x - 16 = 0$$

The third order polynomial equation above can be grouped and factored as follows:
$$x^2(x + 2) - 8(x + 2) = 0$$
$$\Rightarrow (x + 2)(x^2 - 8) = 0$$

The solutions to the equation are, therefore, $x = -2, \pm 2\sqrt{2}$.
Since the height of the box must be a positive number, we choose the positive solution. Thus the height is $2\sqrt{2}$ inches.

Example: Elly Mae can feed the animals in 15 minutes. Jethro can feed them in 10 minutes. How long will it take them if they work together?

If Elly Mae can feed the animals in 15 minutes, then she could feed 1/15 of them in 1 minute, 2/15 of them in 2 minutes, $x/15$ of them in x minutes. In the same fashion Jethro could feed $x/10$ of them in x minutes. Together they complete 1 job. The equation is:

$$\frac{x}{15} + \frac{x}{10} = 1$$

Multiply each term by the LCD of 30:

$$2x + 3x = 30$$
$$x = 6 \text{ minutes}$$

 Example: A salesman drove 480 miles from Pittsburgh to Hartford. The next day he returned the same distance to Pittsburgh in half an hour less time than his original trip took, because he increased his average speed by 4 mph. Find his original speed.

Since distance = rate x time then time = $\underline{\text{distance}}$
                                                                rate
original time $- 1/2$ hour $=$ shorter return time

$$\frac{480}{x} - \frac{1}{2} = \frac{480}{x+4}$$

Multiplying by the LCD of $2x(x + 4)$, the equation becomes:

$$480\left[2(x+4)\right]-1\left[x(x+4)\right]=480(2x)$$

$$960x + 3840 - x^2 - 4x = 960x$$

$$x^2 + 4x - 3840 = 0$$

$$(x + 64)(x - 60) = 0 \quad \text{Either (x-60=0) or (x+64=0) or both=0}$$

$$x = 60 \qquad\qquad \text{60 mph is the original speed.}$$

This is the solution since the time

$$x + 4 = 64 \qquad\qquad \text{cannot be negative. Check your answer}$$

$$\frac{480}{60} - \frac{1}{2} = \frac{480}{64}$$

$$8 - \frac{1}{2} = 7\frac{1}{2}$$

$$7\frac{1}{2} = 7\frac{1}{2}$$

<u>Example:</u> For a cone of height h and radius r, the slant height is given by $s = \sqrt{r^2 + h^2}$. The lateral surface area is πrs and the area of the base is πr^2.

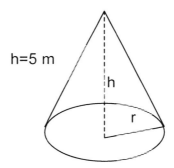

h=5 m

If the lateral surface area of a cone is twice that of its base and the height of the cone is 5m, find the radius.

The problem given may be modeled using the following radical equation:

$$\pi r\sqrt{25 + r^2} = 2\pi r^2$$

Canceling the common factor πr from both sides and squaring both sides we get

$$25 + r^2 = 4r^2$$
$$\Rightarrow 3r^2 = 25$$
$$\Rightarrow r = \sqrt{25/3} = 2.9$$

Thus, the radius of the cone is 2.9m.

All of the above examples essentially involve polynomial functions since the rational and radical equations were simplified to yield polynomial equations. There are many other kinds of nonlinear functions as well. For examples of problems modeled using exponential functions see Skill **6C**. Examples using logarithmic and trigonometric functions are given below.

Example: The water, w, in an open container is evaporating. The number of ounces remaining after h hours is shown in the table below:

Hours (h)	2	5	10	15	19	30
Water (w)	13	11	9	8.5	7.5	6.5

We construct a scatter plot for this data and find a logarithmic regression equation to model the data.

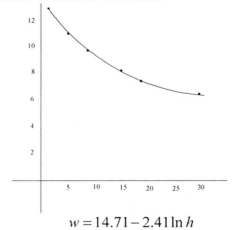

$$w = 14.71 - 2.41 \ln h$$

Using this regression equation predict how many ounces of water are remaining in the container after 48 hours.

$$w = 14.71 - 2.41\ln(48)$$
$$w = 14.71 - 2.41(3.87)$$
$$w = 14.71 - 9.33$$
$$w = 5.4$$

Trigonometric functions have a cyclical (or **periodic**) behavior that is suited to modeling periodic phenomena. For instance, the height of a point marked on a wheel, tracked as the wheel rolls, can be modeled using trigonometric functions. The key to modeling such periodic phenomena is identification of the amplitude, period and phase (if necessary) of the phenomenon. This information allows expression of some parameter of the phenomenon as an equation involving a trigonometric function.

Example: Write an equation for the height of sea waves whose crests pass every 5 seconds and whose peaks are 10 feet above their troughs.

In this case, phase information is not needed since there is no fixed position to form a point of comparison (or origin). Thus, either a sine or cosine function can be used. The amplitude of the waves are half the distance between the peaks and troughs, or 5 feet. The period is simply the inverse of the time between peaks: 0.2 sec^{-1}. The equation for the height h of the waves with respect to time t is then the following:

$$h = 5\sin(0.2t)\,\text{feet}$$

where t is measured in seconds.

Competency 007   **The teacher uses and understands the conceptual foundations of calculus related to topics in middle school mathematics**

This competency explains basic concepts of calculus such as limits, slope and area under the curve and their application to topics familiar to middle school students.

7A.   **Relate topics in middle school mathematics to the concept of limit in sequences and series**

A **limit** is the value that a function approaches as a variable of the function approaches a certain value. Thus, the limit L of a function $f(x)$ as x approaches some value c is written as follows:

$$\lim_{x \to c} f(x) = L$$

This concept can be understood through graphical illustrations, as with the following example. The graph shows a plot of $y = 2x$. A limit in this case might be the limit of y as x approaches 3. Graphically, this involves tracing the plot of the function to the point at $x = 3$.

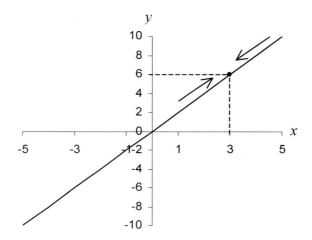

The limit in this case is clearly 6. The limit can be considered either from the right or left (that is, considering x decreasing toward 3 or x increasing toward 3). In the simple example above, the limit is the same from either direction, but, in some cases, the limit may be different from different directions or the function may not even exist on one side of the limit.

For simple functions, evaluating the limit may simply involve calculating $f(c)$ (according to the limit definition given above), but, for other functions, a more subtle approach may be required. In some instances, such as where the limit of the function differs depending on whether c is approached from the left or right, or where the limit of the function is positive or negative infinity, the limit of $f(x)$ at $x = c$ does not exist.

The **continuity** of a function is easily understood graphically as the absence of any missing points or any breaks in the plot of the function. A more rigorous definition can be formulated, however. A function $f(x)$ is continuous at a point c if all of the following apply:

1. The function $f(x)$ is defined at $x = c$.
2. The limit $\lim_{x \to c} f(x)$ exists.
3. The limit can be found by substitution: $\lim_{x \to c} f(x) = f(c)$.

A function can then be called **continuous** for an open interval (a, b) if the above definition applies to the function for every point c in the interval. The function is also continuous at the points $x = a$ and $x = b$ if $\lim_{x \to a^+} f(x) = f(a)$ and $\lim_{x \to b^-} f(x) = f(b)$ both exist. (The +/– notation simply signifies approaching the limiting value from either the right or left, respectively.) If both of these conditions apply, then the function is continuous for the closed interval $[a, b]$.

Example: Determine if the function shown in the graph is continuous at $x = 2$.

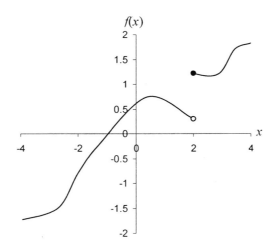

By inspection, it can be seen that the limits of the function as x approaches 2 from the right and left are not equal.

$$\lim_{x \to 2^+} f(x) \neq \lim_{x \to 2^-} f(x)$$

As a result, the function does not meet all of the criteria for continuity at $x = 2$ and is therefore discontinuous.

A sequence is a list of numbers that follow a specific pattern. For example, the following list of numbers represents a sequence defined by the formula $\dfrac{n}{n+1}$.

$$\frac{1}{2}, \frac{2}{3}, \frac{3}{4}, \frac{4}{5}, \frac{5}{6}, \dots \frac{99}{100}, \dots$$

Thus we can think of a sequence as a function whose domain consists of the positive integers $1, 2, \dots, n$.

We say that the limit of the above sequence is 1, because as n approaches infinity, the sequence approaches 1. Thus, **a limit is the upper or lower boundary of a sequence**; the value that the sequence will never pass.

A series is a sum of numbers. **Convergent series possess a numerical limit**. For example, the sum of the series $\dfrac{1}{2^n}$ starting with n = 1, has a limit of 1. We represent the series as follows:

$$\sum_{n=1}^{\infty} \frac{1}{2^n} = \frac{1}{2} + \frac{1}{4} + \frac{1}{8} + \frac{1}{16} + \frac{1}{32} + \dots$$

The symbol $\sum$ (sigma) represents summation and the numbers to the right of the sigma symbol are the beginning and end values of the series. Note, that no matter how many values we add in the series, the total sum approaches, but never reaches 1.

A **geometric series** is a series whose successive terms are related by a common factor (rather than the common difference of the arithmetic series). Assuming a is the first term of the series and r is the common factor, the general n-term geometric series can be written as follows.

$$a + ar + ar^2 + ar^3 + \dots + ar^{n-1}$$

The sum of a geometric series to *n* terms is given by

$$S_n = a\frac{1-r^n}{1-r}$$

The infinite geometric series is the limit of S_n as *n* approaches infinity.

$$a + ar + ar^2 + \ldots = \lim_{n\to\infty} a\frac{1-r^n}{1-r}$$

For $-1 < r < 1$, rearrange the original form of the limit.

$$\lim_{n\to\infty} a\frac{1-r^n}{1-r} = a\frac{1-r^\infty}{1-r}$$

Since the magnitude of *r* is less than 1, r^∞ must be zero. This yields a closed form for the infinite geometric series, which converges only if $-1 < r < 1$.

$$a + ar + ar^2 + \ldots = \frac{a}{1-r}$$

<u>Example:</u> Evaluate the following series: $1 + \frac{1}{2} + \frac{1}{4} + \frac{1}{8} + \ldots$

Note that this series is an infinite geometric series with *a* = 1 and $r = \frac{1}{2}$ (or 0.5). Use the formula to evaluate the series.

$$1 + \frac{1}{2} + \frac{1}{4} + \frac{1}{8} + \ldots = \frac{a}{1-r} = \frac{1}{1-0.5} = \frac{1}{0.5} = 2$$

The answer is thus 2.

Even though the concepts of limits and continuity were not brought up in the discussion of functions, they were implicit in issues related to the domain of nonlinear functions. In particular, it is clear that the **asymptotes of functions are essentially limits** of the functions as the independent or dependent variable goes to infinity.

7B. **Relate the concept of average rate of change to the slope of the secant line and instantaneous rate of change to the slope of the tangent line**

The rate of change of a function f(x) is equivalent to its slope (change in f(x) for a given change in x). For nonlinear functions, the slope is continuously changing over the domain. The rate of change of a function can be found as an average rate of change over some portion of the domain (a difference quotient), or it can be found at a particular domain value (derivative).

The **difference quotient** is the average rate of change over an interval. For a function *f*, the **difference quotient** is represented by the formula:

$$\frac{f(x+h) - f(x)}{h}.$$

This formula computes the **slope of the secant line** through two points on the graph of *f*. These are the points with *x* coordinates *x* and *x + h*.

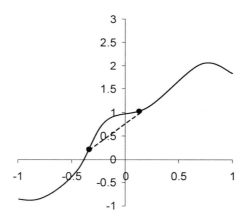

Example: Find the difference quotient for the function
$f(x) = 2x^2 + 3x - 5$.

Use the difference quotient formula and simplify the results.

$$\frac{f(x+h) - f(x)}{h} = \frac{2(x+h)^2 + 3(x+h) - 5 - (2x^2 + 3x - 5)}{h}$$

$$= \frac{2(x^2 + 2hx + h^2) + 3x + 3h - 5 - 2x^2 - 3x + 5}{h}$$

$$= \frac{2x^2 + 4hx + 2h^2 + 3x + 3h - 5 - 2x^2 - 3x + 5}{h}$$

$$= \frac{4hx + 2h^2 + 3h}{h}$$

$$= 4x + 2h + 3$$

The **derivative** is the **slope of a line tangent to a graph** f(x) at x, and is usually denoted $f'(x)$. This is also referred to as the instantaneous rate of change. The derivative of f(x) at x = a is found by taking the limit of the average rates of change (computed by the difference quotient) as h approaches 0.

$$f'(a) = \lim_{h \to 0} \frac{f(a+h) - f(a)}{h}$$

Pick a point (for instance, at x = –3) on the graph of a function and draw a tangent line at that point. Find the derivative of the function and substitute the value x = –3. This result will be the slope of the tangent line.

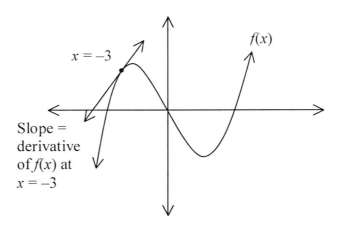

Example: Suppose a company's annual profit (in millions of dollars) is represented by the above function, $f(x) = 2x^2 + 3x - 5$, and x represents the number of years in the interval. Compute the rate at which the annual profit was changing over a period of 2 years.

$$f'(a) = \lim_{h \to 0} \frac{f(a+h) - f(a)}{h}$$
$$= f'(2) = \lim_{h \to 0} \frac{f(2+h) - f(2)}{h}$$

Using the difference quotient we computed previously, $4x + 2h + 3$, yields
$$f'(2) = \lim_{h \to 0}(4(2) + 2h + 3)$$
$$= 8 + 3$$

The annual profit for the company has increased at the average rate of $11 million per year over the two-year period.

7C. **Relate topics in middle school mathematics to the area under a curve**

The formal definition of an **integral** is based on the **Riemann sum**. A Riemann sum is the sum of the areas of a set of rectangles that is used to approximate the area under the curve of a function. Given a function f defined over some closed interval [a, b], the interval can be divided into a set of n arbitrary partitions, each of length Δx_i. Within the limits of each partition, some value $x = c_i$ can be chosen such that Δx_i and $f(c_i)$ define the width and height (respectively) of a rectangle. The sum of the aggregate of all the rectangles defined in this manner over the interval [a, b] is the Riemann sum.

Consider, for example, the function $f(x) = x^2 + 1$ over the interval [0,1]. The plot of the function is shown below.

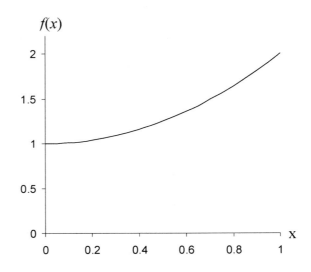

Partition the interval into segments of width 0.2 along the x-axis, and choose the function value $f(c_i)$ at the center of each interval. This function value is the height of the respective rectangle.

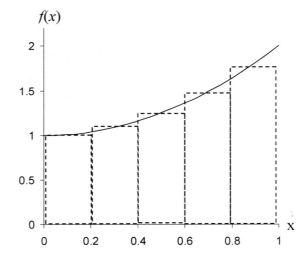

The Riemann sum for this case is expressed below.

$$\sum_{i=1}^{5} 0.2f(0.2i - 0.1) = 1.33$$

This expression is the sum of the areas of all the rectangles shown above. This is an approximation of the area under the curve of the function (and a reasonably accurate one, as well—the actual area is $\frac{4}{3}$).

Generally, the Riemann sum for arbitrary partitioning and selection of the values c_i is the following:

$$\sum_{i=1}^{n} f(c_i) \Delta x_i$$

where c_i is within the closed interval defined by the partition Δx_i.

The **definite integral** is defined as the limit of the Riemann sum as the widths of the partitions Δx_i go to zero (and, consequently, n goes to infinity). Thus, the definite integral can be expressed mathematically as follows:

$$\int_{a}^{b} f(x)\,dx = \lim_{\Delta x_m \to 0} \sum_{i=1}^{n} f(c_i) \Delta x_i$$

where Δx_m is the width of the largest partition. If the partitioning of the interval is such that each partition has the same width, then the definition can be written as follows:

$$\int_{a}^{b} f(x)\,dx = \lim_{\Delta x \to 0} \sum_{i=1}^{n} f(c_i) \Delta x$$

Note that $n = \dfrac{b-a}{\Delta x}$ in this case.

The definite integral, therefore, is the area under the curve of $f(x)$ over the interval $[a, b]$. By taking the limit of the Riemann sum, the number of rectangles used to find the area under the curve becomes infinite and, therefore, the error in the result goes to zero since the width of each rectangle becomes infinitesimal.

Since this is the formal definition of a definite integral, it is helpful to understand the process of deriving the **integrals of algebraic functions** based on this definition. The following example illustrates this process using the Riemann sum. The process can be summarized with the following basic steps.

1. Partition the interval into n segments of equal width.
2. Substitute the value of the function into the Riemann sum using the x value at the center of each subinterval.
3. Write the sum in closed form.
4. Take the limit of the result as n approaches infinity.

<u>Example:</u> For $f(x) = x^2$, find the values of the Riemann sum over the interval [0, 1] using n subintervals of equal width, each evaluated at the right endpoint of each subinterval. Find the limit of the Riemann sum.

Take the interval [0, 1] and subdivide it into n subintervals each of length $\dfrac{1}{n}$.

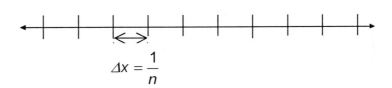

$$\Delta x = \frac{1}{n}$$

The endpoints of the ith subinterval are

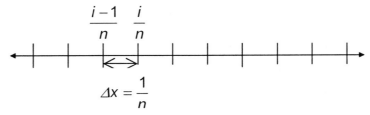

$$\Delta x = \frac{1}{n}$$

Let $x_i = \dfrac{i}{n}$ be the right endpoint. Draw a line of length $f(x_i) = \left(\dfrac{i}{n}\right)^2$ at the right-hand endpoint.

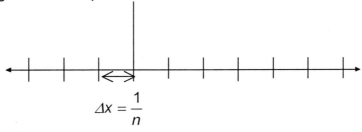

$$\Delta x = \frac{1}{n}$$

Draw a rectangle.

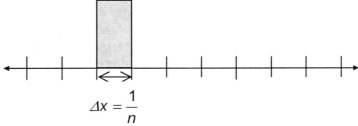

$$\Delta x = \frac{1}{n}$$

The area of this rectangle is $f(x)\Delta x$.

$$f(x)\Delta x = \left(\frac{i}{n}\right)^2 \frac{1}{n} = \frac{i^2}{n^3}$$

Now draw all n rectangles (drawing below not to scale).

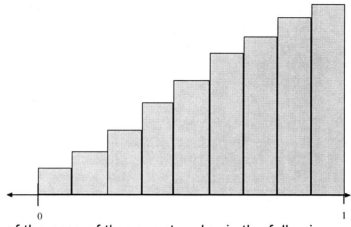

The sum of the area of these rectangles is the following.

$$\sum_{i=1}^{n} \frac{i^2}{n^3} = \frac{1}{n^3} \sum_{i=1}^{n} i^2$$

The sum can be evaluated as follows.

$$\frac{1}{n^3} \sum_{i=1}^{n} i^2 = \frac{1}{n^3} \frac{n(n+1)(2n+1)}{6}$$

This is the Riemann sum for n subdivisions of the interval [0, 1]. Finally, to evaluate the integral, take the limit as n approaches infinity.

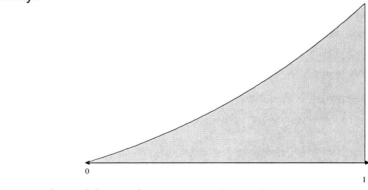

$$\lim_{n \to \infty} \frac{1}{n^3} \frac{n(n+1)(2n+1)}{6} = \frac{1}{6} \lim_{n \to \infty} \frac{2n^3 + 3n^2 + n}{n^3}$$

$$= \frac{1}{6} \lim_{n \to \infty} \left(2 + \frac{3}{n} + \frac{1}{n^2}\right) = \frac{1}{3}$$

This is the correct answer. Thus,

$$\int_{0}^{1} x^2 dx = \frac{1}{3}$$

7D. **Demonstrate an understanding of the use of calculus concepts to answer questions about rates of change, areas, volumes, and properties of functions and their graphs**

Many basic problems using rate of change of a certain quantity may be modeled using differentiation.

If a particle (such as a car, bullet or other object) is moving along a line, then the position of the particle can be expressed as a function of time. The rate of change of position with respect to time is the velocity of the object; thus, the first derivative of the distance function yields the velocity function for the particle. Substituting a value for time into this expression provides the instantaneous velocity of the particle at that time. The absolute value of the derivative is the speed (magnitude of the velocity) of the particle. A positive value for the velocity indicates that the particle is moving forward (that is, in the positive x direction); a negative value indicates the particle is moving backward (that is, in the negative x direction).

The acceleration of the particle is the rate of change of the velocity. The second derivative of the position function (which is also the first derivative of the velocity function) yields the acceleration function. If a value for time produces a positive acceleration, the particle's velocity is increasing; if it produces a negative value, the particle's velocity is decreasing. If the acceleration is zero, the particle is moving at a constant speed.

Example: The motion of a particle moving along a line is according to the equation $s(t) = 20 + 3t - 5t^2$, where s is in meters and t is in seconds. Find the position, velocity and acceleration of the particle at $t = 2$ seconds.

To find the position, simply use $t = 2$ in the given position function. Note that the initial position of the particle is $s(0) = 20$ meters.

$$s(2) = 20 + 3(2) - 5(2)^2$$
$$s(2) = 20 + 6 - 20 = 6\,\text{m}$$

To find the velocity of the particle, calculate the first derivative of $s(t)$ and then evaluate the result for $t = 2$ seconds.

$$s'(t) = v(t) = 3 - 10t$$
$$v(2) = 3 - 10(2) = 3 - 20 = -17\,\text{m/s}$$

Finally, for the acceleration of the particle, calculate the second derivative of $s(t)$ (also equal to the first derivative of $v(t)$) and evaluate for $t = 2$ seconds.

$$s''(t) = v'(t) = a(t) = -10\,\text{m/s}^2$$

Since the acceleration function $a(t)$ is a constant, the acceleration is always -10 m/s^2 (the velocity of the particle decreases every second by 10 meters per second).

Some rate problems may involve functions with different parameters that are each dependent on time. In such a case, implicit differentiation may be required. Often times, related rate problems give certain rates in the description, thus eliminating the need to have specific functions of time for every parameter. Related rate problems are otherwise solved in the same manner as other similar problems.

<u>Example:</u> A spherical balloon is inflated such that its radius is increasing at a constant rate of 1 inch per second. What is the rate of increase of the volume of the balloon when the radius is 10 inches?

First, write the equation for the volume of a sphere in terms of the radius, r.

$$V(r) = \frac{4}{3}\pi r^3$$

Differentiate the function implicitly with respect to time, t, by using the chain rule.

$$\frac{dV(r)}{dt} = \frac{4}{3}\pi\frac{d}{dt}(r^3)$$
$$\frac{dV(r)}{dt} = \frac{4}{3}\pi(3r^2)\frac{dr}{dt} = 4\pi r^2\frac{dr}{dt}$$

To find the solution to the problem, use the radius value $r = 10$ inches and the rate of increase of the radius $\dfrac{dr}{dt} = 1$ in/sec . Calculate the resulting rate of increase of the volume, $\dfrac{dV(r)}{dt}$.

$$\frac{dV(10)}{dt} = 4\pi(10\,\text{in})^2\, 1\,\text{in/sec} = 400\pi\,\text{in}^3/\text{sec} \approx 1257\,\text{in}^3/\text{sec}$$

Taking the integral of a function and evaluating it over some interval on x provides the total **area under the curve** (or, more formally, the **area bounded by the curve and the x-axis**). Thus, the area of geometric figures can be determined when the figure can be cast as a function or set of functions in the coordinate plane. Remember, though, that regions above the x-axis have "positive" area and regions below the x-axis have "negative" area. It is necessary to account for these positive and negative values when finding the area under curves. The boundaries between positive and negative regions are delineated by the roots of the function.

Example: Find the area under the following function on the given interval: $f(x) = \sin x$; $[0, 2\pi]$.

First, find the roots of the function on the interval.

$$f(x) = \sin x = 0$$
$$x = 0, \pi$$

The function $\sin x$ is positive over [0, π] (since $\sin\dfrac{\pi}{2} = 1$) and negative over [π, 2π] (since $\sin\dfrac{3\pi}{2} = -1$). Use these intervals for the integration to find the area A under the curve.

$$A = \int_{0}^{2\pi} |\sin x|\, dx = \left|\int_{0}^{\pi} \sin x\, dx\right| + \left|\int_{\pi}^{2\pi} \sin x\, dx\right|$$

$$A = \left|-\cos x\Big|_{0}^{\pi}\right| + \left|-\cos x\Big|_{\pi}^{2\pi}\right| = \left|-\cos\pi + \cos 0\right| + \left|-\cos 2\pi + \cos\pi\right|$$

$$A = |1+1| + |-1-1| = 2 + 2 = 4$$

Thus, the total area under the curve of $f(x) = \sin x$ on the interval $[0, 2\pi]$ is 4 square units.

Integral calculus, in addition to differential calculus, is a powerful tool for analysis of problems involving linear motion. The derivative of the position (or displacement) function is the velocity function, and the derivative of a velocity function is the acceleration function. As a result, the antiderivative of an acceleration function is a velocity function, and the antiderivative of the velocity function is a position (or displacement) function. Solving word problems of this type involve converting the information given into an appropriate integral expression. To find the constant of integration, use the conditions provided in the problem (such as an initial displacement, velocity or acceleration).

Example: A particle moves along the x-axis with acceleration $a(t) = 3t - 1\dfrac{cm}{sec^2}$. At time $t = 4$ seconds, the particle is moving to the left at 3 cm per second. Find the velocity of the particle at time $t = 2$ seconds.

Evaluate the antiderivative of the acceleration function $a(t)$ to get the velocity function $v(t)$ along with the unknown constant of integration C.

$$v(t) = \int a(t)\,dt = \int (3t - 1)\,dt$$
$$v(t) = \frac{3t^2}{2} - t + C$$

Use the condition that at time $t = 4$ seconds, the particle has a velocity of –3 cm/sec.

$$v(4) = \frac{3(4)^2}{2} - 4 + C = -3$$
$$\frac{48}{2} - 4 + C = -3$$
$$C = -3 + 4 - 24 = -23\frac{cm}{sec}$$

Now evaluate $v(t)$ at time $t = 2$ seconds to get the solution to the problem.

$$v(t) = \frac{3t^2}{2} - t - 23\frac{cm}{sec}$$
$$v(2) = \frac{3(2)^2}{2} - 2 - 23\frac{cm}{sec} = 6 - 25\frac{cm}{sec} = -19\frac{cm}{sec}$$

DOMAIN III. GEOMETRY AND MEASUREMENT

Competency 008   The teacher understands measurement as a process

This competency reviews various concepts associated with the measurement process, including selection of the appropriate units of measurement, dimensional analysis and unit conversion, the Pythagorean theorem, and right triangle trigonometry. An understanding of these concepts is fundamental to the discussion of geometry in later competencies.

8A.   Select and use appropriate units of measurement (e.g., temperature, money, mass, weight, area, capacity, density, percents, speed, acceleration) to quantify, compare, and communicate information

Non-standard units are sometimes used when standard instruments might not be available. For example, students might measure the length of a room by their arm spans. An inch originated as the length of three barley grains placed end to end. Seeds or stones might be used for measuring weight. In fact, the word "carat," used for measuring precious gems, was derived from carob seeds. In ancient times, baskets, jars and bowls were used to measure capacity.

To estimate measurements of familiar objects, it is necessary to first determine the units to be used.

Examples:
Length
1. The coastline of Florida miles or kilometers
2. The width of a ribbon   inches or millimeters
3. The thickness of a bookinches or centimeters
4. The length of a football field   yards or meters
5. The depth of water in a pool   feet or meters

Weight or mass
1. A bag of sugar   pounds or grams
2. A school bus   tons or kilograms
3. A dime   ounces or grams

Capacity
1. Paint to paint a bedroom   gallons or liters
2. Glass of milk   cups or liters
3. Bottle of soda   quarts or liters
4. Medicine for child   ounces or milliliters

The appropriate use of measurement units is further discussed later in this competency.

8B.   Develop, justify, and use conversions within measurement systems

The following skill section discusses the development, use, and justification of conversions between and within measurement systems.

8C.   Apply dimensional analysis to derive units and formulas in a variety of situations (e.g., rates of change of one variable with respect to another) and to find and evaluate solutions to problems

There are many methods for converting measurements among various units within a system or between systems. One method is multiplication of the given measurement by a conversion factor. This conversion factor is the following ratio, which is always equal to unity.

$$\frac{\text{new units}}{\text{old units}} \quad \text{OR} \quad \frac{\text{what you want}}{\text{what you have}}$$

The fundamental feature of **unit analysis** or **dimensional analysis** is that conversion factors can be multiplied together and units can be cancelled in the same way as numerators and denominators of numerical fractions. The following examples help clarify this point.

<u>Example:</u> Convert 3 miles to yards.

Multiply the initial measurement by the conversion factor, cancel the mile units, and solve:

$$\frac{3\text{ miles}}{1} \times \frac{1,760\text{ yards}}{1\text{ mile}} = 5,280\text{ yards}$$

<u>Example:</u> It takes Cynthia 45 minutes to get ready each morning. How many hours does she spend getting ready each week?

Multiply the initial measurement by the conversion factors from minutes to hours and from days to weeks, then cancel the minute and day units and solve:

$$\frac{45 \text{ min}}{1 \text{ day}} \times \frac{1 \text{ hour}}{60 \text{ min}} \times \frac{7 \text{ days}}{1 \text{ week}} = 5.25 \frac{\text{hours}}{\text{week}}$$

Conversion factors for different types of units are listed below:

<u>Measurements of length (English system)</u>

12 inches (in)	=	1 foot (ft)
3 feet (ft)	=	1 yard (yd)
1760 yards (yd)	=	1 mile (mi)

<u>Measurements of length (metric system)</u>

Kilometer (km)	=	1000 meters (m)
Hectometer (hm)	=	100 meters (m)
Decameter (dam)	=	10 meters (m)
Meter (m)	=	1 meter (m)
Decimeter (dm)	=	1/10 meter (m)
Centimeter (cm)	=	1/100 meter (m)
Millimeter (mm)	=	1/1000 meter (m)

<u>Conversion of length from English to metric</u>

1 inch	=	2.54 centimeters
1 foot	≈	30.48 centimeters
1 yard	≈	0.91 meters
1 mile	≈	1.61 kilometers

<u>Measurements of weight (metric system)</u>

kilogram (kg)	=	1000 grams (g)
gram (g)	=	1 gram (g)
milligram (mg)	=	1/1000 gram (g)

<u>Conversion of weight from metric to English</u>

28.35 grams (g)	=	1 ounce (oz)
16 ounces (oz)	=	1 pound (lb)
2000 pounds (lb)	=	1 ton (t) (short ton)
1.1 ton (t)	=	1 metric ton (t)

Conversion of weight from English to metric

1 ounce	≈	28.35 grams
1 pound	≈	0.454 kilogram
1.1 ton	=	1 metric ton

Measurement of volume (English system)

8 fluid ounces (oz)	=	1 cup (c)
2 cups (c)	=	1 pint (pt)
2 pints (pt)	=	1 quart (qt)
4 quarts (qt)	=	1 gallon (gal)

Measurement of volume (metric system)

Kiloliter (kl)	=	1000 liters (l)
Liter (l)	=	1 liter (l)
Milliliter (ml)	=	1/1000 liter (ml)

Conversion of volume from English to metric

1 teaspoon (tsp)	≈	5 milliliters
1 fluid ounce	≈	29.57 milliliters
1 cup	≈	0.24 liters
1 pint	≈	0.47 liters
1 quart	≈	0.95 liters
1 gallon	≈	3.8 liters

Note: (') represents feet and (") represents inches.

Example: Convert 8,750 meters to kilometers.

$$\frac{8,750 \text{ meters}}{1} \times \frac{1 \text{ kilometer}}{1,000 \text{ meters}} = 8.75 \text{ km}$$

Example: 4 mi. = _____ yd.

1760 yd = 1 mi
4 mi × 1760 yd/mi = 7040 yd

Square units can be derived from the basic units of length by squaring the equivalent measurements.

1 square foot (sq. ft. or ft^2) = 144 sq. in.
1 sq. yd. = 9 sq. ft.
1 sq. yd. = 1296 sq. in.

Note that conversion in each case is performed in the following manner.

$$1\,ft^2 = (1\,ft)(1\,ft) = (12\,in)(12\,in) = 144\,in^2$$

Example: 14 sq. yd. = _____ sq. ft.

$$14\,yd^2 = 14\,(1\,yd)(1\,yd) = 14\,(3\,ft)(3\,ft) = 126\,ft^2$$

Example: A car skidded 170 yards on an icy road before coming to a stop. How long is the skid distance in kilometers?

Since 1 yard ≈ 0.9 meters, multiply 170 yards by 0.9 meters/1 yard.

$$170\,yd. \times \frac{0.9\,m}{1\,yd.} = 153\,m$$

Since 1000 meters = 1 kilometer, multiply 153 meters by 1 kilometer/1000 meters.

$$153\,m \times \frac{1\,km}{1000\,m} = 0.153\,km$$

Example: The distance around a race course is exactly 1 mile, 17 feet, and $9\frac{1}{4}$ inches. Approximate this distance to the nearest tenth of a foot.

Convert the distance to feet.

$$1\text{ mile} = 1760\text{ yards} = 1760 \times 3\text{ feet} = 5280\text{ feet.}$$
$$9\frac{1}{4}\text{ in.} = \frac{37}{4}\text{ in.} \times \frac{1\,ft.}{12\,in.} = \frac{37}{48}\,ft. \approx 0.77083\,ft.$$

So 1 mile, 17 ft. and $9\frac{1}{4}$ in. = 5280 ft. + 17 ft. + 0.77083 ft.
$$= 5297.77083 \ ft.$$

The answer rounds to 5297.8 feet.

Example: If the temperature is 90° F, what is it expressed in Celsius units?

To convert between Celsius (C) and Fahrenheit (F), use the following formula.

$$\frac{C}{5} = \frac{F-32}{9}$$

If F = 90, then $C = 5\frac{(90-32)}{9} = \frac{5 \times 58}{9} = 32.2$.

Example: A map shows a scale of 1 inch = 2 miles. Convert this scale to a numerical ratio so that any unit system (such as metric) can be used to measure distances.

The scale is a ratio—1 inch: 2 miles. If either value is converted so that the two values have the same units, then this scale can be converted to a purely numerical ratio. To avoid fractions, convert miles to inches.

$$2mi = 2mi \times \frac{5,280\,ft}{1mi} \times \frac{12\,in}{1ft} = 126,720\,in$$

The ratio is then 1:126,720.

8D. **Describe the precision of measurement and the effects of error on measurement**

Most numbers in mathematics are "exact" or "counted." Measurements are "approximate" and usually involve interpolation or figuring out which mark on the ruler is the closest, for instance. Any measurement obtained with a measuring device is approximate. Variations in measurement are defined in terms of precision and accuracy.

Precision measures the degree of variation in a particular measurement without reference to a true or real value. If a measurement is precise, it can be made repeatedly with little variation in the result. The precision of a measuring device is the smallest fractional or decimal division on the instrument. The smaller the unit or fraction of a unit on the measuring device, the more precisely it can measure.

The **greatest possible error** (ignoring gross human error) of measurement is always equal to one-half the smallest fraction of a unit on the measuring device. For example, if the smallest unit was one millimeter, then the greatest possible error would be ±1/2 mm.

Accuracy is a measure of how close the result of measurement comes to the "true" value. In the game of darts, the true value is the bull's eye. If three darts are tossed and each lands on the bull's eye, the dart thrower is both precise (all land near the same spot) and accurate (the darts all land on the "true" value).

The greatest allowable measure of error allowed is called the **tolerance**. The least acceptable limit is called the lower limit, and the greatest acceptable limit is called the upper limit. The difference between the upper and lower limits is called the **tolerance interval**. For example, a specification for an automobile part might be 14.625 ± 0.005 mm. This means that the smallest acceptable length of the part is 14.620 mm and the largest length acceptable is 14.630 mm. The tolerance interval is 0.010 mm. One can see how it would be important for automobile parts to be within a set of limits in terms of physical dimensions. If the part is too long or too short, it will not fit properly and vibrations may occur, thereby weakening the part and eventually causing damage to other parts.

Error in measurement can also be expressed by a **percentage of error**. For example, a measurement of 12 feet may be said to be off by 2%. This means that the actual measurement could be between

12 − (2% of 12) and 12 + (2% of 12)
12 − (.02)12 and 12 + (.02)12
11.76 ft. and 12.24 feet

To determine the percent error between a measurement of a value and the actual value, use the following formula.

$$\text{Percent Error} = \frac{|\text{Measured} - \text{Actual}|}{\text{Actual}} \times 100$$

Error in measurement may also be indicated by the terms "rounded" or "to the nearest." When rounding to a given place value, it is necessary to look at the number in the next smaller place. If this number is 5 or more, the number in the place to which we are rounding is increased by one and all numbers to the right are changed to zero. If the number is less than 5, the number in the place to which we are rounding stays the same and all numbers to the right are changed to zero. For example, the length of a side of a square to the nearest inch may be 10 inches. This means that the actual length of the side could be between 9.5 inches and 10.4 inches (since all of these values round to 10).

8E. **Apply the Pythagorean theorem, proportional reasoning, and right triangle trigonometry to solve measurement problems**

The Pythagorean Theorem

A **right triangle** is a triangle with one right angle. The side opposite the right angle is called the **hypotenuse**. The other two sides are the **legs**.

The Pythagorean theorem states that, for any right triangle, the square of the length of the hypotenuse is equal to the sum of the squares of the lengths of the legs. Symbolically, this is stated as:

$$c^2 = a^2 + b^2$$

<u>Example:</u> Given the right triangle below, find the missing side.

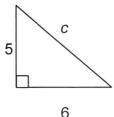

$c^2 = a^2 + b^2$	1. write formula
$c^2 = 5^2 + 6^2$	2. substitute known values
$c^2 = 61$	3. take square root
$c = \sqrt{61}$ or 7.81	4. solve

The Converse of the Pythagorean Theorem states that if the square of one side of a triangle is equal to the sum of the squares of the other two sides, then the triangle is a right triangle.

Example: Given $\triangle XYZ$, with sides measuring 12, 16 and 20 cm. Is this a right triangle?

$$c^2 = a^2 + b^2$$
$$20^2 \ \underline{?} \ 12^2 + 16^2$$
$$400 \ \underline{?} \ 144 + 256$$
$$400 = 400$$

Yes, the triangle is a right triangle.

This theorem can be expanded to determine if triangles are obtuse or acute.

If the square of the longest side of a triangle is greater than the sum of the squares of the other two sides, then the triangle is an obtuse triangle. If the square of the longest side of a triangle is less than the sum of the squares of the other two sides, then the triangle is an acute triangle.

Example: Given $\triangle LMN$ with sides measuring 7, 12, and 14 inches. Is the triangle right, acute, or obtuse?

$$14^2 \ \underline{?} \ 7^2 + 12^2$$
$$196 \ \underline{?} \ 49 + 144$$
$$196 > 193$$

Therefore, the triangle is obtuse.

When an altitude is drawn to the hypotenuse of a right triangle, then the two triangles formed are similar to the original triangle and to each other.

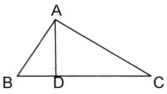

Given right triangle ABC with right angle at A, altitude AD drawn to hypotenuse BD at D, $\triangle ABC \sim \triangle ABD \sim \triangle ACD$.

If a, b and c are positive numbers such that $\dfrac{a}{b} = \dfrac{b}{c}$, then b is called the **geometric mean** between a and c.

The geometric mean is significant when the altitude is drawn to the hypotenuse of a right triangle.

The length of the altitude is the geometric mean between each segment of the hypotenuse. Also, each leg is the geometric mean between the hypotenuse and the segment of the hypotenuse that is adjacent to the leg.

Right Triangle Trigonometry

Trigonometric functions can be related to right triangles: each trigonometric function corresponds to a ratio of certain sides of the triangle with respect to a particular angle. Thus, given the generic right triangle diagram below, the following functions can be specified.

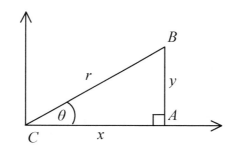

$$\sin\theta = \frac{y}{r} \qquad \csc\theta = \frac{r}{y}$$

$$\cos\theta = \frac{x}{r} \qquad \sec\theta = \frac{r}{x}$$

$$\tan\theta = \frac{y}{x} \qquad \cot\theta = \frac{x}{y}$$

Based on these definitions, the unknown characteristics of a particular right triangle can be calculated based on certain known characteristics. For instance, if the hypotenuse and one of the adjacent angles are both known, the lengths of the other two sides of the triangle can be calculated.

Proportional Reasoning

The use of such concepts as similarity (discussed above for geometric figures) is part of proportional reasoning. Often, it is helpful to find an unknown parameter in a problem through comparison to a known parameter. This approach can be applied to triangle similarity (discussed in **Competency 010**), for instance.

Competency 009 **The teacher understands the geometric relationships and axiomatic structure of Euclidean geometry**

Euclidean geometry is (in many ways) an intuitive geometric system, and it is the foundation of the way in which many people learn the fundamental concepts of geometry. This competency presents the basic constructs of Euclidean geometry, including points, lines, and planes, and then discusses parallel and perpendicular lines, congruent triangles, classical constructions, and using the axiomatic structure of Euclidean geometry to prove and justify theorems.

9A. **Understand concepts and properties of points, lines, planes, angles, lengths, and distances**

A **point** is a dimensionless location and has no length, width or height.

A **line** connects a series of points and continues "straight" infinitely in two directions. Lines extend in one dimension. A line is defined by any two points that fall on the line; therefore a line may have multiple names.

A **line segment** is a portion of a line. A line segment is the shortest distance between two endpoints and is named using those end points. Line segments therefore have exactly two names (i.e., $\overline{AB}$ or $\overline{BA}$). Because line segments have two endpoints, they have a defined length or distance.

A **ray** is a portion of a line that has only one end point and continues infinitely in one direction. Rays are named using the endpoint as the first point and any other point on the ray as the second.

Note that the symbol for a line includes two arrows (indicating infinite extent in both directions), the symbol for a ray includes only one arrow (indicating that it has one end point) and the symbol for a line segment has no arrows (indicating two end points).

<u>Example:</u> Use the diagram below, calculate the length of $\overline{AB}$ given $\overline{AC}$ is 6 cm and $\overline{BC}$ is twice as long as $\overline{AB}$.

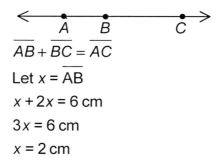

$\overline{AB} + \overline{BC} = \overline{AC}$

Let $x = \overline{AB}$

$x + 2x = 6$ cm

$3x = 6$ cm

$x = 2$ cm

An **angle** is formed by the intersection of two rays.

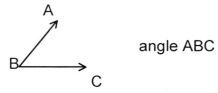

angle ABC

Angles are measured in degrees. $1° = \dfrac{1}{360}$ of a circle.

A **right angle** measures 90°.

An **acute angle** measures more than 0° and less than 90°.

An **obtuse angle** measures more than 90° and less than 180°.

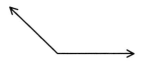

A **straight angle** measures 180°.

A **reflexive angle** measures more than 180° and less than 360°.

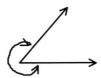

A **plane** is a flat surface defined by three points. Planes extend indefinitely in two dimensions. A common example of a plane is *x-y* plane used in the Cartesian coordinate system.

In geometry, the point, line, and plane are key concepts and can be discussed in relation to each other.

collinear points
are all on the same line

non-collinear points
are not on the same line

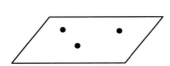

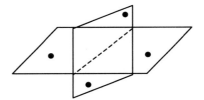

coplanar points
are on the same plane

non-coplanar points
are not on the same plane

Problems throughout this competency illustrate the use of these various geometric elements in the solution of problems.

9B. Analyze and apply the properties of parallel and perpendicular lines

Parallel lines in two dimensions can be sufficiently defined as lines that do not intersect. In three dimensions, however, this definition is insufficient. **Parallel lines** in three dimensions are defined as lines for which every pair of nearest points on the lines has a fixed distance.

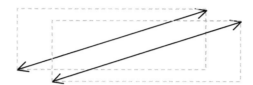

Lines in three dimensions that do not intersect and are not parallel are called **skew lines**. Parallel lines are coplanar, skew lines are not.

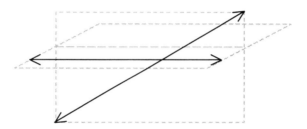

Two planes intersect on a single line. If two planes do not intersect, then they are parallel. Parallel and non-parallel planes are shown in the diagram below.

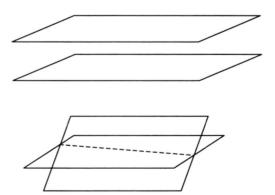

Parallelism between two planes may also be defined in the same way as parallel lines: the distance between any pair of nearest points (one point on each plane) is constant.

Perpendicularity of lines and planes in three dimensions is largely similar to that of two dimensions. Two lines are **perpendicular**, in two or three dimensions, if they intersect at a point and form 90° angles between them. Consequently, perpendicular lines are always coplanar.

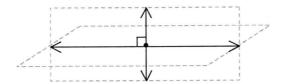

Notice that, for any line and coincident point on that line, there are an infinite number of perpendicular lines to the line through that point. In two dimensions, there is only one.

Two planes are perpendicular if they intersect and the angles formed between them are 90°. For any given plane and line on that plane, there is only one perpendicular plane.

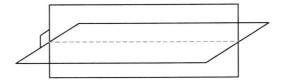

Properties of Parallel Lines

The **Parallel Postulate** in Euclidean planar geometry states that if a line *l* is crossed by two other lines *m* and *n* (where the crossings are not at the same point on *l*), then *m* and *n* intersect on the side of *l* where the sum of the interior angles α and β is less than 180°. This scenario is illustrated below.

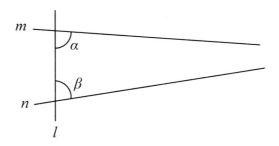

Based on this definition, a number of implications and equivalent formulations can be derived. First, note that the lines m and n intersect on the right-hand side of l above only if $\alpha + \beta < 180°$. This implies that if α and β are both 90° and, therefore, $\alpha + \beta = 180°$, then the lines do not intersect on either side. This is illustrated below.

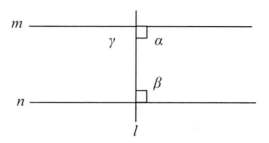

The supplementary angles formed by the intersection of l and m (and the intersection of l and n) must sum to 180°:

$$\alpha + \gamma = 180° \qquad\qquad \beta + \delta = 180°$$

Since these sums are both equal to 180°, the lines m and n do not intersect on either side of l. That is to say, these lines are **parallel**.

Let the non-intersecting lines m and n used in the above discussion remain parallel, but adjust l such that the interior angles are no longer right angles.

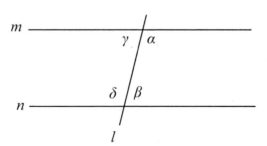

The Parallel Postulate still applies, and it is therefore still the case that $\alpha + \beta = 180°$ and $\gamma + \delta = 180°$. Combined with the fact that $\alpha + \gamma = 180°$ and $\beta + \delta = 180°$, the **Alternate Interior Angle Theorem** can be justified. This theorem states that if two parallel lines are cut by a transversal, the alternate interior angles are congruent.

By manipulating the four relations based on the above diagram, the relationships between alternate interior angles (γ and β form one set of alternate interior angles, and α and δ form the other) can be established.

$$\alpha = 180° - \beta$$
$$\alpha + \gamma = 180° = 180° - \beta + \gamma$$
$$-\beta + \gamma = 0$$
$$\gamma = \beta$$

By the same reasoning,

$$\gamma = 180° - \delta$$
$$\beta + \delta = 180° = \beta + 180° - \delta$$
$$\beta = \delta$$

One of the consequences of the Parallel Postulate, in addition the Alternate Interior Angle Theorem, is that **corresponding angles** are equal. If two parallel lines are cut by a transversal line, then the corresponding angles are equal. The diagram below illustrates one set of corresponding angles (α and β) for the parallel lines m and n cut by l.

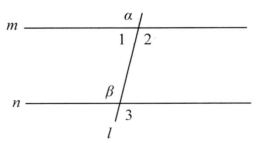

That α and β are equal can be proven as follows.

$\angle\beta = \angle 2$	Alternate Interior Angle Theorem
$\angle 1 + \angle 2 = 180°$	Supplementary angles
$\angle 2 = 180° - \angle 1$	
$\angle 1 + \angle\alpha = 180°$	Supplementary angles
$\angle\alpha = 180° - \angle 1$	
$\angle 2 = 180° - \angle 1 = \angle\alpha$	
$\angle 2 = \angle\alpha$	
$\angle\beta = \angle 2 = \angle\alpha$	
$\angle\beta = \angle\alpha$	

Thus, it has been proven that corresponding angles are equal.

Note, also, that the above proof also demonstrates that vertical angles are equal ($\angle 2 = \angle \alpha$). Thus, opposite angles formed by the intersection of two lines (called **vertical angles**) are equal. Furthermore, **alternate exterior angles** (angles α and 1 in the diagram above) are also equal.

$\angle \beta = \angle 3$	Vertical angles
$\angle \alpha = \angle 2$	Vertical angles
$\angle \beta = \angle 2$	Alternate Interior Angle Theorem
$\angle \alpha = \angle 2 = \angle \beta = \angle 3$	
$\angle \alpha = \angle 3$	

9C. Use the properties of congruent triangles to explore geometric relationships and prove theorems

Congruence

Congruent figures have the same size and shape; i.e., if one of the figures is superimposed on the other, the boundaries coincide exactly. Congruent line segments have the same length; congruent angles have equal measures. The symbol $\cong$ is used to indicate that two figures, line segments or angles are congruent.

The **reflexive, symmetric** and **transitive** properties described for algebraic equality relationships may also be applied to congruence. For instance, if $\angle A \cong \angle B$ and $\angle A \cong \angle D$, then $\angle B \cong \angle D$ (transitive property).

The polygons (pentagons) *ABCDE* and *VWXYZ* shown below are congruent since they are exactly the same size and shape.

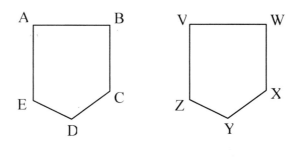

$$ABCDE \cong VWXYZ$$

Corresponding parts are congruent angles and congruent sides. For the polygons shown above:

corresponding angles
∠A ↔ ∠V
∠B ↔ ∠W
∠C ↔ ∠X
∠D ↔ ∠Y
∠E ↔ ∠Z

corresponding sides
AB ↔ VW
BC ↔ WX
CD ↔ XY
DE ↔ YZ
AE ↔ VZ

Two triangles are congruent if each of the three angles and three sides of one triangle match up in a one-to-one fashion with congruent angles and sides of the second triangle. To see how the sides and angles match up, it is sometimes necessary to imagine rotating or reflecting one of the triangles so the two figures are oriented in the same position.

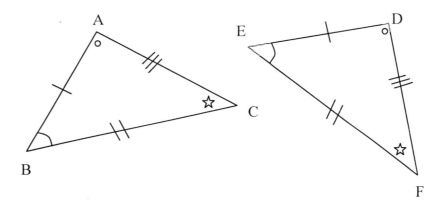

In the example above, the two triangles ABC and DEF are congruent if these 6 conditions are met:

1. ∠A ≅ ∠D
2. ∠B ≅ ∠E
3. ∠C ≅ ∠F
4. $\overline{AB} \cong \overline{DE}$
5. $\overline{BC} \cong \overline{EF}$
6. $\overline{AC} \cong \overline{DF}$

The congruent angles and segments "correspond" to each other.

It is not always necessary to demonstrate all of the above six conditions to prove that two triangles are congruent. There are several "shortcut" methods described below.

The **SAS Postulate** (side-angle-side) states that if two sides and the included angle of one triangle are congruent to two sides and the included angle of another triangle, then the two triangles are congruent.

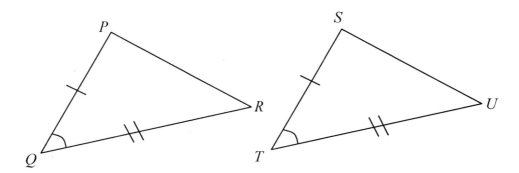

To see why this is true, imagine moving the triangle PQR (shown above) in such a way that the point P coincides with the point S, and line segment PQ coincides with line segment ST. Point Q will then coincide with T since PQ ≅ ST. Also, segment QR will coincide with TU, because ∠Q ≅ ∠T. Point R will coincide with U, because QR ≅ TU. Since P and S coincide and R and U coincide, line PR will coincide with SU because two lines cannot enclose a space. Thus the two triangles match perfectly point for point and are congruent.

<u>Example</u>: Are the following triangles congruent?

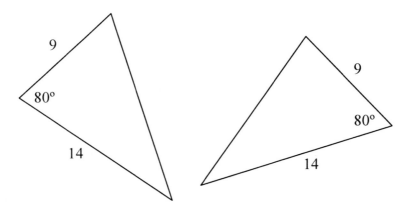

Each of the two triangles has a side that is 14 units and another that is 9 units. The angle included in the sides is 80° in both triangles. Therefore, the triangles are congruent by SAS.

The **SSS Postulate** (side-side-side) states that if three sides of one triangle are congruent to three sides of another triangle, then the two triangles are congruent.

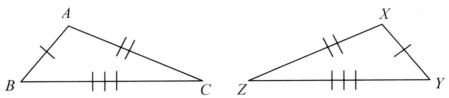

Since $AB \cong XY$, $BC \cong YZ$ and $AC \cong XZ$, then $\triangle ABC \cong \triangle XYZ$.

<u>Example</u>: Given isosceles triangle ABC with D being the midpoint of base AC, prove that the two triangles ABD and ADC are congruent.

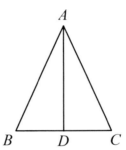

<u>Proof:</u>

1. Isosceles triangle ABC, D midpoint of base AC	Given
2. $AB \cong AC$	An isosceles triangle has two congruent sides
3. $BD \cong DC$	Midpoint divides a line into two equal parts
4. $AD \cong AD$	Reflexive property
5. $\triangle ABD \cong \triangle BCD$	SSS

The **ASA Postulate** (angle-side-angle) states that if two angles and the included side of one triangle are congruent to two angles and the included side of another triangle, the triangles are congruent.

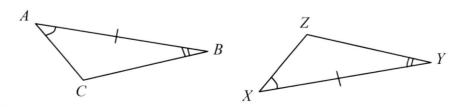

$\angle A \cong \angle X$, $\angle B \cong \angle Y$, $AB \cong XY$ then $\triangle ABC \cong \triangle XYZ$ by ASA

<u>Example:</u> Given two right triangles with one leg (*AB* and *KL*) of each measuring 6 cm and the adjacent angle 37º, prove the triangles are congruent.

<u>Proof:</u>

1. Right $\triangle ABC$ and $\triangle KLM$
    $AB = KL = 6$ cm
    $\angle A = \angle K = 37º$
	Given

2. $AB \cong KL$ $\angle A \cong \angle K$	Figures with the same measure are congruent
3. $\angle B \cong \angle L$	All right angles are congruent.
4. $\triangle ABC \cong \triangle KLM$	ASA

<u>Example:</u> What method could be used to prove that triangles ABC and ADE are congruent?

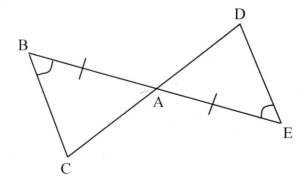

The sides *AB* and *AE* are given as congruent, as are $\angle BAC$ and $\angle DAE$. $\angle BAC$ and $\angle DAE$ are vertical angles and are therefore congruent. Thus triangles $\triangle ABC$ and $\triangle ADE$ are congruent by the ASA postulate.

The **HL Theorem** (hypotenuse-leg) is a congruence shortcut that can only be used with right triangles. According to this theorem, if the hypotenuse and leg of one right triangle are congruent to the hypotenuse and leg of the other right triangle, then the two triangles are congruent.

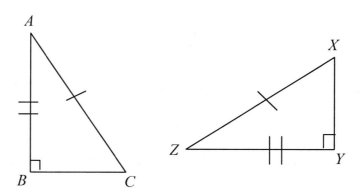

If $\angle B$ and $\angle Y$ are right angles and $AC \cong XZ$ (hypotenuse of each triangle), $AB \cong YZ$ (corresponding leg of each triangle), then $\triangle ABC \cong \triangle XYZ$ by HL.

Proof:

1. $\angle B \cong \angle Y$
   $AB \cong YZ$
   $AC \cong XZ$ Given

2. $BC = \sqrt{AC^2 - AB^2}$ Pythagorean theorem
3. $XY = \sqrt{XZ^2 - YZ^2}$ Pythagorean theorem
4. $XY = \sqrt{AC^2 - AB^2} = BC$ Substitution ($XZ \cong AC$, $YZ \cong AB$)

5. $\triangle ABC \cong \triangle XYZ$ SAS ($AB \cong YZ$, $\angle B \cong \angle Y$, $BC \cong XY$)

9D. **Describe and justify geometric constructions made using a compass and straight edge and other appropriate technologies**

Classical construction refers to the use of a straightedge and compass for creating geometrical figures that match certain criteria. A construction consists of only segments, arcs, and points. Typical constructions includes the replication of line segments, angles or shapes, bisection of angles and lines, drawing lines that are parallel or perpendicular to a given line, as well as drawing different kinds of polygons and circles.

Duplication of line segments and angles

The easiest construction to make is to **duplicate a given line segment**. Given segment AB, construct a segment equal in length to segment AB by following these steps.

1. Place a point anywhere in the plane to anchor the duplicate segment. Call this point S.

2. Open the compass to match the length of segment AB. Keeping the compass rigid, swing an arc from S.

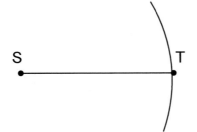

3. Draw a segment from S to any point on the arc. This segment will be the same length as AB.

To construct an angle congruent to a given angle:

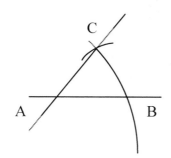

1. Given the angle A, draw an arc with any radius such that it intersects the sides of the angle at B and C.

2. On a working line *w*, select a point A' as the vertex of the angle to be drawn. With A' as the center and the same radius as the previous arc, draw an arc that intersects the line *w* in B'.

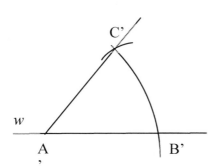

3. With B' as the center and radius equal to BC (measured off by placing ends of compass on B and C), draw a second arc that intersects the first arc at C'.

4. Join points A' and C'. The angle A' is congruent to the given angle A.

Construction of parallel lines

Angle duplication may be used to construct a line parallel to a given line AB through point W as shown below:

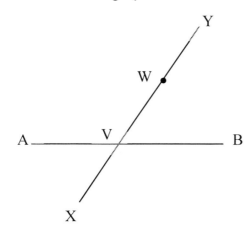

1. Draw a line XY through W intersecting AB in V.

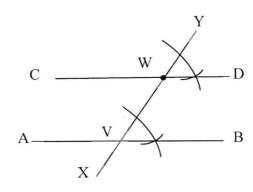

2. Construct angle YWD congruent to angle WVB. Then CD is the line parallel to AB.

Construction of perpendicular lines and bisectors

Given a line such as line l and a point P not on l, follow these steps to construct a **perpendicular line to l that passes through P.**

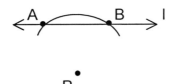

1. Swing an arc of any radius from P so that the arc intersects line l in two points A and B.

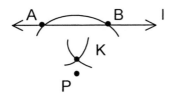

2. Open the compass to any length and swing two arcs of the same radius, one from A and the other from B. These two arcs will intersect at a new point K.

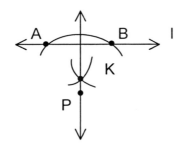

3. Connect K and P to form a line perpendicular to line l that passes through P.

Given a line segment with two endpoints such as A and B, follow these steps to **construct the line that both bisects and is perpendicular** to the line given segment.

1. Swing an arc of any radius from point A. Swing another arc of the same radius from B. The arcs will intersect at two points. Label these points C and D.

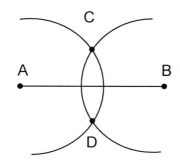

2. Connect C and D to form the perpendicular bisector of segment

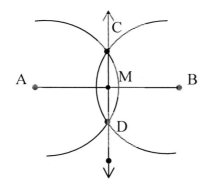

3. The point M where line CD and segment AB intersect is the midpoint of segment AB.

Construction of angle bisectors

To **bisect a given angle** such as angle *FUZ*, follow these steps.

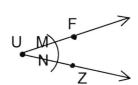

1. Swing an arc of any length with its center at point U. This arc will intersect rays *UF* and *UZ* at M and N.

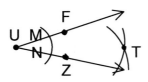

2. Open the compass to any length and swing one arc from point M and another arc of the same radius from point N. These arcs will intersect in the interior or angle *FUZ* at point T.

3. Connect U and T for the ray which bisects angle *FUZ*. Ray *UT* is the angle bisector of angle *FUZ*

Replicating shapes

The constructions we have done so far provide the building blocks of different shapes we may want to replicate. A shape consisting of a square topped by an equilateral triangle (shown below) may be replicated by following these steps:

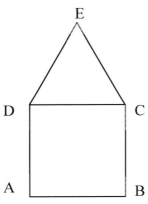

1. Draw a horizontal working line *w*.

2. Draw a line *l* perpendicular to the line *w* such that it intersects w in A'.

3. With A as center draw an arc with radius AB such that it intersects line w in B' and line l in D'.

4. Draw line *m* parallel to line A'B' through D'.

5. With D as center draw an arc that cuts line m in C'.

6. Join B'C' to complete the square.

7. With D' and C' as centers and radius equal to DE draw two arcs that intersect in E'.

8. Join D'E' and C'E' to complete the triangle.

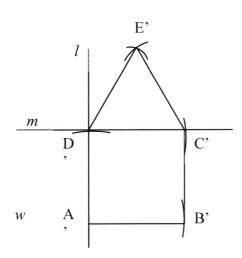

Construction of regular polygons

Not all regular polygons can be constructed with a compass and straightedge. The mathematician Gauss showed that a regular polygon with n sides can be constructed using a compass and ruler only if n is a product of a power of 2 and any number of distinct Fermat primes. Since the only known small Fermat primes are 3, 5, and 27, **a regular polygon can be constructed only if it has one of the following number of sides: 3, 4, 5, 6, 8, 10, 12, 15, 16, 17, 20, 24,**.. and so on.

We have already constructed an **equilateral triangle** and **square** in replicating a shape. Constructing a regular hexagon and **regular** octagon within a circle is also relatively simple. For construction of a **regular hexagon**, draw a diameter (AB in the figure below) in a circle. Then using the end points of the diameter A and B as centers, draw arcs with radius equal to the radius of the circle to intersect the circle in four points (C&D from A, E&F from B) that are the other vertices of the hexagon.

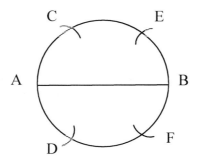

A **regular octagon** may be constructed by drawing two perpendicular diameters within a circle followed by lines that bisect the angles formed by the diameters. The points where all these lines intersect the circle are the vertices of a regular octagon.

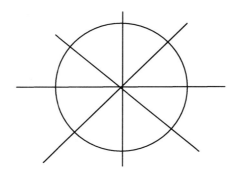

Construction of a **regular pentagon** is a little more involved. One method of construction is described below:

Make a circle with your compass, use the ruler to draw a line through the center of the circle (diameter). Then using compass and ruler, draw a vertical perpendicular line to the diameter (a radii). Next, using the same two tools, find the midpoint between point B and the center, point C, of the circle and draw another line from the midpoint of $\overline{BC}$ to point D. Next bisect $\angle a$ in half to a point on $\overline{DC}$.

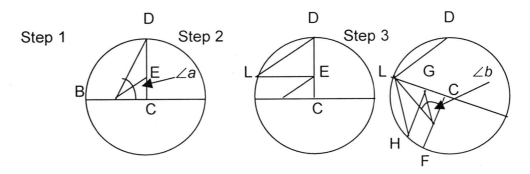

In Step 2, draw a line from point E to the edge of the circle that is parallel to $\overline{BC}$ and then connect points L and D with a line- this is the first side of your regular pentagon: $\overline{LD}$. To construct the second side, simply draw a line from point L through the center, point C to the other side of the circle that we'll call point F. Repeat the entire process of Steps 1 and 2 to find the second side of our regular pentagon: from the midpoint of $\overline{FC}$, draw a line to point L, then bisect $\angle b$ to a point on $\overline{LC}$ which we'll call point G. Once again, draw a line that is parallel to $\overline{FC}$ from point G to the circle's edge, which can be called point H. Connect point L and point H and you have created the second side of the regular pentagon. Repeat these steps until all five sides have been drawn and to created a regular pentagon (all sides equal and all angles = 108°) just by using a compass and ruler.

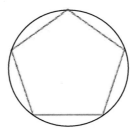

9E. **Apply knowledge of the axiomatic structure of Euclidean geometry to justify and prove theorems**

Deductive thinking is the process of arriving at a conclusion based on other statements that are all known to be true, such as theorems, axioms or postulates. Valid mathematical arguments are deductive in nature.

A **direct proof** demonstrates a proposition by beginning with the given information and showing that it leads to the proposition through logical steps. An **indirect proof** of a proposition can be carried out by demonstrating that the opposite of the proposition is untenable.

A proof of a geometrical proposition is typically presented in a format with two columns side by side. In a **two-column proof** of this type, the left column consists of the given information or statements that can be proved by deductive reasoning. The right column consists of the reasons used to justify each statement on the left. The right side should identify given information or state the theorems, postulates, definitions or algebraic properties used to show that the corresponding steps are valid.

The following **algebraic postulates** are frequently used as justifications for statements in two-column geometric proofs:

Addition Property:	If $a = b$ and $c = d$, then $a + c = b + d$.
Subtraction Property:	If $a = b$ and $c = d$, then $a - c = b - d$.
Multiplication Property:	If $a = b$, then $ac = bc$.
Division Property:	If $a = b$ and $c \neq 0$, then $a/c = b/c$.
Reflexive Property:	$a = a$
Symmetric Property:	If $a = b$, then $b = a$.
Transitive Property:	If $a = b$ and $b = c$, then $a = c$.
Distributive Property:	$a(b + c) = ab + ac$
Substitution Property:	If $a = b$, then b may be substituted for a in any other expression (a may also be substituted for b).

Euclidean geometry (as well as other geometric systems) are based on certain **axioms** that are unprovable, but are accepted as true. Based on these fundamental tenets, conclusions are derived deductively according to the general rules of logic and mathematical reasoning. These conclusions, in so far as they rely on the axioms of the geometric system, only apply where the axioms are accepted as true. In other systems with different axioms, such conclusions may not be true. For instance, one consequence of the axioms of Euclidean geometry is that there is only one line that connects two particular points; in other geometric systems (such as spherical geometry, for instance), there may be multiple lines that connect two points.

Thus, the discussion of the Parallel Postulate presented above applies only where the axioms that underlie Euclidean geometry are accepted. The Parallel Postulate therefore has a different formulation (and different consequences) in systems with different axioms. These variations illustrate the nature of an axiomatic system. The preceding skill sections in this competency illustrate particular instances of reasoning to the end of justifying and proving theorems and other conclusions.

Competency 010   The teacher analyzes the properties of two- and three-dimensional figures.

This competency reviews the properties of polygons, circles, and other two-dimensional figures and also reviews the properties of three-dimensional figures. Volume, area, perimeter, and other properties are discussed, as are the concepts of similarity, nets, and cross-sections.

10A.   Use and understand the development of formulas to find lengths, perimeters, areas, and volumes of basic geometric figures

A polygon is a simple closed figure composed of line segments. Here we will consider only **convex polygons**, i.e. polygons for which the measure of each internal angle is less than 180°. Of the two polygons shown below, the one on the left is a convex polygon.

A **regular polygon** is one for which all sides are the same length and all interior angles are the same measure.

The sum of the measures of the **interior angles** of a polygon can be determined using the following formula, where n represents the number of angles in the polygon.

Sum of $\angle s = 180(n - 2)$

The measure of each angle of a regular polygon can be found by dividing the sum of the measures by the number of angles.

Measure of $\angle = \dfrac{180(n - 2)}{n}$

Example: Find the measure of each angle of a regular octagon. Since an octagon has eight sides, each angle equals:

$$\frac{180(8-2)}{8} = \frac{180(6)}{8} = 135°$$

The sum of the measures of the **exterior angles** of a polygon, taken one angle at each vertex, equals 360°.

The measure of each exterior angle of a regular polygon can be determined using the following formula, where n represents the number of angles in the polygon.

Measure of exterior $\angle$ of regular polygon

$$= 180 - \frac{180(n-2)}{n} = \frac{360}{n}$$

Example: Find the measure of the interior and exterior angles of a regular pentagon.

Since a pentagon has five sides, each exterior angle measures:

$$\frac{360}{5} = 72°$$

Since each exterior angle is supplementary to its interior angle, the interior angle measures 180 – 72 or 108°.

A **quadrilateral** is a polygon with four sides. The sum of the measures of the angles of a convex quadrilateral is 360°.

A **trapezoid** is a quadrilateral with exactly <u>one</u> pair of parallel sides. The two parallel sides of a trapezoid are called the bases, and the two non-parallel sides are called the legs. If the two legs are the same length, then the trapezoid is called isosceles.

The segment connecting the two midpoints of the legs is called the median. The median has the following two properties:

1. The median is parallel to the two bases.
2. The length of the median is equal to one-half the sum of the length of the two bases.

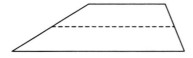

In an **isosceles trapezoid**, the non-parallel sides are congruent.

An isosceles trapezoid has the following properties:

1. The diagonals of an isosceles trapezoid are congruent.
2. The base angles of an isosceles trapezoid are congruent.

Example: An isosceles trapezoid has a diagonal of 10 and a base angle measure of 30°. Find the measure of the other 3 angles.

Based on the properties of trapezoids, the measure of the other base angle is 30° and the measure of the other diagonal is 10. The other two angles have a measure of

$$360 = 30(2) + 2x$$
$$x = 150°$$

The other two angles measure 150° each.

A **parallelogram** is a quadrilateral with two pairs of parallel sides and has the following properties:

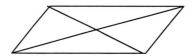

1. The diagonals bisect each other.
2. Each diagonal divides the parallelogram into two congruent triangles.
3. Both pairs of opposite sides are congruent.
4. Both pairs of opposite angles are congruent.
5. Two adjacent angles are supplementary.

Example: Find the measures of the other three angles of a parallelogram if one angle measures 38°.

Since opposite angles are equal, there are two angles measuring 38°. Since adjacent angles are supplementary, 180 − 38 = 142.

Hence the other two angles measure 142° each.

<u>Example:</u> The measures of two adjacent angles of a parallelogram are $3x + 40$ and $x + 70$. Find the measures of each angle.

$$2(3x + 40) + 2(x + 70) = 360$$
$$6x + 80 + 2x + 140 = 360$$
$$8x + 220 = 360$$
$$8x = 140$$
$$x = 17.5$$
$$3x + 40 = 92.5$$
$$x + 70 = 87.5$$

Thus the angles measure 92.5º, 92.5º, 87.5º, and 87.5º.

A **rectangle** is a parallelogram with a right angle. Since a rectangle is a special type of parallelogram, it exhibits all the properties of a parallelogram. All the angles of a rectangle are right angles because of congruent opposite angles. Additionally, the diagonals of a rectangle are congruent.

A **rhombus** is a parallelogram with all sides equal in length. A rhombus also has all the properties of a parallelogram. Additionally, its diagonals are perpendicular to each other and they bisect its angles.

A **square** is a rectangle with all sides equal in length. A **square** has all the properties of a rectangle <u>and</u> a rhombus.

<u>Example:</u> True or false?

All squares are rhombuses.	True
All parallelograms are rectangles.	False - <u>some</u> parallelograms are rectangles
All rectangles are parallelograms.	True

Some rhombuses are squares.	True
Some rectangles are trapezoids.	False - only <u>one</u> pair of parallel sides
All quadrilaterals are parallelograms.	False -some quadrilaterals are parallelograms
Some squares are rectangles.	False - all squares are rectangles
Some parallelograms are rhombuses.	True

<u>Example:</u> In rhombus *ABCD* side *AB* = 3*x* - 7 and side *CD* = *x* + 15. Find the length of each side.

Since all the sides are the same length, $3x - 7 = x + 15$
$$2x = 22$$
$$x = 11$$

Since $3(11) - 7 = 25$ and $11 + 15 = 25$, each side measures 25 units.

The **perimeter** of any polygon is the sum of the lengths of the sides. The **area** of a polygon is the number of square units covered by the figure or the space that a figure occupies. In the area formulae below, *b* refers to the base and *h* to the height or altitude of a figure. For a trapezoid, *a* and *b* are the two parallel bases.

FIGURE	AREA FORMULA	PERIMETER FORMULA
Rectangle	LW	$2(L + W)$
Triangle	$\frac{1}{2}bh$	$a + b + c$
Parallelogram	bh	sum of lengths of sides
Trapezoid	$\frac{1}{2}h(a + b)$	sum of lengths of sides

Even though different figures have different area formulae, the formulae are connected and one can be easily converted from one to another. For instance, it is easy to see from the diagram below that the area of the triangle ABD is half that of rectangle EABD and the area of triangle ADC is half that of rectangle AFDC. Thus, the area of triangle ABC is half that of rectangle EFBC and is equal to

$$\frac{1}{2}BC \cdot EB = \frac{1}{2}BC \cdot AD$$

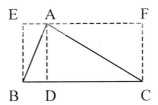

The area of a parallelogram may similarly be shown to be equal to that of an equivalent rectangle. Since triangles ACE and BDF are congruent in the diagram below (AE and BF are altitudes), parallelogram ABCD is equal in area to rectangle AEFB that has the same base (CD=EF) and height.

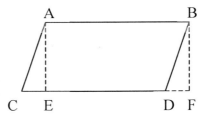

The area of a trapezoid is the sum of the areas of two triangles each of which has one of the parallel sides as a base. In the diagram below,

area of trapezoid ABCD = area of ABC + area of ACD

$$= \frac{1}{2}BC \cdot AE + \frac{1}{2}AD \cdot CF$$

$$= \frac{1}{2}AE(BC + AD) \quad \text{(Since AE = CF)}$$

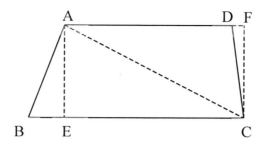

Example: A farmer has a piece of land shaped as shown below. He wishes to fence this land at an estimated cost of $25 per linear foot. What is the total cost of fencing this property to the nearest foot?

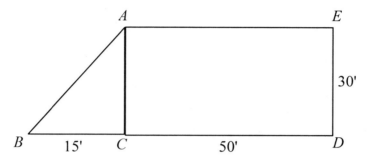

From the right triangle ABC, AC = 30 and BC = 15.

Since $(AB) = (AC)^2 + (BC)^2$, $(AB) = (30)^2 + (15)^2$. So, *AB* is $\sqrt{1{,}125}$ feet, or about 33.5 feet. To the nearest foot, AB = 34 feet. The perimeter of the piece of land is

$$AB + BC + CD + DE + EA = 34 + 15 + 50 + 30 + 50 = 179 \text{ feet}$$

The cost of fencing is $25 x 179 = $4,475.00

The area of any regular polygon having *n* sides can be expressed as a sum of the areas of *n* congruent triangles. If each side of the polygon is of length *a*, and the apothem (distance from center of polygon to one side) is *h*, area of the polygon = $n \times \dfrac{1}{2} \times a \times h$ (*n* times the area of one triangle)

Since *n* x *a* is the perimeter of the polygon, we can also write

$$\text{area of the polygon} = \frac{1}{2} \times \text{perimeter} \times \text{apothem}$$

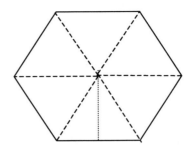

Three-Dimensional Figures

Three-dimensional figures require slightly more complicated mathematical manipulations to derive or apply such properties as surface area and volume. In some instances, two-dimensional concepts can be applied directly. In other instances, a more rigorous approach is needed.

To represent three-dimensional objects in a coordinate system, three coordinates are required. Thus, a point in three dimensions must be represented as (*x*, *y*, *z*), instead of simply (*x*, *y*) as is used in the two-dimensional representation.

The **volume** and **surface area** of three-dimensional figures can be derived most clearly (in some cases) using integral calculus. (See **Competency 007** for more information on integrals.)

An area, bounded by a curve (or curves), that is revolved about a line is called a **solid of revolution**. To find the volume of such a solid, the **disc method** (called the **washer method** if the solid has an empty interior of some form) works in most instances. Imagine slicing through the solid perpendicular to the line of revolution. The cross section should resemble either a disc or a washer. The washer method involves finding the sum of the volumes of all "washers" that compose the solid, using the following general formula:

$$V = \pi \left(r_1^2 - r_2^2 \right) t$$

where *V* is the volume of the washer, r_1 and r_2 are the interior and exterior radii and *t* is the thickness of the washer.

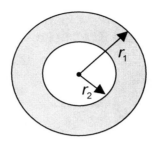

Depending on the situation, the radius is the distance from the line of revolution to the curve; or if there are two curves involved, the radius is the difference between the two functions. The thickness is dx if the line of revolution is parallel to the x-axis and dy if the line of revolution is parallel to the y-axis. The integral is then the following, where dV is the differential volume of a washer.

$$\int dV = \int \pi \left(r_1^2 - r_2^2 \right) dt$$
$$V = \pi \int \left(r_1^2 - r_2^2 \right) dt$$

It is assumed here that r_1 is the outer radius and r_2 is the inner radius. For the disc method, where only one radius is needed, $r_2 = 0$.

For instance, the volume of a **sphere** of radius r can be derived by revolving a semicircular area around the axis defined by its diameter.

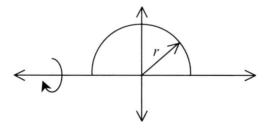

The result of this revolution is a solid sphere of radius r. To perform the integral, use the function $f(x)$ for the semicircle of radius r.

$$f(x) = \sqrt{r^2 - x^2}$$

$$V = \pi \int_{-r}^{r} \left[\sqrt{r^2 - x^2} \right]^2 dx$$

$$V = \pi \int_{-r}^{r} \left(r^2 - x^2 \right) dx$$

$$V = \pi \left[r^2 x - \frac{x^3}{3} \right]_{-r}^{r} = \pi \left[\left(r^3 + r^3 \right) - \left(\frac{r^3}{3} + \frac{r^3}{3} \right) \right]$$

$$V = \pi \left[2r^3 - \frac{2r^3}{3} \right] = \frac{4}{3} \pi r^3$$

The surface area can also be found by a similar integral that calculates the surface of revolution around the diameter, but there is a simpler method. Note that the differential change in volume of a sphere (dV) for a differential change in the radius (dr) is an infinitesimally thin spherical shell.

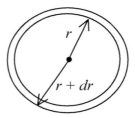

This infinitesimally thin shell is simply a surface with an area, but no volume. Find the derivative of the volume with respect to the radius to get the surface area. (Alternatively, this can be viewed as the differential volume of a thin spherical shell divided by the differential change in radius, which leads to an area.)

$$S = \frac{dV}{dr} = \frac{d}{dr} \frac{4}{3} \pi r^3$$

$$S = 4\pi r^2$$

The volume and surface area of a **right cone**, use an approach similar to that of the sphere. In this case, however, a line segment, rather than a semicircle, is revolved around the horizontal axis. The cone has a height h and a base radius r.

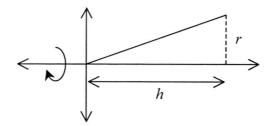

The function $f(x)$ that defines the line segment in this case is

$$f(x) = \frac{r}{h}x$$

from $x = 0$ to $x = h$.

$$V = \pi \int_0^h \left(\frac{r}{h}x\right)^2 dx$$

$$V = \pi \left(\frac{r}{h}\right)^2 \int_0^h x^2 dx = \pi \left(\frac{r}{h}\right)^2 \left[\frac{x^3}{3}\right]_0^h$$

$$V = \pi \left(\frac{r}{h}\right)^2 \frac{h^3}{3} = \frac{\pi r^2 h}{3}$$

To find the **lateral surface area** (which excludes the flat end of the cone), an integral must be used to find the surface of revolution. This integral uses $f(x)$ as follows (which is based on the arc length integral derived later in this section).

$$S = 2\pi \int_0^h f(x)\sqrt{1 + \left[f'(x)\right]^2}\, dx$$

$$f'(x) = \frac{r}{h}$$

$$S = 2\pi \sqrt{1 + \left(\frac{r}{h}\right)^2} \frac{r}{h}\int_0^h x\, dx = \frac{2\pi r}{h}\sqrt{1 + \left(\frac{r}{h}\right)^2}\left[\frac{x^2}{2}\right]_0^h$$

$$S = \frac{2\pi r}{h}\sqrt{1 + \left(\frac{r}{h}\right)^2}\left[\frac{h^2}{2}\right] = \pi r h\left(\frac{1}{h}\right)\sqrt{r^2 + h^2}$$

$$S = \pi r\sqrt{r^2 + h^2}$$

For right circular cylinders, the volume is simply the area of a cross section (a circle of radius r) multiplied by the height h of the cylinder. The lateral surface area (the surface area excluding the area on the ends of the figure) is simply the circumference of the circular cross section multiplied by the height h.

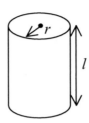

$$V = \pi r^2 h$$
$$S = 2\pi rh$$

The volumes and surface areas of these figures are summarized below.

Figure	Volume	Lateral Surface Area
Right Cylinder	$\pi r^2 h$	$2\pi rh + 2\pi r^2$
Right Cone	$\dfrac{\pi r^2 h}{3}$	$\pi r\sqrt{r^2 + h^2} + \pi r^2$
Sphere	$\dfrac{4}{3}\pi r^3$	$4\pi r^2$

For figures such as pyramids and prisms, the volume and surface areas must be derived by breaking the figure into portions for which these values can be calculated easily. For instance, consider the following figure.

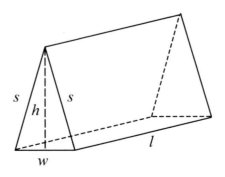

The volume of this figure can be found by calculating the area of the triangular cross section and then multiplying by *l*.

$$V = \frac{1}{2}hwl$$

The lateral surface area can be found by adding the areas of each side.

$$S = 2sl + lw$$

Similar reasoning applies to other figures composed of sides that are defined by triangles, quadrilaterals and other planar or linear elements.

The **arc length** of a curve is another useful application of integration. The arc length is the distance traversed by a curve over a given interval. Geometrically, the distance *d* between two points (x_1, y_1) and (x_2, y_2) is given by the following formula.

$$d = \sqrt{(x_2 - x_1)^2 + (y_2 - y_1)^2}$$

If the points are only an infinitesimal distance apart (*ds*, which is the differential arc length), then the above expression can be written as follows in differential form.

$$ds = \sqrt{dx^2 + dy^2}$$

Factor out the *dx* term:

$$ds = \sqrt{1 + \left(\frac{dy}{dx}\right)^2}\, dx$$

But $\frac{dy}{dx}$ is simply the derivative of a function *y(x)* (which can be expressed as *f(x)* instead). Thus, the integral of the above expression over the interval [*a*, *b*] yields the formula for the arc length.

$$\int ds = s = \int_a^b \sqrt{1 + \left[f'(x)\right]^2}\, dx$$

<u>Example:</u> Find the distance traversed by the function

$f(x) = \ln(\cos x)$ on the interval $\left[-\dfrac{\pi}{4}, \dfrac{\pi}{4} \right]$.

Use the formula for arc length s, applying trigonometric identities as appropriate.

$$s = \int \sqrt{1 + \left[\dfrac{d}{dx} \ln(\cos x) \right]^2} = \int \sqrt{1 + \left[\dfrac{\sin x}{\cos x} \right]^2} \, dx$$

$$s = \int \sqrt{1 + [\tan x]^2} \, dx = \int \sqrt{1 + \tan^2 x} \, dx = \int \sqrt{\sec^2 x} \, dx$$

$$s = \int \sqrt{1 + [\tan x]^2} \, dx = \int \sqrt{1 + \tan^2 x} \, dx = \int \sec x \, dx$$

Evaluate the integral over the limits of integration.

$$s = \int_{-\pi/4}^{\pi/4} \sec x \, dx = \ln(\sec x + \tan x) \Big|_{-\pi/4}^{\pi/4}$$

$$s = \ln\left(\sec \dfrac{\pi}{4} + \tan \dfrac{\pi}{4} \right) - \ln\left(\sec\left[-\dfrac{\pi}{4} \right] + \tan\left[\dfrac{\pi}{4} \right] \right)$$

$$s = \ln\left(\sqrt{2} + 1 \right) - \ln\left(\sqrt{2} - 1 \right) \approx 1.763$$

The result is approximately 1.763 units.

<u>Example:</u> Find the height of a box whose volume is 120 cubic meters and the area of the base is 30 square meters.

$$V = Bh$$
$$120 = 30h$$
$$h = 4 \text{ meters}$$

<u>Example:</u> How much material is needed to make a basketball that has a diameter of 15 inches? How much air is needed to fill the basketball?

Draw and label a sketch:

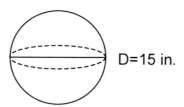

D=15 in.

Surface Area

$SA = 4\pi r^2$

$= 4\pi (7.5)^2$

$= 706.858 \text{ in}^2$

3. solve

Volume

$V = \dfrac{4}{3}\pi r^3$

$= \dfrac{4}{3}\pi (7.5)^3$

$= 1767.1459 \text{ in}^3$

1. write formula

2. substitute

Similar solids share the same shape but are not necessarily the same size. The ratio of any two corresponding measurements of similar solids is the scale factor. For example, the scale factor for two square pyramids, one with a side measuring 2 inches and the other with a side measuring 4 inches, is 2:4.

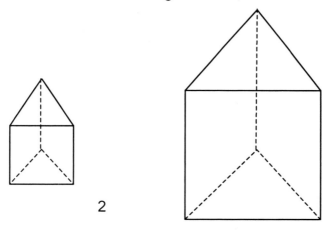

2

4

The base perimeter, the surface area, and the volume of similar solids are directly related to the scale factor. If the scale factor of two similar solids is a:b, then

ratio of base perimeters = a:b
ratio of areas = a^2:b^2
ratio of volumes = a^3:b^3

Thus, for the above example,

> ratio of base perimeters = 2:4
> ratio of areas = $2^2:4^2$ = 4:16
> ratio of volumes = $2^3:4^3$ = 8:64

Example: What happens to the volume of a square pyramid when the length of the sides of the base are doubled?

> scale factor = a:b = 1:2
> ratio of volume = $1^3:2^3$ = 1:8 (The volume is increased 8 times.)

Example: Given the following measurements for two similar cylinders with a scale factor of 2:5 (cylinder A to cylinder B), determine the height, radius, and volume of each cylinder.

> cylinder A: $r = 2$
> cylinder B: $h = 10$

For cylinder A,

$$\frac{h_a}{10} = \frac{2}{5}$$
$$5h_a = 20 \qquad \text{Solve for } h_a$$
$$h_a = 4$$

Volume of cylinder A = $\pi r^2 h = \pi(2)^2 4 = 16\pi$

For cylinder B,

$$\frac{2}{r_b} = \frac{2}{5}$$
$$2r_b = 10 \qquad \text{Solve for } r_b$$
$$r_b = 5$$

Volume of cylinder B = $\pi r^2 h = \pi(5)^2 10 = 250\pi$

Example: A water glass of height 6" and an inner radius of 2" is filled to the top with water. How high would a conical glass with inner sides meeting at 45° have to be to hold the same amount of water?

This question requires comparing volumes. First, find the volume V_c of the cylindrical glass.

$$V_c = \pi r^2 h = \pi (2 \text{ in})^2 (6 \text{ in}) = 24\pi \text{ in}^3 \approx 75.4 \text{ in}^3$$

Next, write the volume of the cone in terms of the radius r. The relationship between the height h of the cone and the radius r is the following (since the sides meet at 45° at the apex):

$$\frac{r}{h} = \tan 22.5° \approx 0.414$$
$$r = 0.414h$$

The volume of a cone is

$$V = \frac{\pi r^2 h}{3}$$

In this case,

$$V \approx \frac{\pi h}{3}(0.414h)^2 \approx 0.057\pi h^3$$

After equating the volume of the conical glass with that of the cylindrical glass, the height of the cone that holds the same volume can be calculated.

$$75.4 \text{ in}^3 = 0.057\pi h^3$$
$$h^3 = \frac{75.4 \text{ in}^3}{0.057\pi} \approx 421.1 \text{ in}^3$$
$$h \approx 7.50 \text{ in}$$

Thus, the cone must be about 7.5 inches high.

10B. Apply relationships among similar figures, scale, and proportion and analyzes how changes in scale affect area and volume measurements

Similarity

Two figures that have the same shape are **similar**. To be the same shape, corresponding angles must be equal. Therefore, polygons are similar if and only if there is a one-to-one correspondence between their vertices such that the corresponding angles are congruent. For similar figures, the lengths of corresponding sides are proportional. The symbol ~ is used to indicate that two figures are similar.

The polygons *ABCDE* and *VWXYZ* shown below are similar.

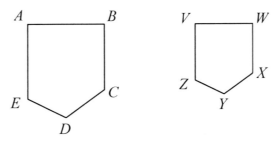

ABCDE ~ VWXYZ

Corresponding angles: $\angle A = \angle V$, $\angle B = \angle W$, $\angle C = \angle X$, $\angle D = \angle Y$, $\angle E = \angle Z$

Corresponding sides: $\dfrac{AB}{VW} = \dfrac{BC}{WX} = \dfrac{CD}{XY} = \dfrac{DE}{YZ} = \dfrac{AE}{VZ}$

<u>Example:</u> Given two similar quadrilaterals, find the lengths of sides *x, y,* and *z*.

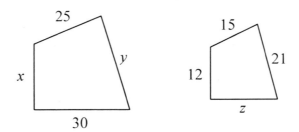

Since corresponding sides are proportional, 15/25 = 3/5, so the scale factor is 3/5.

$$\frac{12}{x} = \frac{3}{5} \qquad\qquad \frac{21}{y} = \frac{3}{5} \qquad\qquad \frac{z}{30} = \frac{3}{5}$$
$$3x = 60 \qquad\qquad 3y = 105 \qquad\qquad 5z = 90$$
$$x = 20 \qquad\qquad y = 35 \qquad\qquad z = 18$$

Just as for congruence, there are shortcut methods that can be used to prove similarity.

According to the **AA Similarity Postulate**, if two angles of one triangle are congruent to two angles of another triangle, then the triangles are similar. It is obvious that if two of the corresponding angles are congruent, the third set of corresponding angles must be congruent as well. Hence, showing AA is sufficient to prove that two triangles are similar.

The **SAS Similarity Theorem** states that, if an angle of one triangle is congruent to an angle of another triangle and the sides adjacent to those angles are in proportion, then the triangles are similar.

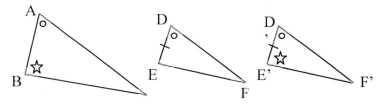

If $\angle A = \angle D$ and $\dfrac{AB}{DE} = \dfrac{AC}{DF}$, $\sqcup ABC \sqcup DEF$.

Example: A graphic artist is designing a logo containing two triangles. The artist wants the triangles to be similar. Determine whether the artist has created similar triangles.

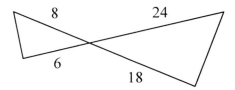

The sides are proportional $\dfrac{8}{24} = \dfrac{6}{18} = \dfrac{1}{3}$ and vertical angles are congruent. The two triangles are therefore similar by the SAS similarity theorem.

According to the **SSS Similarity Theorem**, if the sides of two triangles are in proportion, then the triangles are similar.

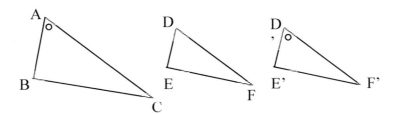

If $\dfrac{AB}{DE} = \dfrac{AC}{DF} = \dfrac{BC}{EF}$, ⊔ABC ⊔DEF

Example: Tommy draws and cuts out 2 triangles for a school project. One of them has sides of 3, 6, and 9 inches. The other triangle has sides of 2, 4, and 6. Is there a relationship between the two triangles?

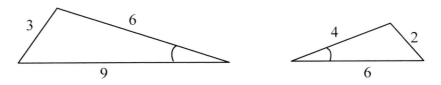

Determine the proportions of the corresponding sides.

$$\frac{2}{3} \qquad\qquad \frac{4}{6} = \frac{2}{3} \qquad\qquad \frac{6}{9} = \frac{2}{3}$$

The smaller triangle is 2/3 the size of the large triangle, therefore they are similar triangles by the SSS similarity theorem.

Some of the problems in the above skill section on formulas for geometric figures treat cases where dimensions of figures or solids are changed, resulting in changes to certain other parameters.

10C. Use a variety of representations (e.g., numeric, verbal, graphic, symbolic) to analyze and solve problems involving two- and three-dimensional figures such as circles, triangles, polygons, cylinders, prisms, and spheres

A polygon is a simple closed figure composed of line segments. Here we will consider only **convex polygons**, i.e. polygons for which the measure of each internal angle is less than 180°. Of the two polygons shown below, the one on the left is a convex polygon.

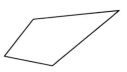 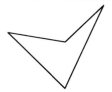

A **regular polygon** is one for which all sides are the same length and all interior angles are the same measure.

The sum of the measures of the **interior angles** of a polygon can be determined using the following formula, where n represents the number of angles in the polygon.

Sum of $\angle s = 180(n - 2)$

The measure of each angle of a regular polygon can be found by dividing the sum of the measures by the number of angles.

Measure of $\angle = \dfrac{180(n - 2)}{n}$

Example: Find the measure of each angle of a regular octagon. Since an octagon has eight sides, each angle equals:

$$\dfrac{180(8 - 2)}{8} = \dfrac{180(6)}{8} = 135^\circ$$

The sum of the measures of the **exterior angles** of a polygon, taken one angle at each vertex, equals 360º.

The measure of each exterior angle of a regular polygon can be determined using the following formula, where n represents the number of angles in the polygon.

Measure of exterior $\angle$ of regular polygon
$$= 180 - \dfrac{180(n - 2)}{n} = \dfrac{360}{n}$$

Example: Find the measure of the interior and exterior angles of a regular pentagon.

Since a pentagon has five sides, each exterior angle measures:

$$\dfrac{360}{5} = 72^\circ$$

Since each exterior angle is supplementary to its interior angle, the interior angle measures 180 – 72 or 108°.

A **quadrilateral** is a polygon with four sides. The sum of the measures of the angles of a convex quadrilateral is 360°.

A **trapezoid** is a quadrilateral with exactly <u>one</u> pair of parallel sides. The two parallel sides of a trapezoid are called the bases, and the two non-parallel sides are called the legs. If the two legs are the same length, then the trapezoid is called isosceles.

The segment connecting the two midpoints of the legs is called the median. The median has the following two properties:

1. The median is parallel to the two bases.
2. The length of the median is equal to one-half the sum of the length of the two bases.

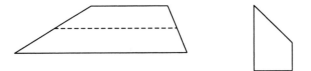

In an **isosceles trapezoid**, the non-parallel sides are congruent.

An isosceles trapezoid has the following properties:

1. The diagonals of an isosceles trapezoid are congruent.
2. The base angles of an isosceles trapezoid are congruent.

<u>Example:</u> An isosceles trapezoid has a diagonal of 10 and a base angle measure of 30°. Find the measure of the other 3 angles.

Based on the properties of trapezoids, the measure of the other base angle is 30° and the measure of the other diagonal is 10. The other two angles have a measure of

$$360 = 30(2) + 2x$$
$$x = 150°$$

The other two angles measure 150° each.

A **parallelogram** is a quadrilateral with <u>two</u> pairs of parallel sides and has the following properties:

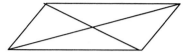

1. The diagonals bisect each other.
2. Each diagonal divides the parallelogram into two congruent triangles.
3. Both pairs of opposite sides are congruent.
4. Both pairs of opposite angles are congruent.
5. Two adjacent angles are supplementary.

<u>Example:</u> Find the measures of the other three angles of a parallelogram if one angle measures 38°.

Since opposite angles are equal, there are two angles measuring 38°. Since adjacent angles are supplementary, 180 − 38 = 142. Hence the other two angles measure 142° each.

<u>Example:</u> The measures of two adjacent angles of a parallelogram are 3x + 40 and x + 70. Find the measures of each angle.

$$2(3x + 40) + 2(x + 70) = 360$$
$$6x + 80 + 2x + 140 = 360$$
$$8x + 220 = 360$$
$$8x = 140$$
$$x = 17.5$$
$$3x + 40 = 92.5$$
$$x + 70 = 87.5$$

Thus the angles measure 92.5°, 92.5°, 87.5°, and 87.5°.

A **rectangle** is a parallelogram with a right angle. Since a rectangle is a special type of parallelogram, it exhibits all the properties of a parallelogram. All the angles of a rectangle are right angles because of congruent opposite angles. Additionally, the diagonals of a rectangle are congruent.

A **rhombus** is a parallelogram with all sides equal in length. A rhombus also has all the properties of a parallelogram. Additionally, its diagonals are perpendicular to each other and they bisect its angles.

A **square** is a rectangle with all sides equal in length. A **square** has all the properties of a rectangle <u>and</u> a rhombus.

<u>Example:</u> True or false?

All squares are rhombuses.	True
All parallelograms are rectangles.	False - <u>some</u> parallelograms are rectangles
All rectangles are parallelograms.	True
Some rhombuses are squares.	True
Some rectangles are trapezoids.	False - only <u>one</u> pair of parallel sides
All quadrilaterals are parallelograms.	False -some quadrilaterals are parallelograms
Some squares are rectangles.	False - all squares are rectangles
Some parallelograms are rhombuses.	True

<u>Example:</u> In rhombus *ABCD* side *AB* = 3x - 7 and side *CD* = x + 15. Find the length of each side.

Since all the sides are the same length, $3x - 7 = x + 15$
$$2x = 22$$
$$x = 11$$

Since $3(11) - 7 = 25$ and $11 + 15 = 25$, each side measures 25 units.

Circles

The distance around a circle is the **circumference**. The ratio of the circumference to the diameter is represented by the Greek letter pi, where $\pi \approx 3.14$. The circumference of a circle is given by the formula $C = 2\pi r$ or $C = \pi d$ where r is the radius of the circle and d is the diameter. The **area** of a circle is given by the formula $A = \pi r^2$.

We can extend the area formula of a regular polygon to get the area of a circle by considering the fact that a circle is essentially a regular polygon with an infinite number of sides. The radius of a circle is equivalent to the apothem of a regular polygon. Thus, applying the area formula for a regular polygon to a circle we get

$$\frac{1}{2} \times perimeter \times apothem = \frac{1}{2} \times 2\pi r \times r = \pi r^2$$

If two circles have radii that are in a ratio of $a : b$, then the following ratios also apply to the circles:

1. The diameters are in the ratio $a : b$.
2. The circumferences are in the ratio $a : b$.
3. The areas are in the ratio $a^2 : b^2$, or the ratio of the areas is the square of the ratio of the radii.

If you draw two radii in a circle, the angle they form with the center as the vertex is a **central angle**. The piece of the circle "inside" the angle is an arc. Just like a central angle, an arc can have any degree measure from 0 to 360. The measure of an arc is equal to the measure of the central angle that forms the arc. Since a diameter forms a semicircle and the measure of a straight angle like a diameter is 180°, the measure of a semicircle is also 180°.

Given two points on a circle, the two points form two different arcs. Except in the case of semicircles, one of the two arcs will always be greater than 180° and the other will be less than 180°. The arc less than 180° is a **minor arc** and the arc greater than 180° is a **major arc**.

Example: If $m\angle BAD = 45°$, what is the measure of the major arc BD?

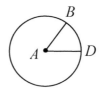

The minor arc BD is the same as $m\angle BAD = 45°$. Since the sum of the minor and major arcs formed by two points on a circle always add to 360º, the major arc BD must be 360º – 45º = 315º.

Example: If $\overline{AC}$ is a diameter of the circle below, what is the measure of $\angle BDC$?

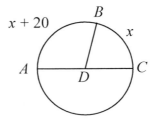

Since the diameter forms a semicircle ABC with a measure of 180º, the following expression applies.

$(x + 20) + x = 180°$

Solving for x yields

$2x + 20 = 180°$
$2x = 160°$
$x = 80°$

Finally, since the measure of an arc is the same as the measure of the central angle,

$\angle BDC = x = 80°$

Although an arc has a measure associated with the degree measure of the corresponding central angle, it also has a length that is a fraction of the circumference of the circle. For each central angle and its associated arc, there is a sector of the circle that resembles a pie piece. The area of such a sector is a fraction of the area of the circle. The fractions used for the area of a sector and length of its associated arc are both equal to the ratio of the central angle to 360°.

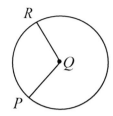

$$\frac{\angle PQR}{360°} = \frac{\text{length of arc RP}}{\text{circumference of circle}} = \frac{\text{area of sector PQR}}{\text{area of circle}}$$

<u>Example:</u> Circle A as a radius of 4 cm. What is the length of arc *ED*?

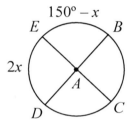

Because arcs *BE* and *ED* form a semicircle, arc *BED* is 180°. Use this to write an equation and solve for *x*.

$(150° - x) + 2x = 180°$
$x = 30°$

The angle corresponding to arc *ED* is thus $2x = 60°$. The ratio of this arc to that of the entire circle (360°) must be the same as the ratio of the arc length (labeled *L*) to the circumference of the circle, as shown below.

$$\frac{60°}{360°} = \frac{L}{2\pi(4\text{cm})}$$

$$L = \frac{1}{6}2\pi(4\text{cm}) = \frac{4}{3}\pi \text{ cm} \approx 4.19\text{cm}$$

<u>Example</u>: The radius of circle M is 3 cm. The length of arc *PF* is 2π cm. What is the area of sector *MPF*?

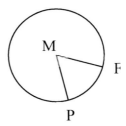

The circumference of the circle is 2π(3 cm), making the circumference equal to 6π cm. The total area of the circle is π(3 cm)^2, or 9π cm^2. The ratio of the arc length *PF* to the circumference of the circle must be the same as the ratio of the area of sector *MPF* (labeled *A*) to the total area of the circle. Thus,

$$\frac{A}{9\pi \text{ cm}^2} = \frac{2\pi}{6\pi}$$

$$A = \frac{1}{3}9\pi \text{ cm}^2 = 3\pi \text{ cm}^2 \approx 9.42 \text{ cm}^2$$

A **tangent line** intersects or touches a circle in exactly one point. If a radius is drawn to that point, the radius will be perpendicular to the tangent.

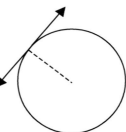

A **secant line** intersects a circle in two points and includes a **chord** which is a segment with endpoints on the circle. If a radius or diameter is perpendicular to a chord, the radius will cut the chord into two equal parts and vice-versa.

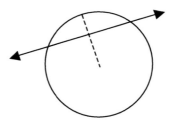

If **two chords** in the same circle have the same length, the two chords will have arcs that are the same length, and the two chords will be equidistant from the center of the circle. Distance from the center to a chord is measured by finding the length of a segment from the center perpendicular to the chord.

Example: $\overline{DB}$ is tangent to circle C at A. If $m\square ADC = 40°$, find x.

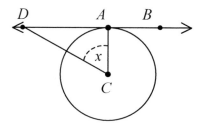

Since segment AC is perpendicular to the tangent line DB, angle DAC must be a right angle. Since $m\square ADC = 40°$ and since the sum of the angles in a triangle must be 180°,

$$90° + 40° + x = 180°$$
$$x = 50°$$

An **inscribed angle** is an angle whose vertex is on the circumference circle. Such an angle could be formed by two chords, two diameters, two secants, or a secant and a tangent. An inscribed angle has one arc of the circle in its interior. The measure of the inscribed angle is one-half the measure of its intercepted arc. If two inscribed angles intercept the same arc, the two angles are congruent (i.e., their measures are equal). If an inscribed angle intercepts an entire semicircle, the angle is a right angle.

When two chords intersect inside a circle, two sets of vertical angles are formed in the interior if the circle. Each set of vertical angles intercepts two arcs that are across from each other. The measure of an angle formed by two chords in a circle is equal to one-half the sum of the arc intercepted by the angle and the arc intercepted by its vertical angle.

If an angle has its vertex outside of the circle and each side of the angle intersects the circle, then the angle contains two different arcs. The measure of the angle is equal to one-half the difference of the two arcs.

<u>Example:</u> Find *x* and *y* for the circle below.

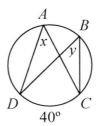

Since ∠ *DAC* and ∠ *DBC* are both inscribed angles, each has a measure equal to one-half of the measure of arc *DC*, or 20°. Thus, both *x* and *y* are equal to 20°.

<u>Example:</u> Find the measure of arc BC if the measure of arc DE is 30° and angle BAC is 20°.

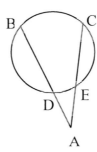

Use the following expression that relates the angle *BAC* to the lengths of the arcs *BC* and *DE*.

$$m\angle BAC = \frac{1}{2}(BC - DE)$$
$$2(20°) = 40° = BC - 30°$$
$$BC = 70°$$

If **two chords intersect inside a circle**, each chord is divided into two smaller segments. The product of the lengths of the two segments formed from one chord equals the product of the lengths of the two segments formed from the other chord.

If **two tangent segments intersect outside of a circle**, the two segments have the same length.

If **two secant segments intersect outside a circle**, a portion of each segment will lie inside the circle and a portion (called the exterior segment) will lie outside the circle. The product of the length of one secant segment and the length of its exterior segment equals the product of the length of the other secant segment and the length of its exterior segment.

If **a tangent segment and a secant segment intersect outside a circle**, the square of the length of the tangent segment equals the product of the length of the secant segment and its exterior segment.

Example: If $\overline{AB}$ and $\overline{CD}$ are chords and $CE = 10$, $ED = x$, $AE = 5$, and $EB = 4$, find x.

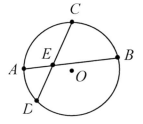

Because the chords intersect inside the circle, the product of the segment lengths for chord CD is equal to the product of the segment lengths for chord AB. Thus,

$(AE)(EB) = (CE)(ED)$
$(5)(4) = (10)(x)$
$10x = 20$
$x = 2$

The length of x (or segment ED) is 2.

Example: Find the lengths of chords AB and CB if $AB = x^2 + x - 2$ and $BC = x^2 - 3x + 5$.

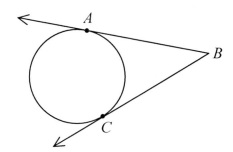

These chords are both tangent to the circle. Because intersecting tangents are equal in length, find x by setting the two quadratic expressions equal to one another:

$$x^2 + x - 2 = x^2 - 3x + 5$$
$$4x = 7$$
$$x = \frac{7}{4} = 1.75$$

Using this result, the lengths of the segments can be found by substitution.

$$AB = (1.75)^2 + (1.75) - 2 = 3.0625 + 1.75 - 2 = 2.8125$$
$$BC = (1.75)^2 - 3(1.75) + 5 = 3.0625 - 5.25 + 5 = 2.1825$$

10D. Analyze the relationship among three-dimensional figures and related two-dimensional representations (e.g., projections, cross-sections, nets) and use these representations to solve problems

If a three-dimensional object is intersected by a plane, it forms a cross section. In the picture below, the striped portion is a cross section of a cube.

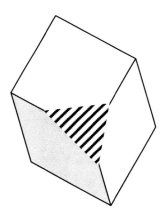

A conic section (e.g., a circle, ellipse, parabola, or hyperbola), for instance, is formed by the intersection of a cone with a plane.

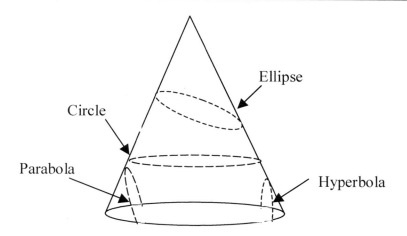

Circles and ellipses are both closed figures. The plane creating the circle cross-section in intersection with the cone is parallel to the base of the cone. Parabolas and hyperbolas are open figures. The plane creating the parabola cross-section in intersection with the cone is parallel to the slant side of the cone.

A **net** is a two-dimensional figure that can be cut out and folded up to make a three-dimensional solid. Below are models of some regular solids with their corresponding face polygons and nets. Nets clearly show the shape and number of faces of a solid.

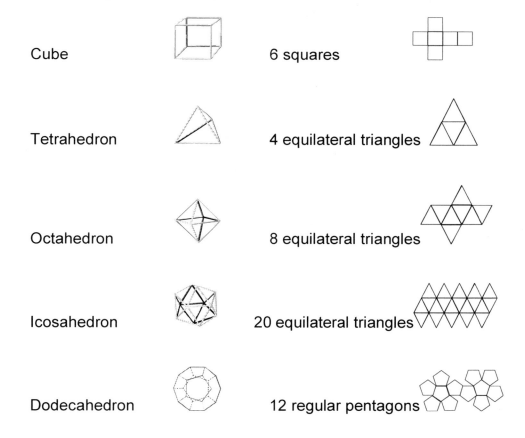

Cube   6 squares

Tetrahedron   4 equilateral triangles

Octahedron   8 equilateral triangles

Icosahedron   20 equilateral triangles

Dodecahedron   12 regular pentagons

There can be more than one possible net for a particular three-dimensional figure. For instance, here are two more nets for a tetrahedron.

 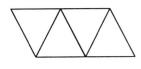

For a polyhedron, the numbers of vertices (*V*), faces (*F*), and edges (*E*) are related by **Euler's Formula**: $V + F = E + 2$.

Example: How many edges are in a pentagonal pyramid?

A pentagonal pyramid has six vertices and six faces. Using Euler's Formula, compute the number of edges:

$$V + F = E + 2$$
$$6 + 6 = E + 2$$
$$E = 10$$

Thus, the figure has 10 edges.

Example: Draw the net of a triangular prism and identify the polygons that make up the faces. How many vertices and edges do triangular prisms have?

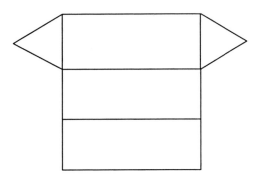

Two triangles and three rectangles are the faces of the figure. There are nine edges (three between the rectangle faces and three on each side where the triangle faces meet the rectangle faces). There are six vertices at the vertices of the two triangle faces.

Competency 011 **The teacher understands transformational geometry and relates algebra to geometry and trigonometry using the Cartesian coordinate system.**

This competency presents transformational geometry and the relationships between algebra, geometry, and trigonometry in the context of the Cartesian plane. Various geometric transformations are discussed, as are the use of transformations in exploring symmetry and the use of coordinates to explore trigonometry.

11A. **Describe and justify geometric constructions made using a reflection device and other appropriate technologies**

Reflection devices and other technologies, like overhead projectors, transform geometric constructions in predictable ways. Students should have the ability to recognize the patterns and properties of geometric constructions made with these technologies. The most common reflection device is a mirror. Mirrors reflect geometric constructions across a given axis. For example, if we place a mirror on the side AC of the triangle (below) the composite image created by the original figure and the reflection is a square.

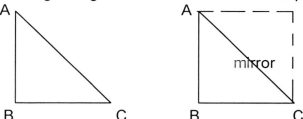

Projection devices, like overhead projectors, often expand geometric figures proportionally, meaning the ratio of the measures of the figure remains the same. Consider the following projection.

Light Source

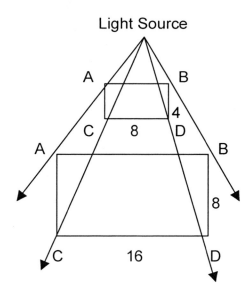

Competency 009 extensively discusses the description and justification of geometric constructions using other methods.

11B. **Use translations, reflections, glide-reflections, and rotations to demonstrate congruence and to explore the symmetries of figures**

Transformational geometry is the study of manipulating objects through movement, rotation and scaling. The transformation of an object is called its *image.* If the original object was labeled with letters, such as *ABCD*, the image can be labeled with the same letters followed by a prime symbol: *A'B'C'D'*. Transformations can be characterized in different ways.

An **isometry** is a linear transformation that maintains the dimensions of a geometric figure. **Symmetry** is exact similarity between two parts or halves, as if one were a mirror image of the other. A **translation** is a transformation that "slides" an object a fixed distance in a given direction. The original object and its translation have the same shape and size, and they face in the same direction.

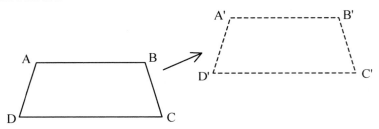

A **rotation** is a transformation that turns a figure about a fixed point, which is called the center of rotation. An object and its rotation are the same shape and size, but the figures may be oriented in different directions. Rotations can occur in either a clockwise or a counterclockwise direction.

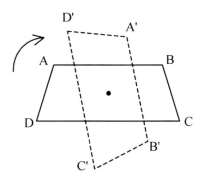

An object and its **reflection** have the same shape and size, but the figures face in opposite directions. The line (where a hypothetical mirror may be placed) is called the **line of reflection**. The distance from a point to the line of reflection is the same as the distance from the point's image to the line of reflection.

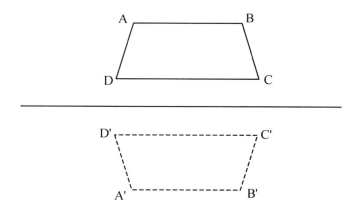

A **glide reflection** involves a combined translation along and a reflection across a single specified line. The characteristic that defines a glide reflection as opposed to a simple combination of an arbitrary translation and arbitrary reflection is that the direction of translation is parallel with the line of reflection. An example of a glide reflection is shown below.

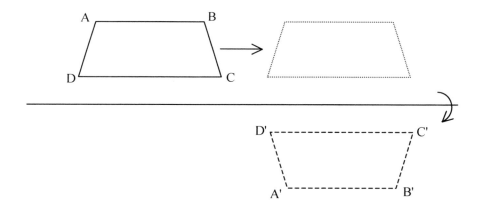

The examples of a translation, rotation, reflection, and glide reflection given above are for polygons, but the same principles apply to the simpler geometrical elements of points and lines. In fact, a transformation performed on a polygon can be viewed equivalently as the same transformation performed on the set of points (vertices) and lines (sides) that compose the polygon. Thus, to perform complicated transformations on a figure, it is helpful to perform the transformations on all the points (or vertices) of the figure, then reconnect the points with lines as appropriate.

A figure has symmetry when there is an isometry that maps the figure onto itself. A figure has **rotational symmetry** if there is a rotation of 180 degrees or less that maps the figure onto itself. **Point symmetry** is where a plane figure can be mapped onto itself by a half-turn or a rotation of 180 degrees around some point. Thus, point symmetry is a specific type of rotational symmetry. An example of a figure with point symmetry is shown below.

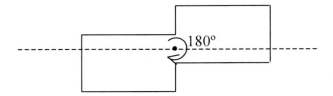

Reflectional or **line symmetry** is an isometry that maps the figure onto itself by reflection across a line. An alternative view is that if the figure is folded along a line of symmetry, the two halves will match perfectly. Examples of figures with line symmetry are shown below, with all the potential lines of symmetry marked as broken lines.

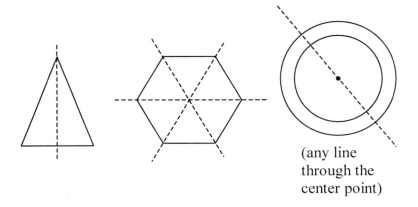

(any line through the center point)

Translational symmetry is where an image can be translated in a specific direction to produce the same image. Necessarily, this requires that the image be infinite in extent and repeating in nature. A **tessellation** is an image with translational symmetry. A tessellation (or tiling) consists of a repeating pattern of figures, which completely cover an area. Below are two example of tessellations in art.

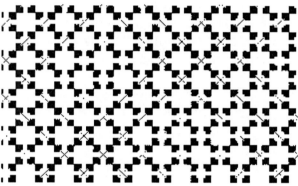

A regular tessellation is made by taking a pattern of polygons that are interlocked and can be extended infinitely. A portion of a tessellation made with hexagons is shown below. This image is made by taking congruent, regular polygons and using them to cover a plane in such a way that *there are no holes or overlaps*. A semi-regular tessellation is made with polygons arranged exactly the same way at every vertex point. Tessellations occur in frequently in nature. A bee's honeycomb is an example of a tessellation found in nature.

11C. Use dilations (expansions and contractions) to illustrate similar figures and proportionality

Dilations involve an expansion of a figure and a translation of that figure (the translation may be for a distance zero). These two transformations are obtained by first defining a **center of dilation**, C, which is some point that acts like an origin for the dilation. The distance from C to each point in a figure is then altered by a **scale factor** s. If the magnitude of s is greater than zero, the size of the figure is increased; if the magnitude of s is less than zero, the size is decreased.

The expansion of a geometric figure is a result of the scale factor, s. For instance, if s = 2, the expanded figure will be twice the size of the original figure. (A dilation maintains the angles and relative proportions of a figure.) The translation of a geometric figure is a result of the location of the center of dilation, C. If C is located at the center of the figure, for instance, the figure is dilated without and translation of its center.

<u>Example:</u> Dilate the figure shown by a scale factor of 2 using the origin of the coordinate system as the center of dilation.

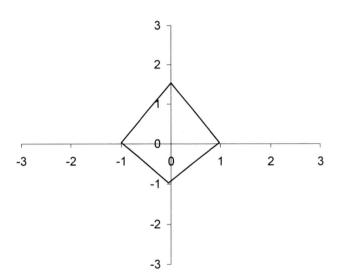

To perform this dilation, the distance between the origin and each point on the figure must be increased by a factor of 2. It is sufficient, however, to simply increase the distance of the vertices of the figure by a factor of 2 and then connect them to form the dilated figure.

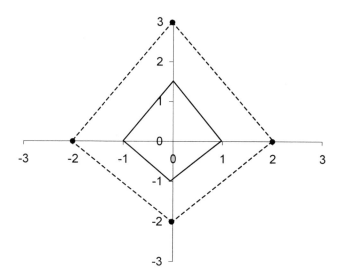

The resulting figure above (dashed line) is the dilation of the original figure.

The points on a figure are dilated by increasing or decreasing their respective distances from a center of dilation C. As a result, each point P on a figure is essentially translated along the line through P and C. To show that a dilation of this type preserves angles, consider some angle formed by two line segments, with a center of dilation at some arbitrary location. The dilation is for some scale factor s.

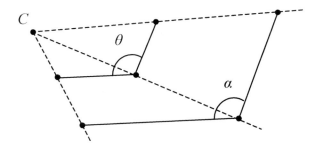

To show that the angles θ and α are equal, it is sufficient to show that the two pairs of overlapping triangles are similar. If they are similar, all the corresponding angles in the figure must be congruent.

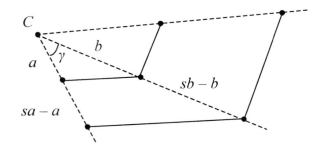

The smaller triangle in this case has sides of lengths a and b and an angle γ between them. The larger triangle has sides of lengths sa (or $sa - a + a = sa$) and sb and an angle γ between them. Thus, by SAS similarity, these two triangles are similar. Once this reasoning is applied to the other pair of overlapping triangles, it can be shown that angles θ and α are equal. Furthermore, due to the fact that these triangles have been shown to be similar, it is also true that line segments must scale by a factor s (this is necessary to maintain the similarity of the triangles above).

As a result of this reasoning, it can be shown that figures that are dilated using an arbitrary scale factor s and center of dilation C must maintain all angles through the dilation, and all line segments (or sides) of the figure must also scale by s. As a result, figures that are dilated are **similar** to the original figures.

Since dilations are transformations that maintain similarity of the figures being dilated, they can also be viewed as **changes of scale** about C. For instance, a dilation of a portion of a map would simply result in a change of the scale of the map.

11D. **Use symmetry to describe tessellations and show how they can be used to illustrate geometric concepts, properties, and relationships**

Tessellations are discussed in detail in **Skill 11B.**

11E. **Apply concepts and properties of slope, midpoint, parallelism, and distance in the coordinate plane to explore properties of geometric figures and solve problems**

Coordinate geometry involves the application of algebraic methods to geometry. The locations of points in space are expressed in terms of coordinates on a Cartesian plane. The relationships between the coordinates of different points are expressed as equations.

Proofs using coordinate geometry techniques employ the following commonly used formulae and relationships:

1. **Midpoint formula**: The midpoint (x, y) of the line joining points (x_1, y_1) and (x_2, y_2) is given by

$$(x, y) = \left(\frac{x_1 + x_2}{2}, \frac{y_1 + y_2}{2} \right)$$

2. **Distance formula:** The distance between points (x_1, y_1) and (x_2, y_2) is given by

$$D = \sqrt{(x_2 - x_1)^2 + (y_2 - y_1)^2}$$

3. **Slope formula:** The slope m of a line passing through the points (x_1, y_1) and (x_2, y_2) is given by

$$m = \frac{y_2 - y_1}{x_2 - x_1}$$

4. **Equation of a line**: The equation of a line is given by $y = mx + b$, where m is the slope of the line and b is the y-intercept, i.e. the y-coordinate at which the line intersects the y-axis.

5. **Parallel and perpendicular lines**: Parallel lines have the same slope. The slope of a line perpendicular to a line with slope m is $-1/m$.

Example: Prove that quadrilateral ABCD with vertices A(–3,0), B(–1,0), C(0,3) and D(2,3) is in fact a parallelogram using coordinate geometry:

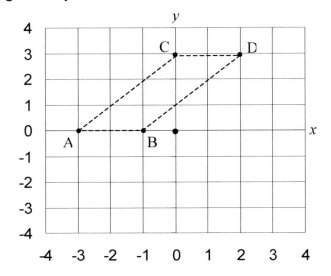

By definition, a parallelogram has diagonals that bisect each other. Using the midpoint formula, $(x,y) = \left(\dfrac{x_1 + x_2}{2}, \dfrac{y_1 + y_2}{2} \right)$, find the midpoints of $\overline{AD}$ and $\overline{BC}$.

The midpoint of $\overline{BC} = \left(\dfrac{-1+0}{2}, \dfrac{0+3}{2} \right) = \left(\dfrac{-1}{2}, \dfrac{3}{2} \right)$

The midpoint of $\overline{AD} = \left(\dfrac{-3+2}{2}, \dfrac{0+3}{2} \right) = \left(\dfrac{-1}{2}, \dfrac{3}{2} \right)$

Since the midpoints of the diagonals are the same, the diagonals bisect each other. Hence the polygon is a parallelogram.
In the above example the proof involved a specific geometrical figure with given coordinates. Coordinate geometry can also be used to prove more general results.

Example: Prove that the diagonals of a rhombus are perpendicular to each other.

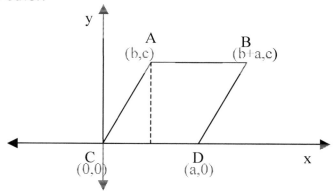

Draw a rhombus ABCD with side of length a such that the vertex C is at the origin and the side CD lies along the x-axis. The coordinates of the corners of the rhombus can then be written as shown above.

The slope m_1 of the diagonal AD is given by $m_1 = \dfrac{c}{b-a}$.

The slope m_2 of the diagonal BC is given by $m_2 = \dfrac{c}{b+a}$.

The product of the slopes is $m_1 \cdot m_2 = \dfrac{c}{b-a} \cdot \dfrac{c}{b+a} = \dfrac{c^2}{b^2-a^2}$.

The length of side AC = $\sqrt{b^2 + c^2} = a$ (since each side of the rhombus is equal to a). Therefore,

$$b^2 + c^2 = a^2$$
$$\Rightarrow b^2 - a^2 = -c^2$$
$$\Rightarrow \frac{c^2}{b^2 - a^2} = -1$$

Thus the product of the slopes of the diagonals $m_1 \cdot m_2 = -1$. Hence the two diagonals are perpendicular to each other.

Example: Prove that the line joining the midpoints of two sides of a triangle is parallel to and half of the third side.

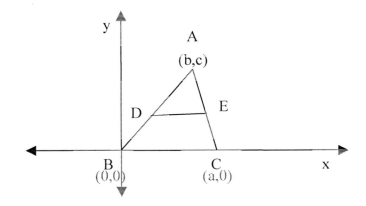

Draw triangle ABC on the coordinate plane in such a way that the vertex B coincides with the origin and the side BC lies along the x-axis. Let point C have coordinates (a,0) and A have coordinates (b,c). D is the midpoint of AB and E is the midpoint of AC.
We need to prove that DE is parallel to BC and is half the length of BC.

Using the midpoint formula,

$$\text{coordinates of D} = \left(\frac{b}{2}, \frac{c}{2}\right); \quad \text{coordinates of E} = \left(\frac{b+a}{2}, \frac{c}{2}\right)$$

The slope of the line DE is then given by $\dfrac{\dfrac{c}{2} - \dfrac{c}{2}}{\dfrac{b+a}{2} - \dfrac{b}{2}} = 0$, which is

equal to the slope of the x-axis. Thus DE is parallel to BC.

The length of the line segment DE =

$$\sqrt{\left(\frac{b+a}{2} - \frac{b}{2}\right)^2 + \left(\frac{c}{2} - \frac{c}{2}\right)^2} = \sqrt{\left(\frac{a}{2}\right)^2} = \frac{a}{2}$$

Thus the length of DE is half that of BC.

11F. Apply transformations in the coordinate plane

Applications of transformations in the coordinate plane do not involve any new concepts. The discussion of dilations presented above offers an example in the context of the coordinate plane. An additional example is presented below in the context of compositions of transformations.

Multiple transformations (or **compositions of transformations**) can be performed on a geometrical figure. The order of these transformations may or may not be important. For instance, multiple translations can be performed in any order, as can multiple rotations (around a single fixed point) or reflections (across a single fixed line). The order of the transformations becomes important when several types of transformations are performed or when the point of rotation or the line of reflection change among transformations. For example, consider a translation of a given distance upward and a clockwise rotation by 90° around a fixed point. Changing the order of these transformations changes the result.

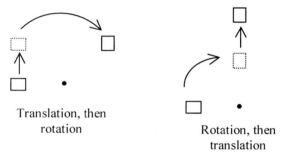

Translation, then
rotation

Rotation, then
translation

As shown, the final position of the box is different, depending on the order of the transformations. Thus, it is crucial that the proper order of transformations (whether determined by the details of the problem or some other consideration) be followed.

Example: Find the final location of a point at (1, 1) that undergoes the following transformations: rotate 90° counter-clockwise about the origin; translate distance 2 in the negative y direction; reflect about the x-axis.

First, draw a graph of the *x*- and *y*-axes and plot the point at (1, 1).

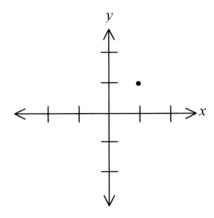

Next, perform the rotation. The center of rotation is the origin and is in the counter-clockwise direction. In this case, the even value of 90° makes the rotation simple to do by inspection. Next, perform a translation of distance 2 in the negative *y* direction (down). The results of these transformations are shown below.

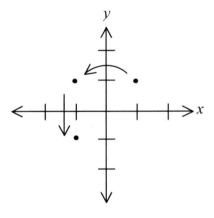

Finally, perform the reflection about the x-axis. The final result, shown below, is a point at (1, −1).

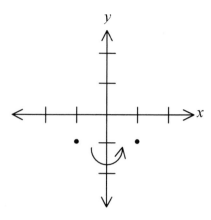

Using this approach, polygons can be transformed on a point-by-point basis.

11G. Use the unit circle in the coordinate plane to explore properties of trigonometric functions

The unit circle is a circle with a radius of one centered at (0,0) on the coordinate plane. Thus, any ray from the origin to a point on the circle forms a right triangle with a hypotenuse measuring one unit. Applying the Pythagorean theorem, $x^2 + y^2 = 1$. Because the reflections of the triangle about both the x- and y-axis are on the unit circle and $x^2 = (-x)^2$ for all x values, the formula holds for all points on the unit circle.

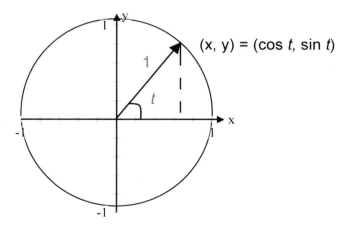

$(x, y) = (\cos t, \sin t)$

Note that, because the length of the hypotenuse of the right triangle formed in the unit circle is one, the point on the unit circle that forms the triangle is (cos t, sin t) where t is the angle the ray forms with the positive x-axis. In other words, for any point on the unit circle, the x value represents the cosine of t, the y value represents the sine of t, and the ratio of the y-coordinate to the x-coordinate is the tangent of t.

The unit circle illustrates several properties of trigonometric functions. For example, applying the Pythagorean theorem to the unit circle yields the equation $\cos^2(t) + \sin^2(t) = 1$. In addition, the unit circle reveals the periodic nature of trigonometric functions. When we increase the angle t by 2π radians or 360 degrees, the values of x and y coordinates on the unit circle remain the same.

Thus, the sine and cosine values repeat with each revolution. The unit circle also reveals the range of the sine and cosine functions. The values of sine and cosine are always between one and negative one. Finally, the unit circle shows that when the x coordinate of a point on the circle is zero, the tangent function is undefined. Thus, tangent is undefined at the angles $\frac{\pi}{2}, \frac{3\pi}{2}$ and the corresponding angles in all subsequent revolutions.

DOMAIN IV.   **PROBABILITY AND STATISTICS**

Competency 012   **The teacher understands how to use graphical and numerical techniques to explore data, characterize patterns, and describe departures from patterns.**

This competency reviews basic statistical concepts for analyzing and appropriately describing data distributions. Methods of displaying data are discussed, followed by quantitative measures of central tendency and dispersion, and other considerations focusing on the use and application of statistics.

12A.   **Organize and display data in a variety of formats (e.g., tables, frequency distributions, stem-and-leaf plots, box-and-whisker plots, histograms, pie charts)**

There are many graphical ways in which to represent data, such as line plots, line graphs, scatter plots, stem and leaf plots, histograms, bar graphs, pie charts, and pictographs.

A **line plot** organizes data in numerical order along a number line. An x is placed above the number line for each occurrence of the corresponding number. Line plots allow viewers to see at a glance a range of data and where typical and atypical data falls. These plots are generally used to summarize relatively small sets of data.

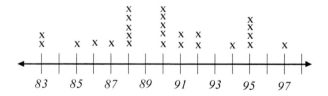

A **line graph** compares two variables, and each variable is plotted along an axis. A line graph highlights trends by drawing connecting lines between data points. This representation is particularly appropriate for data that varies continuously. Line graphs are sometimes referred to as **frequency polygons**.

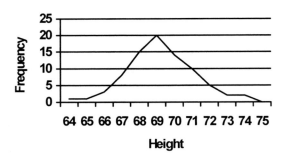

Bar graphs are similar to histograms. However, bar graphs are often used to convey information about categorical data where the horizontal scale represents a non-numeric attributes such as cities or years. Another difference is that the bars in bar graphs rarely touch. Bar graphs are also useful in comparing data about two or more similar groups of items.

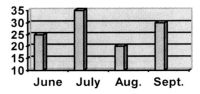

A **pie chart**, also known as a **circle graph**, is used to represent relative amounts of a whole.

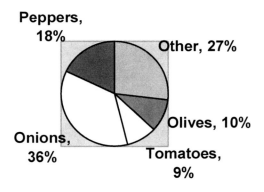

Scatter plots compare two characteristics of the same group of things or people and usually consist of a large body of data. They show how much one variable is affected by another. The relationship between the two variables is their **correlation**. The closer the data points come to making a straight line when plotted, the closer the correlation.

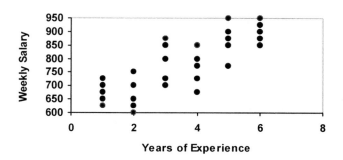

Stem and leaf plots are visually similar to line plots. The **stems** are the digits in the greatest place value of the data values, and the **leaves** are the digits in the next greatest place values. Stem and leaf plots are best suited for small sets of data and are especially useful for comparing two sets of data. The following is an example using test scores:

4	9
5	4 9
6	1 2 3 4 6 7 8 8
7	0 3 4 6 6 6 7 7 7 8 8 8 8
8	3 5 5 7 8
9	0 0 3 4 5
10	0 0

A **box-and-whisker plot** displays five statistics: a minimum and maximum score (neither of which should be considered outliers) and three quartiles. The box is composed of the first quartile, the median (or second quartile) and the third quartile, as shown in the example below. The (non-outlier) minimum and maximum values are shown at the end of the "whiskers" attached to the box.

The above box-and-whisker example summarizes the scores on a mathematics test for the students in Class I. It indicates that the lowest score is 60 and the highest score is 100. Twenty-five percent of the class scored 68 or lower (the first quartile), 50% scored 76 or lower (the second quartile), and 25% scored 90 or higher (the third quartile).

Histograms are used to summarize information from large sets of data that can be naturally grouped into intervals. The vertical axis indicates **frequency** (the number of times any particular data value occurs), and the horizontal axis indicates data values or ranges of data values. The number of data values in any interval is the **frequency of the interval**.

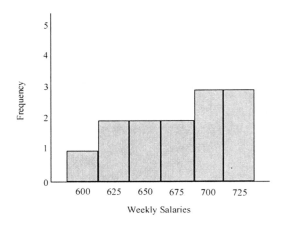

A **pictograph** uses small figures or icons to represent data. Pictographs are used to summarize relative amounts, trends, and data sets, and they are useful in comparing quantities.

Monarch Butterfly Migration to the U.S.
in millions

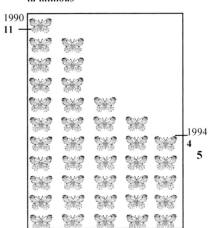

The data in this graph is not accurate. It is for illustration purposes only.

12B. Apply concepts of center, spread, shape, and skewness to describe a data distribution

Application of statistical concepts such as center, spread, shape, and skewness are made in example problems and discussions throughout this competency. See **Skill 12D** in particular.

12C. Support arguments, make predictions, and draw conclusions using summary statistics and graphs to analyze and interpret one-variable data

Statistics are cited almost invariably, in one form or another, in studies and publications that seek to prove a point about people, animals, food, drugs, or any number of other subjects. Using summary statistics and graphs appropriately to support conclusions and predictions is a crucial skill to this end.

Summary statistics and graphs for one-variable data include the types of information (mean, median, mode, variance, etc.) and methods of display (the various types of data plots and diagrams) discussed above. Appropriate application of these statistics and methods of display requires a knowledge of the particular area to which they are being applied as well as how well each aspect of the statistics represents the information. For example, consider the following frequency data distribution presented in histogram form. The frequencies (vertical axis) are shown for several discrete values (horizontal axis).

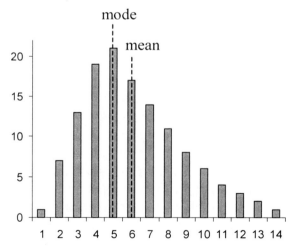

The (weighted) mean and mode of the data are labeled in the plot. Note that the use of the mean for describing the data distribution is somewhat descriptive, it does not seem to be the best way to describe the data since it is off center. In some situations, this seemingly minor difference could drastically affect the conclusions or predictions made based on the data. Thus, means (or averages) can be deceptive or can lead to incorrect conclusions when they are used as summary statistics. If an appropriate graph or other method of displaying the data is included, however, the use of the mean as a measure of central tendency could be a little less deceptive or otherwise misleading.

As can be seen from the preceding example, then, selecting the appropriate set of numbers and visual displays for a given set of data is necessary to accurately summarize a set of data. Such accurate summary statistics are necessary to making proper predictions and to drawing warranted conclusions. The same considerations applied to measures of central tendency in the example also apply to data spread and distribution shape or skewness.

In addition, arguments based on hypothesis testing require appropriate selection of test statistics. For more on hypothesis testing and some potential statistical tests that can be performed, see **Competency 014**.

12D. **Demonstrate an understanding of measures of central tendency (e.g., mean, median, mode) and dispersion (e.g., range, interquartile range, variance, standard deviation)**

Measures of Central Tendency

The mean, median and mode are **measures of central tendency** (i.e., the average or typical value) in a data set. They can be defined both for discrete and continuous data sets. A **discrete variable** is one that can only take on certain specific values. For instance, the number of students in a class can only be a whole number (e.g., 15 or 16, but not 15.5). A **continuous variable**, such as the weight of an object, can take on a continuous range of values.

For discrete data, the **mean** is the average of the data items, or the value obtained by adding all the data values and dividing by the total number of data items. For a data set of n items with data values $x_1, x_2, x_3, \ldots, x_n$, the mean is given by

$$\overline{x} = \frac{x_1 + x_2 + x_3 + \ldots + x_n}{n}$$

The **median** is found by putting the data in order from smallest to largest and selecting the item in the middle (or the average of the two values in the middle if the number of data items is even). The **mode** is the most frequently occurring datum. There can be more than one mode in a data set.

Example: Find the mean, median, and mode of the test scores listed below:

85	77	65
92	90	54
88	85	70
75	80	69
85	88	60
72	74	95

Mean: sum of all scores ÷ number of scores = 78
Median: put numbers in order from smallest to largest. Pick the middle number.

54, 60, 65, 69, 70, 72, 74, 75, 77, 80, 85, 85, 85, 88, 88, 90, 92, 95

Both values are in the middle.

Therefore, median is average of two numbers in the middle, or 78.5. The mode, or most frequent number is 85.

Discrete data is typically displayed in a table as shown in the example above. If the data set is large, it may be expressed in compact form as a **frequency distribution**. The number of occurrences of each data point is the **frequency** of that value. The **relative frequency** is defined as the frequency divided by the total number of data points. Since the sum of the frequencies equals the number of data points, the relative frequencies add up to 1. The relative frequency of a data point, therefore, represents the probability of occurrence of that value. Thus, a distribution consisting of relative frequencies is known as a **probability distribution**.

For data expressed as a frequency distribution, the mean is given by

$$\overline{x} = \frac{\sum x_i f_i}{\sum f_i} = \sum x_i f_i'$$

where x_i represents a data value, f_i the corresponding frequency and f_i' the corresponding relative frequency.

The **cumulative frequency** of a data point is the sum of the frequencies from the beginning up to that point. The median of a frequency distribution is the point at which the cumulative frequency reaches half the value of the total number of data points.

The mode is the point at which the frequency distribution reaches a maximum. There can be more than one mode in which case the distribution is **multimodal**.

Example: The frequency distribution below shows the summary of some test results where people scored points ranging from 0 to 45 in increments of 5. One person scored 5 points, 4 people scored 10 points and so on. Find the mean, median and mode of the data set.

Points	Frequency	Cumulative Frequency	Relative Frequency
5	1	1	0.009
10	4	5	0.035
15	12	17	0.105
20	22	39	0.193
25	30	69	0.263
30	25	94	0.219
35	13	107	0.114
40	6	113	0.053
45	1	114	0.009

The mean score is the following:
(5x1+10x4+15x12+20x22+25x30+30x25+35x13+40x6+45x1)/114
= (5+40+180+440+750+750+455+240+45)/114 = 25.5.

The median score (the point at which the cumulative frequency reaches or surpasses the value 57) is 25.

The mode (or value with the highest frequency) is 25.

The frequency distribution from the above example is displayed below as a histogram.

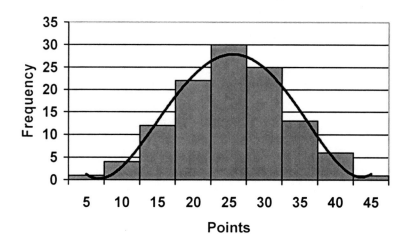

The histogram shows the reason why the mean, median and mode of this distribution are practically identical. This is due to the distribution being symmetric with one peak exactly in the middle. A trend line has been added to the histogram. Notice that this approximates the most common **continuous distribution**, a **normal or bell curve** for which the mean, median and mode are identical.

A frequency distribution may also be created by subdividing the range of the data into sub-ranges. In this case, the count in each subdivision or **bin** is the frequency. Discrete as well as continuous data may be represented in this way.

A large data set of continuous data is often represented using a **probability distribution** expressed as a **probability density function.** The integral of the probability density function over a certain range gives the probability of a data point being in that range of values. The integral of the probability density function over the whole range of values is equal to 1.

The **mean** value for a distribution of a variable x represented by a probability density function $f(x)$ is given by

$$\int_{-\infty}^{+\infty} xf(x)dx$$

(Compare this with its discrete counterpart $\overline{x} = \sum x_i f_i'$).

The **median** is the upper bound for which the integral of the probability density function is equal to 0.5; i.e., if $\int_{-\infty}^{a} f(x)dx = 0.5$, then a is the median of the distribution.

The **mode** is the maximum value or values of the probability density function within the range of the function.

As mentioned before, the mean and median are very close together for symmetric distributions. **If the distribution is skewed to the right, the mean is greater than the median. If the distribution is skewed to the left, the mean is smaller than the median.** Distributions can also be described in terms of a center (a distribution has a clear center if it is symmetric about some vertical line), spread (a distribution may be relatively flat, or it may be sharply peaked), and shape (a distribution can have a single peak, multiple peaks, or a variety of other shapes).

<u>Example</u>: Find the mean, median and mode for the distribution given by the probability density function

$$f(x) = \begin{cases} 4x(1-x^2) & 0 \le x \le 1 \\ 0 & \text{otherwise} \end{cases}$$

Mean = $\int_{0}^{1} 4x^2(1-x^2)dx = \frac{4x^3}{3}\Big|_0^1 - \frac{4x^5}{5}\Big|_0^1 = \frac{4}{3} - \frac{4}{5} = \frac{20-12}{15} = \frac{8}{15} = 0.53$

If $x = a$ is the median, then

$$\int_{0}^{a} 4x(1-x^2)dx = 0.5$$

$$\Rightarrow \frac{4x^2}{2}\Big|_0^a - \frac{4x^4}{4}\Big|_0^a = 0.5$$

$$\Rightarrow 2a^2 - a^4 = 0.5$$

$$\Rightarrow 2a^4 - 4a^2 + 1 = 0$$

Solving for *a* yields

$$a^2 = \frac{4 \pm \sqrt{16-8}}{4} = 1 \pm \frac{2\sqrt{2}}{4} = 1 - \frac{\sqrt{2}}{2} \text{ (to keep } x \text{ within the range 0 to 1)}$$

$$a = \sqrt{1 - \frac{1}{\sqrt{2}}} = 0.54$$

The mode is obtained by taking the derivative of the probability density function and setting it to zero as shown below. (Notice that the second derivative is negative at $x = 0.58$, and, hence, this is clearly a maximum.)

$$\frac{d}{dx}(4x - 4x^3) = 4 - 12x^2 = 0$$

$$\Rightarrow 12x^2 = 4$$

$$\Rightarrow x^2 = \frac{1}{3}$$

$$\Rightarrow x = \frac{1}{\sqrt{3}} = 0.58$$

Measures of Dispersion

The following discussion reviews measures of data dispersion, such as standard deviation, variance, skewness, and interquartile range. These characteristics are considered for both discrete and continuous distributions.

Statistics for Discrete Distributions

Range is a measure of variability that is calculated by subtracting the smallest value from the largest value in a set of discrete data.

The **variance** and **standard deviation** are measures of the "spread" (or **dispersion**) of data around the mean. It is noteworthy that descriptive statistics involving such parameters as variance and standard deviation can be applied to a set of data that spans the entire population (parameters, typically represented using Greek symbols) or to a set of data that only constitutes a portion of the population (sample statistics, typically represented by Latin letters).

The mean of a set of data, whether for a population (μ) or for a sample ($\bar{x}$), uses the formula discussed above, and it can be represented as either a set of individual data or as a set of data with associated frequencies. The variance and standard deviation for the population differ slightly from those of a sample. The population variance (σ^2) and the population standard deviation (σ) are as follows.

$$\sigma^2 = \frac{1}{n}\sum(x_i - \mu)^2$$
$$\sigma = \sqrt{\sigma^2}$$

Another statistic is the so-called skewness (here represented by the symbol γ), which is calculated according to the following formula.

$$\gamma = \frac{1}{n}\sum\left(\frac{x_i - \mu}{\sigma}\right)^3$$

Skewness quantifies the asymmetry of a distribution. A normal distribution, for instance, is symmetric about its mean and would therefore have a skewness of zero.

Example: Calculate and describe the skewness of the following ordered data set (consider this set a population rather than a sample): {2, 5, 8, 14, 7, 4, 3, 2, 1, 0}.

To describe qualitatively the skewness, prepare a plot of the data. In this case, a histogram is one possibility:

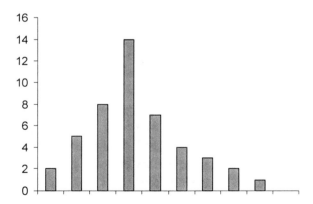

Qualitatively, this data set is skewed to the left, since the peak is off center and the general trend is asymmetric. To calculate the skewness quantitatively, use the skewness formula above. First, calculate the mean, μ, and the standard deviation, σ. Since the data set is simply described as "ordered," simply assume that each datum receives an equal weight.

$$\mu = \frac{2+5+8+14+7+4+3+2+1+0}{10} = 4.6$$

$$\sigma^2 = \frac{1}{n}\sum (x_i - \mu)^2 = \frac{1}{10}\left\{(2-4.6)^2 + (5-4.6)^2 + \ldots + (0-4.6)^2\right\}$$

$$\sigma^2 \approx 15.64$$

$$\sigma = \sqrt{\sigma^2} \approx \sqrt{15.64} \approx 3.95$$

Using this information, the skewness, γ, can now be calculated.

$$\gamma = \frac{1}{n}\sum \left(\frac{x_i - \mu}{\sigma}\right)^3 = \frac{1}{10}\left\{\left(\frac{2-4.6}{3.95}\right)^3 + \ldots + \left(\frac{0-4.6}{3.95}\right)^3\right\}$$

$$\gamma \approx 1.13$$

Thus, the data distribution has a skewness of about 1.13 to the left (as shown on the histogram).

For a sample, the data does not include the entire population. As a result, it should be expected that the sample data might not be perfectly representative of the population. To account for this shortcoming in the sample variance (s^2) and standard deviation (s), the sum of the squared differences between the data and the mean is divided by ($n - 1$) instead of just n. This increases the variance and standard deviation slightly, which in turn increases slightly the data spread to account for the possibility that the sample may not accurately represent the population.

$$s^2 = \frac{1}{n-1}\sum (x_i - \bar{x})^2$$

$$s = \sqrt{s^2}$$

Example: Calculate the range, variance and standard deviation for the following data set: {3, 3, 5, 7, 8, 8, 8, 10, 12, 21}.

The range is simply the largest data value minus the smallest. In this case, the range is 21 − 3 = 18.

To calculate the variance and standard deviation, first calculate the mean. If it is not stated whether a data set constitutes a population or sample, assume it is a population. (In this case, if the data was labeled "ages of the 10 people in a room," this would be a population. If the data was labeled "ages of males at a crowded circus event," the data would be a sample.)

$$\mu = \frac{3+3+5+7+8+8+8+10+12+21}{10} = 8.5$$

Use this mean to calculate the variance.

$$\sigma^2 = \frac{1}{10}\sum(x_i - 8.5)^2$$
$$\sigma^2 = \frac{1}{10}\left\{(3-8.5)^2 + (3-8.5)^2 + (5-8.5)^2 + \ldots + (21-8.5)^2\right\}$$
$$\sigma^2 = \frac{246.5}{10} = 24.65$$

The standard deviation is

$$\sigma = \sqrt{\sigma^2} = \sqrt{24.65} \approx 4.96$$

The **interquartile range** is a measure of dispersion that uses **quartiles**, which divide the data into four segments. To find the quartile of a particular datum, first determine the median of the data set (which is labeled Q2), then find the median of the upper half (labeled Q3) and the median of the lower half (labeled Q1) of the data set. There is some confusion in determining the upper and lower quartile, and statisticians do not agree on the appropriate method to use. Tukey's method for finding the quartile values is to find the median of the data set, then find the median of the upper and lower halves of the data set. If there are an odd number of values in the data set, include the median value in both halves when finding the quartile values. For example, consider the following data set:

$$\{1, 4, 9, 16, 25, 36, 49, 64, 81\}$$

First, find the median value, which is 25. This is the value Q2. Since there is an odd number of values in the data set (nine), include the median in both halves. To find the quartile values, find the medians of the two sets

$$\{1, 4, 9, 16, 25\} \text{ and } \{25, 36, 49, 64, 81\}$$

Since each of these subsets has an odd number of elements (five), use the middle value. Thus, the lower quartile value (Q1) is 9 and the upper quartile value (Q3) is 49.

Another method to find quartile values (if the total data set has an odd number of values) excludes the median from both halves when finding the quartile values. Using this approach on the data set above, exclude the median (25) from each half. To find the quartile values, find the medians of

{1, 4, 9, 16} and {36, 49, 64, 81}

Since each of these data sets has an even number of elements (four), average the middle two values. Thus the lower quartile value (Q1) is (4+9)/2 = 6.5 and the upper quartile value (Q3) is (49+64)/2 = 56.5. The middle quartile value (Q2) remains 25.

Other methods for calculating quartiles also exist, but these two methods are the most straightforward. To calculate the interquartile range (R_{IQ}), simply subtract Q1 from Q3. Thus,

$$R_{IQ} = Q1 - Q3$$

Statistics for Continuous Distributions

The range for a continuous data distribution is the same as that for a discrete distribution: the largest value minus the smallest value. Calculation of the mean, variance and standard deviation are similar, but slightly different. Since a continuous distribution does not permit a simple summation, integrals must be used. The mean μ of a distribution function $f(x)$ is expressed below (and is discussed previously in this section).

$$\mu = \int_{-\infty}^{\infty} x f(x)\, dx$$

The variance σ^2 over also has an integral form, and has a form similar to that of a discrete distribution.

$$\sigma^2 = \int_{-\infty}^{\infty} (x - \mu)^2 f(x)\, dx$$

The standard deviation σ is simply

$$\sigma = \sqrt{\sigma^2}$$

The skewness of a continuous distribution is given below.

$$\gamma = \int_{-\infty}^{\infty} \left(\frac{x - \mu}{\sigma}\right)^3 f(x)\,dx$$

The interquartile range can also be found for continuous distributions. Quartiles are typically applied to discrete data distributions, but application to continuous distributions is also possible. In such a case, quartiles would be calculated by dividing the area under the curve of the distribution into four even (or approximately even) segments. The boundaries of these segments are the quartile values. Thus, formula for interquartile range (I_{QR}) in the case of continuous distributions is the same as that for discrete distributions.

$$I_{QR} = Q1 - Q3$$

Example: Calculate the standard deviation of a data distribution function $f(x)$ where

$$f(x) = \begin{cases} 0 & x < 1 \\ -2x^2 + 2 & -1 \le x \le 1 \\ 0 & x > 1 \end{cases}$$

First calculate the mean of the function. Since the function is zero except between 1 and −1, the integral can likewise be evaluated from −1 to 1. (For further discussion of integrals, see **Competency 007**.)

$$\mu = \int_{-1}^{1} \left(-2x^2 + 2\right) x \, dx$$

$$\mu = -2 \int_{-1}^{1} \left(x^3 - x\right) dx$$

$$\mu = -2 \left[\frac{x^4}{4} - \frac{x^2}{2}\right]_{x=-1}^{x=1}$$

$$\mu = -2 \left\{\left[\frac{(1)^4}{4} - \frac{(1)^2}{2}\right] - \left[\frac{(-1)^4}{4} - \frac{(-1)^2}{2}\right]\right\} = 0$$

The mean can also be seen clearly by the fact that the graph of the function $f(x)$ is symmetric about the y-axis, indicating that its center (or mean) is at $x = 0$. Next, calculate the variance of f.

$$\sigma^2 = \int_{-1}^{1} (x - 0)^2 \left(-2x^2 + 2\right) dx = -2 \int_{-1}^{1} x^2 \left(x^2 - 1\right) dx$$

$$\sigma^2 = -2 \int_{-1}^{1} \left(x^4 - x^2\right) dx$$

$$\sigma^2 = -2 \left[\frac{x^5}{5} - \frac{x^3}{3}\right]_{x=-1}^{x=1} = -2 \left\{\left[\frac{(1)^5}{5} - \frac{(1)^3}{3}\right] - \left[\frac{(-1)^5}{5} - \frac{(-1)^3}{3}\right]\right\}$$

$$\sigma^2 = -2 \left\{\frac{1}{5} - \frac{1}{3} - \left(-\frac{1}{5}\right) + \left(-\frac{1}{3}\right)\right\} = -2 \left(\frac{2}{5} - \frac{2}{3}\right)$$

$$\sigma^2 = \frac{8}{15} \approx 0.533$$

The standard deviation is

$$\sigma = \sqrt{\sigma^2} = \sqrt{\frac{8}{15}} \approx 0.730$$

12E. Analyze connections among concepts of center and spread, data clusters and gaps, data outliers, and measures of central tendency and dispersion

The connections among statistical concepts such as measures of central tendency and dispersion are considered throughout the discussion in this competency and are illustrated in the various example problems.

12F. Calculate and interpret percentiles and quartiles

Quartiles are discussed in detail in the preceding skill sections. **Percentiles** are similar, but they divide the data in a slightly different manner—they divide data into 100 equal parts. A datum that falls in the nth percentile means that this datum exceeds (by whatever measure) n percent of the other data and that $(100 - n)$ percent of the data exceed this datum. For instance, a person whose score on a test falls in the 65th percentile has outperformed 65 percent of all those who took the test. This does not mean that the score was 65 percent out of 100, nor does it mean that 65 percent of the questions answered were correctly. Instead, this score means that the grade was higher than 65 percent of all those who took the test.

Percentiles and quartiles are typically applied to discrete data distributions, but application to continuous distributions is also possible. In such a case, percentiles and quartiles would be calculated by dividing the area under the curve of the distribution into either 100 (for percentile) or 4 (for quartile) even or approximately even segments. The boundaries of these segments are the percentile or quartile values.

Example: Find the percentile of a student who scored 80 on an exam, where the distribution of scores for the entire class is {68, 72, 73, 75, 78, 80, 81, 85, 92, 96}.

The total number of test scores is 10. Find the number of scores that were less than or equal to 80. In this case, the result is 6. The percentile is

$$\frac{6}{10} 100\% = 60\%$$

Thus, the student who scored 80 on the test is in the 60th percentile. Notice that the student's score is, in this case, much higher than the percentile. Thus, percentile is a relative scoring mechanism. (Conceivably, a student with an almost-perfect score could rank in a very low percentile, assuming all or most of the other students received a perfect score.)

Stanine "standard nine" scores combine the understandability of percentages with the properties of the normal curve of probability. Stanines divide the bell curve into nine sections, the largest of which stretches from the 40th to the 60th percentile and is the "Fifth Stanine" (the average of taking into account error possibilities).

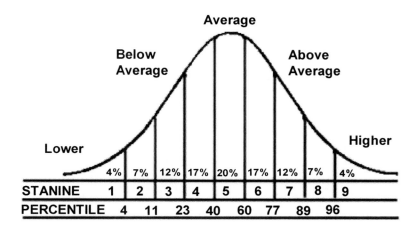

Competency 013   The teacher understands the theory of probability.

This competency presents the basics of probability theory, followed by the application of these concepts to problems involving permutations, combinations, and geometric probability. Finally, the use of various probability distributions is presented.

13A. Explore concepts of probability through data collection, experiments, and simulations

Simulations of random events or variables can be helpful in making informal inferences about theoretical probability distributions. Although simulations can involve use of physical situations that bear some similarity to the situation of interest, often times simulations involve computer modeling.

One of the crucial aspects of modeling probability using a computer program is the need for a random number that can be used to "randomize" the aspect of the program that corresponds to the event or variable. Although there is no function on a computer that can provide a truly random number, most programming languages have some function designed to produce a **pseudorandom number**. A pseudorandom number is not truly random, but it is sufficiently unpredictable that it can be used as a random number in many contexts.

Pseudorandom numbers can serve as the basis for simulation of rolling a die, flipping a coin, selecting an object from a collection of different objects, and a range of other situations. If, for instance, the pseudorandom number generator produces a number between zero and 1, simply divide up that range in accordance with the probabilities of each particular outcome. (For instance, assign 0 to 0.5 as heads and 0.5 to 1 as tails for the flip of a fair coin.) By performing a number of simulated trials and tallying the results, empirical probability distributions can be created.

Ideally, as the number of trials goes to infinity, the empirical probability distribution should approach the theoretical distribution. As a result, by performing a sufficiently large number of trials (this number must be at least somewhat justified for the particular situation) should allow informal inferences based on that data. Such inferences, however, must take into account the limitations of the computer, such as the inability to perform an infinite number of trials in finite time and the numerical inaccuracies that are an inherent part of computer programming.

The use of probability models to represent various situations is illustrated through the various example problems throughout this competency.

13B. Use the concepts and principles of probability to describe the outcome of simple and compound events

The **probability** of an outcome, given a random experiment (a structured, repeatable experiment where the outcome cannot be predicted—or, alternatively, where the outcome is dependent on "chance"), is the relative frequency of the outcome. The relative frequency of an outcome is the number of times an experiment yields that outcome for a very large (ideally, infinite) number of trials. For instance, if a "fair" coin is tossed a very large number of times, then the relative frequency of a "heads-up" outcome is 0.5, or 50% (that is, one out of every two trials, on average, should be heads up). The probability is this relative frequency.

In probability theory, the **sample space** is a list of all possible outcomes of an experiment. For example, the sample space of tossing two coins is the set {HH, HT, TT, TH}, where H is heads and T is tails, and the sample space of rolling a six-sided die is the set {1, 2, 3, 4, 5, 6}. When conducting experiments with a large number of possible outcomes, it is important to determine the size of the sample space. The size of the sample space can be determined by using the fundamental counting principles and the rules of combinations and permutations.

A **random variable** is a function that corresponds to the outcome of some experiment or event, which is in turn dependent on "chance." For instance, the result of a tossed coin is a random variable: the outcome is either heads or tails, and each outcome has an associated probability. A **discrete variable** is one that can only take on certain specific values. For instance, the number of students in a class can only be a whole number (e.g., 15 or 16, but not 15.5). A **continuous variable**, such as the weight of an object, can take on a continuous range of values.

The probabilities for the possible values of a random variable constitute the **probability distribution** for that random variable. Probability distributions can be discrete, as with the case of the tossing of a coin (there are only two possible distinct outcomes), or they can be continuous, as with, for instance, the outside temperature at a given time of day. In this latter case, the probability is represented as a continuous function over a range of possible temperatures, and finite probabilities can only be measured in terms of ranges of temperatures rather than specific temperatures. This is to say that, for a continuous distribution, it is not meaningful to say "the probability that the outcome is x"; instead, only "the probability that the outcome is between x and Δx" is meaningful. (Note that if each potential outcome in a continuous distribution has a non-zero probability, then the sum of all the probabilities would be greater than one, since there are an infinite number of potential outcomes.) Specific probability distributions are presented later in this discussion.

<u>Example:</u> Find the sample space and construct a probability distribution for a six-sided die (with numbers 1 through 6) where the even numbers are twice as likely as the odd numbers to come up on a given roll (assume the even numbers are equally likely and the odd numbers are equally likely).

The sample space is simply the set of all possible outcomes that can arise in a given trial. For this die, the sample space is {1, 2, 3, 4, 5, 6}. To construct the associated probability distribution, note first that the sum of the probabilities must equal 1. Let the probability of rolling an odd number (1, 3, or 5) be x; the probability of rolling an even number (2, 4, or 6) is then $2x$.

$$1 = p(1) + p(2) + p(3) + p(4) + p(5) + p(6) = 3x + 6x = 9x$$
$$x = \frac{1}{9}$$

The probability distribution can be shown as a histogram below.

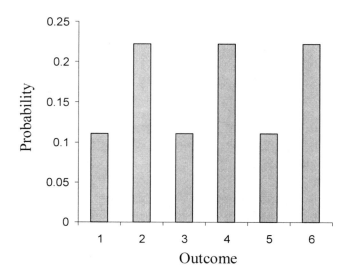

The sum of the probabilities for all the possible outcomes of a discrete distribution (or the integral of the continuous distribution over all possible values) must be equal to unity. The **expected value** of a probability distribution is the same as the **mean value** of a probability distribution. (See below for more discussion of mean values.) The expected value is thus a measure of the central tendency or average value for a random variable with a given probability distribution.

A **Bernoulli trial** is an experiment whose outcome is random and can be either of two possible outcomes, which are called "success" or "failure." Tossing a coin would be an example of a Bernoulli trial. The probability of success is represented by p, with the probability of failure being $q = 1 - p$. Bernoulli trials can be applied to any real-life situation in which there are only two possible outcomes. For example, concerning the birth of a child, the only two possible outcomes for the sex of the child are male or female.

Probability can also be expressed in terms of **odds**. Odds are defined as the ratio of the number of favorable outcomes to the number of unfavorable outcomes. The sum of the favorable outcomes and the unfavorable outcomes should always equal the total possible outcomes.

For example, given a bag of 12 red marbles and 7 green marbles, compute the odds of randomly selecting a red marble.

$$\text{Odds of red} = \frac{12}{7}$$

$$\text{Odds of not getting red} = \frac{7}{12}$$

In the case of flipping a coin, it is equally likely that a head or a tail will be tossed. The odds of tossing a head are 1:1. This is called **even odds**.

A **simple event** is one that describes a single outcome, whereas a **compound event** is made-up of two or more simple events. The following discussion uses the symbols $\cap$ to mean "and," $\cup$ to mean "or" and $P(x)$ to mean "the probability of x." Also, $N(x)$ means "the number of ways that x can occur."

Dependent and Independent Events

Dependent events occur when the probability of the second event depends on the outcome of the first event. For example, consider the two events: the home team wins the semifinal round (event A) and the home team wins the final round (event B). The probability of event B is contingent on the probability of event A. If the home team fails to win the semifinal round, it has a zero probability of winning in the final round. On the other hand, if the home team wins the semifinal round, then it may have a finite probability of winning in the final round. Symbolically, the probability of event B given event A is written $P(B|A)$. The conditional probability can be calculated according to the following definition.

$$P(B|A) = \frac{P(A \cap B)}{P(A)}$$

Consider a pair of dice: one red and one green. First the red die is rolled, followed by the green die. It is apparent that these events do not depend on each other, since the outcome of the roll of the green die is not affected by the outcome of the roll of the red die. The total probability of the two independent events can be found by multiplying the separate probabilities.

$$P(A \cap B) = P(A)P(B)$$

$$P(A \cap B) = \left(\frac{1}{6}\right)\left(\frac{1}{6}\right) = \frac{1}{36}$$

In many instances, however, events are not independent. Suppose a jar contains 12 red marbles and 8 blue marbles. If a marble is selected at random and then replaced, the probability of picking a certain color is the same in the second trial as it is in the first trial. If the marble is *not* replaced, then the probability of picking a certain color is *not* the same in the second trial, because the total number of marbles is decreased by one. This is an illustration of conditional probability. If R_n signifies selection of a red marble on the nth trial and B_n signifies selection of a blue marble on the nth trial, then the probability of selecting a red marble in two trials *with replacement* is

$$P(R_1 \cap R_2) = P(R_1)P(R_2) = \left(\frac{12}{20}\right)\left(\frac{12}{20}\right) = \frac{144}{400} = 0.36$$

The probability of selecting a red marble in two trials *without replacement* is

$$P(R_1 \cap R_2) = P(R_1)P(R|R_1) = \left(\frac{12}{20}\right)\left(\frac{11}{19}\right) = \frac{132}{360} \approx 0.367$$

Example: A car has a 75% probability of traveling 20,000 miles without breaking down. It has a 50% probability of traveling 10,000 additional miles without breaking down if it first makes it to 20,000 miles without breaking down. What is the probability that the car reaches 30,000 miles without breaking down?

Let event A be that the car reaches 20,000 miles without breaking down.

$$P(A) = 0.75$$

Event B is that the car travels an additional 10,000 miles without breaking down (assuming it didn't break down for the first 20,000 miles). Since event B is contingent on event A, write the probability as follows:

$$P(B|A) = 0.50$$

Use the conditional probability formula to find the probability that the car travels 30,000 miles $(A \cap B)$ without breaking down.

$$P(B|A) = \frac{P(A \cap B)}{P(A)}$$

$$0.50 = \frac{P(A \cap B)}{0.75}$$

$$P(A \cap B) = (0.50)(0.75) = 0.375$$

Thus, the car has a 37.5% probability of traveling 30,000 consecutive miles without breaking down.

13C. Generate, simulate, and use probability models to represent a situation

Throughout this competency, probability theory is applied and examples are presented in a way that illustrates the creation of probability models. In addition, the use of simulations for probability models is also discussed (see **Skill 13A**).

13D. Determine probabilities by constructing sample spaces to model situations

The concept and use of sample spaces is discussed in **Skill 13B**.

13E. Solve a variety of probability problems using combinations, permutations, and geometric probability (i.e., probability as the ratio of two areas)

A **permutation** is the number of possible arrangements of items, without repetition, where order of selection is important.

A **combination** is the number of possible arrangements, without repetition, where order of selection is not important.

<u>Example:</u> If any two numbers are selected from the set {1, 2, 3, 4}, list the possible permutations and combinations.

Combinations	Permutations
12, 13, 14, 23, 24, 34	12, 21, 13, 31, 14, 41, 23, 32, 24, 42, 34, 43,
six ways	twelve ways

Note that the list of permutations includes 12 and 21 as separate possibilities since the order of selection is important. In the case of combinations, however, the order of selection is not important and, therefore, 12 is the same combination as 21. Hence, 21 is not listed separately as a possibility.

The number of permutations and combinations may also be found by using the formulae given below.

The number of possible permutations in selecting r objects from a set of n is given by

$$_nP_r = \frac{n!}{(n-r)!}$$

The notation $_nP_r$ is read "the number of permutations of n objects taken r at a time."

In our example, two objects are being selected from a set of four.

$$_4P_2 = \frac{4!}{(4-2)!}$$

Substitute known values.

$$_4P_2 = 12$$

The number of possible combinations in selecting r objects from a set of n is given by

$$_nC_r = \frac{n!}{(n-r)!r!}$$

The number of combinations when r objects are selected from n objects.

In our example,

$$_4C_2 = \frac{4!}{(4-2)!2!}$$

Substitute known values.

$$_4C_2 = 6$$

It can be shown that $_nP_n$, the number of ways n objects can be arranged in a row, is equal to $n!$. We can think of the problem as n positions being filled one at a time. The first position can be filled in n ways using any one of the n objects. Since one of the objects has already been used, the second position can be filled only in $n-1$ ways. Similarly, the third position can be filled in $n-2$ ways and so on. Hence, the total number of possible arrangements of n objects in a row is given by

$$_nP_n = n(n-1)(n-2)........1 = n!$$

Example: Five books are placed in a row on a bookshelf. In how many different ways can they be arranged?

The number of possible ways in which 5 books can be arranged in a row is $5! = 1 \times 2 \times 3 \times 4 \times 5 = 120$.

The formula given above for $_nP_r$, **the number of possible permutations of r objects selected from n objects** can also be proven in a similar manner. If r positions are filled by selecting from n objects, the first position can be filled in n ways, the second position can be filled in $n-1$ ways and so on (as shown before). The rth position can be filled in $n-(r-1) = n-r+1$ ways. Hence,

$$_nP_r = n(n-1)(n-2).....(n-r+1) = \frac{n!}{(n-r)!}$$

The formula for the **number of possible combinations of r objects selected from n, $_nC_r$**, may be derived by using the above two formulae. For the same set of r objects, the number of permutations is $r!$. All of these permutations, however, correspond to the same combination. Hence,

$$_nC_r = \frac{_nP_r}{r!} = \frac{n!}{(n-r)!r!}$$

The number of permutations of n objects in a ring is given by $(n-1)!$. This can be demonstrated by considering the fact that the number of permutations of n objects in a row is $n!$. When the objects are placed in a ring, moving every object one place to its left will result in the same arrangement. Moving each object two places to its left will also result in the same arrangement. We can continue this kind of movement up to n places to get the same arrangement. Thus the count $n!$ is n times too many when the objects are arranged in a ring. Hence, the number of permutations of n objects in a ring is given by $\dfrac{n!}{n} = (n-1)!$.

Example: There are 20 people at a meeting. Five of them are selected to lead a discussion. How many different combinations of five people can be selected from the group? If the five people are seated in a row, how many different seating permutations are possible? If the five people are seated around a circular table, how many possible permutations are there?

The number of possible combinations of 5 people selected from the group of 20 is

$$_{20}C_5 = \frac{20!}{15!5!} = \frac{16 \times 17 \times 18 \times 19 \times 20}{1 \times 2 \times 3 \times 4 \times 5} = \frac{1860480}{120} = 15504$$

The number of possible permutations of the five seated in a row is

$$_{20}P_5 = \frac{20!}{15!} = 16 \times 17 \times 18 \times 19 \times 20 = 1860480$$

The number of possible permutations of the five seated in a circle is

$$\frac{_{20}P_5}{5} = \frac{20!}{5 \times 15!} = \frac{16 \times 17 \times 18 \times 19 \times 20}{5} = 372096$$

If the set of n objects contains some objects that are exactly alike, the number of permutations will again be different than $n!$. For instance, if n_1 of the n objects are exactly alike, then switching those objects among themselves will result in the same arrangement. Since we already know that n_1 objects can be arranged in $n_1!$ ways, $n!$ must be reduced by a factor of $n_1!$ to get the correct number of permutations. Thus, the number of permutations of n objects of which n_1 are exactly alike is given by $\dfrac{n!}{n_1!}$. Generalizing this, we can say that **the number of different permutations of n objects of which n_1 are alike, n_2 are alike,... n_j are alike, is**

$$\frac{n!}{n_1!n_2!...n_j!} \text{ where } n_1 + n_2..... + n_j = n$$

Example: A box contains 3 red, 2 blue and 5 green marbles. If all the marbles are taken out of the box and arranged in a row, how many different permutations are possible?

The number of possible permutations is

$$\frac{10!}{3!2!5!} = \frac{6\times7\times8\times9\times10}{6\times2} = 2520$$

Geometric probability describes situations that involve shapes and measures. For example, given a 10-inch string, we can determine the probability of cutting the string so that one piece is at least 8 inches long. If the cut occurs in the first or last two inches of the string, one of the pieces will be at least 8 inches long.

Thus, the probability of such a cut is $\dfrac{2+2}{10} = \dfrac{4}{10} = \dfrac{2}{5}$ or 40%.

Other geometric probability problems involve the ratio of areas. For example, to determine the likelihood of randomly hitting a defined area of a dartboard (pictured below) we determine the ratio of the target area to the total area of the board.

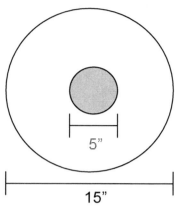

Given that a randomly thrown dart lands somewhere on the board, the probability that it hits the target area is the ratio of the areas of the two circles. Thus, the probability, P, of hitting the target is

$$P = \frac{(2.5)^2 \pi}{(7.5)^2 \pi} \times 100 = \frac{6.25}{56.25} \times 100 = 11.1\% .$$

Likewise, probabilities can be represented using the **Venn diagram**, which represents events or sets of events as shapes that depict the relationships of these events by overlapping (or not overlapping). For example, let the rectangle below represent all the possible outcomes of the random selection of a card from a standard deck. Let oval *A* be the all the outcomes for which a spade is chosen, and let oval *B* be all the outcomes for which a jack is chosen. Since there is one choice that falls within both of these categories (the jack of spades), the ovals overlap.

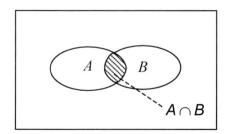

If the shapes correspond to areas that are to scale with their probabilities, then a Venn diagram can be used to calculate probabilities using ratios of these areas. Consider, for instance, the flip of a fair coin. The diagram for this case is shown below. (Although this may not strictly be considered a Venn diagram, depending on the definition of such, it does relay the same idea.)

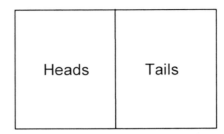

Notice that the total area A is divided evenly between "heads" ($A/2$) and "tails" ($A/2$). Thus, the probability of heads (or tails) is

$$\frac{A/2}{A} = \frac{1}{2}$$

Another Venn diagram is shown below for a six-sided die.

1	4
2	5
3	6

Again, the possibility of a particular outcome or range of outcomes can be found by using ratios of the associated areas. In both the cases above, there are no possible outcomes beyond those shown, so the Venn diagram does not show any area outside these outcomes.

13F. Use the binomial, geometric, and normal distributions to solve problems

The following discussion presents three common probability distributions and examples that illustrate their application. These distributions are the normal distribution, the binomial distribution and the geometric distribution.

The Normal Distribution

A **normal distribution** is the distribution associated with most sets of real-world data. It is frequently called a **bell curve**. A normal distribution has a **continuous random variable** X with mean μ and variance σ^2. The normal distribution has the following form.

$$f(x) = \frac{1}{\sigma\sqrt{2\pi}} e^{-\frac{1}{2}\left(\frac{x-\mu}{\sigma}\right)^2}$$

The total area under the normal curve is one. Thus,

$$\int_{-\infty}^{\infty} f(x)\,dx = 1$$

Since the area under the curve of this function is one, the distribution can be used to determine probabilities through integration. If a continuous random variable x follows the normal distribution, then the probability that x has a value between a and b is

$$P(a < X \le b) = \int_a^b f(x)\,dx = F(b) - F(a)$$

Since this integral is difficult to evaluate analytically, tables of values are often used. Often, however, the tables use the integral

$$\frac{1}{\sqrt{2\pi}} \int_a^b e^{-\frac{t^2}{2}}\,dt = F(b) - F(a)$$

To use this form, simply convert x values to t values using

$$t = \frac{x_i - \mu}{\sigma}$$

where x_i is a particular value for the random variable X. This formula is often called the **z-score**.

<u>Example</u>: Albert's Bagel Shop's morning customer load follows a normal distribution, with **mean** (average) 50 and **standard deviation** 10. Determine the probability that the number of customers on a particular morning will be less than 42.

First, convert to a form that allows use of normal distribution tables:

$$t = \frac{x - \mu}{\sigma} = \frac{42 - 50}{10} = -0.8$$

Next, use a table to find the probability corresponding to the z-score. The actual integral in this case is

$$P(X < 42) = \frac{1}{\sqrt{2\pi}} \int_{-\infty}^{-0.8} e^{-\frac{t^2}{2}} dt$$

The table gives a value for $x = 0.8$ of 0.7881. To find the value for $x < -0.8$, subtract this result from one.

$$P(X < 42) = 1 - 0.7881 = 0.2119$$

This means that there is about a 21.2% chance that there will be fewer than 42 customers in a given morning.

Example: The scores on Mr. Rogers' statistics exam follow a normal distribution with mean 85 and standard deviation 5. A student is wondering what is the probability that she will score between a 90 and a 95 on her exam.

To compute $P(90 < x < 95)$, first compute the z-scores for each raw score.

$$z_{90} = \frac{90 - 85}{5} = 1$$
$$z_{95} = \frac{95 - 85}{5} = 2$$

Use the tables to find $P(1 < z < 2)$. To do this, subtract as follows.

$$P(1 < z < 2) = P(z < 2) - P(z < 1)$$

The table yields

$$P(1 < z < 2) = 0.9772 - 0.8413 = 0.1359$$

It can then be concluded that there is a 13.6% chance that the student will score between a 90 and a 95 on her exam.

The Binomial Distribution

The **binomial distribution** is a probability distribution for discrete random variables and is expressed as follows.

$$f(x) = \binom{n}{x} p^x q^{n-x}$$

where a sequence of n trials of an experiment are performed and where p is the probability of "success" and q is the probability of "failure." The value x is the number of times the experiment yields a successful outcome. Notice that this probability function is the product of p^x (the probability of successful outcomes in x trials) and q^{n-x} (the probability of unsuccessful outcomes in the remainder of the trials). The factor $\binom{n}{x}$ indicates that the x successful trials can be chosen $\binom{n}{x}$ ways (combinations) from the n total trials. (In other words, the successful trials may occur at different points in the sequence.)

Example: A loaded coin has a probability 0.6 of landing heads up. What is the probability of getting three heads in four successive tosses?

Use the binomial distribution. In this case, p is the probability of the coin landing heads up, and $q = 1 - p$ is the probability of the coin landing tails up. Also, the number of "successful" trials (heads up) is 3. Then,

$$f(3) = \binom{4}{3}(0.6)^3 (1-0.6)^{4-3}$$

$$f(3) = \frac{4!}{3!(4-3)!}(0.6)^3 (0.4)^1$$

$$f(3) = \frac{24}{6(1)}(0.216)(0.4) = 0.3456$$

Thus, there is a 34.56% chance that the loaded coin will land heads up three out of four times.

The Geometric Distribution

The geometric distribution is defined given probability $p < 1$ and $q = 1 - p$. The distribution function is given below. for $x = 0, 1, 2,...$

$$f(x) = pq^x$$

The geometric distribution can be interpreted as the probability of one success in $x + 1$ Bernoulli trials. Note that both p and q are less than unity, so the function p decreases with increasing x.

Example: If a damaged engine has a 25% chance of starting on any particular attempt, how many attempts are necessary to ensure that the engine will start 50% of the time for that number of attempts?

This problem requires the use of the geometric distribution. The probability of success is $p = 0.25$, and the probability of failure is $q = 1 - p = 0.75$. The probability P that the engine will start within x attempts is the following:

$$P(x) = \sum_{i=1}^{x} pq^x$$

Thus, using the values of p and q derived from the information given in the problem statement, find the number x such that $P(x) \geq .50$. This can be done by trial and error; start with $x = 1$.

$$P(1) = pq = .1875$$
$$P(2) = pq + pq^2 = 0.1875 + 0.1406 = 0.3281$$
$$P(3) = pq + pq^2 + pq^3 = 0.3281 + 0.1055 = 0.4336$$
$$P(4) = pq + pq^2 + pq^3 + pq^4 = 0.4366 + 0.1055 = 0.5127$$

Thus, the engine will start just over 50% of the time (51.3%) within four attempts.

The following example problems provide some further reinforcement of the concepts presented above.

Example: If the height of a certain population follows a normal distribution and has a mean of 5'6" and a standard deviation of 4", what is the probability that a randomly selected individual is taller than 6'?

Use the formula for the normal probability density distribution, which is given below, and a mean value μ = 66" and a standard deviation value σ = 4". Define X as the continuous random variable associated with height.

$$f(x) = \frac{1}{\sigma\sqrt{2\pi}} e^{-\frac{1}{2}\left(\frac{x-\mu}{\sigma}\right)^2} = \frac{1}{4\sqrt{2\pi}} e^{-\frac{1}{2}\left(\frac{x-66}{4}\right)^2}$$

The probability that a person is taller than 6' (or 72") is expressed as follows:

$$P(X \geq 72'') = \int_{72''}^{\infty} f(x)\,dx$$

Using the previously defined probability density function and a table of values to evaluate the integral yields the resulting probability, where t has been defined as $\dfrac{x-66}{4}$ (thus, $dt = dx/4$):

$$P(X \geq 72'') = \int_{72''}^{\infty} \frac{1}{4\sqrt{2\pi}} e^{-\frac{1}{2}\left(\frac{x-66}{4}\right)^2} dx = \frac{1}{4\sqrt{2\pi}} 4 \int_{72''}^{\infty} e^{-\frac{1}{2}t^2} dt$$

The probability integral is expressed in two slightly different forms since many tables list the integral from −∞ to certain values of t.

$$P(X \geq 72'') = \frac{1}{\sqrt{2\pi}} \int_{1.5}^{\infty} e^{-\frac{1}{2}(t)^2} dt = 1 - \frac{1}{\sqrt{2\pi}} \int_{-\infty}^{1.5} e^{-\frac{1}{2}(t)^2} dt$$

$$P(X \geq 72'') \approx 1 - 0.9332 = 0.0668$$

Thus, there is only a 6.68% probability that a person selected at random from the population will be taller than 6'.

Example: A six-sided die is loaded to roll an even number 60% of the time. If each even number has an equal likelihood of being rolled and each odd has an equal likelihood of being rolled, what is the probability that exactly three out of four consecutive rolls will be greater than 3?

This problem involves a discrete random variable: the roll of a die. First, use the information presented in the problem statement to find the probability that a single roll yields a number greater than 3. Note that the evens are equally likely, and the odds are equally likely. If the probability of an even roll is 0.6, then the probability of numbers 2, 4, and 6 is 0.2 each. For the odd numbers, where the total probability is $1 - 0.6 = 0.4$, the probability of rolling numbers 1, 3, and 5 is 4/30 each.

The total probability that a number greater than 3 (4, 5, or 6) is rolled is then the sum of the individual probabilities of these numbers.

$$P(4, 5, \text{or } 6) = \frac{2}{10} + \frac{4}{30} + \frac{2}{10} = \frac{16}{30} = \frac{8}{15}$$

Thus, the probability of a "successful" roll (a number greater than 3) is 8/15, and the probability of a "failed" roll (a number 3 or less) is $1 - 8/15 = 7/15$. Next, apply the binomial distribution probability function for three successful trials out of four.

$$P(3 \text{ out of } 4) = \binom{4}{3}\left(\frac{8}{15}\right)^3\left(\frac{7}{15}\right)^1$$

$$P(3 \text{ out of } 4) = 4\left(\frac{8}{15}\right)^3\left(\frac{7}{15}\right)^1 = \frac{4 \cdot 8^3 \cdot 7}{15^4} = \frac{14{,}336}{50{,}625} \approx 0.283$$

Thus, the probability for three out of four rolls greater than 3 is about 0.283.

Competency 014 **The teacher understands the relationship among probability theory, sampling, and statistical inference, and how statistical inference is used in making and evaluating predictions.**

This competency presents various concepts associated with probability and statistics in the context of sample statistics, confidence intervals, probability distributions, and linear regression. The information discussed here relies heavily on an understanding of the concepts in **Competency 012** and **Competency 013**.

14A. Apply knowledge of designing, conducting, analyzing, and interpreting statistical experiments to investigate real-world problems

The concepts presented throughout this and preceding competencies in this domain provide insight into the design, conducting, analysis, and interpretation of statistical experiments.

14B. Demonstrate an understanding of random samples, sample statistics, and the relationship between sample size and confidence intervals

Random sampling is the process of studying an aspect of a population by selecting and gathering data from a segment of that population and making inferences and generalizations based on the results. Two main types of random sampling are simple and stratified. With simple random sampling, each member of the population has an equal chance of selection to the sample group. With stratified random sampling, each member of the population has a known but unequal chance of selection to the sample group, as the study selects a random sample from each population demographic. In general, stratified random sampling is more accurate because it provides a more representative sample group. **Sample statistics** are important generalizations about the entire sample such as mean, median, mode, range, and sampling error (standard deviation). Various factors affect the accuracy of sample statistics and the generalizations made from them about the larger population. Sample statistics are discussed further in **Competency 012**.

Sample size is one important factor in the accuracy and reliability of sample statistics. As sample size increases, sampling error (standard deviation) decreases. Sampling error is the main determinant of the size of the confidence interval. Confidence intervals decrease in size as sample size increases. A **confidence interval** gives an estimated range of values, which is likely to include a particular population parameter. The confidence level associated with a confidence interval is the probability that the interval contains the population parameter. For example, a poll reports 60% of a sample group prefers candidate A with a margin of error of ±3% and a confidence level of 95%. In this poll, there is a 95% chance that the preference for candidate A in the whole population is between 57% and 63%.

The ultimate goal of sampling is to make generalizations about a population based on the characteristics of a random sample. Estimators are sample statistics used to make such generalizations. For example, the mean value of a sample is the estimator of the population mean. Unbiased estimators, on average, accurately predict the corresponding population characteristic. Biased estimators, on the other hand, do not exactly mirror the corresponding population characteristic. Although most estimators contain some level of bias, limiting bias to achieve accurate projections is the goal of statisticians.

14C. Apply knowledge of the use of probability to make observations and draw conclusions from single variable data and to describe the level of confidence in the conclusion

A method of determining, to within a certain confidence level, whether a particular conclusion can be accepted according to a certain set of data is called **statistical hypothesis testing**.

The first step of hypothesis testing is to formulate the so-called **null hypothesis**, which is assumed to be true and is to be accepted unless sufficient evidence warrants its rejection. Thus, the null hypothesis is often a simple or readily accepted statement, and it is typically labeled H_0. The opposite of the null hypothesis is the so-called alternate hypothesis, which is typically labeled H_1 or H_a. If the null hypothesis is rejected, the alternate hypothesis is then accepted.

The next step involves computing some test statistic using the associated sample data. Comparison of this data with a critical value for the test statistic (which is a threshold value for a given confidence) allows determination of whether to accept or reject the null hypothesis.

Common test statistics include the t-test, the z-test, and the χ^2 (chi-square) "goodness of fit" test.

The (Student's) **t-test** is the most commonly used method to evaluate the difference in means between two groups. The t-test assesses whether the means of two groups are statistically different from each other. The formula for the t-test is a ratio: the numerator of the ratio is the difference between the two means or averages, and the denominator is a measure of the variability or dispersion of the scores.

$$\frac{\text{difference between group means}}{\text{variability of groups}} = \frac{\overline{X}_T - \overline{X}_C}{SE\left(\overline{X}_T - \overline{X}_C\right)} = \text{t-value}$$

In this example T refers to a treatment group and C refers to a control group. To compute the numerator of the formula, find the difference between the means. The denominator is called the **standard error of the difference**. To compute this quantity, take the variance for each group and divide it by the population of that group. Add these two values and then take the square root of the sum.

$$SE\left(\overline{X}_T - \overline{X}_C\right) = \sqrt{\frac{\text{var}_T}{n_T} + \frac{\text{var}_C}{n_C}}$$

The final formula for the t-test is

$$t = \frac{\overline{X}_T - \overline{X}_C}{\sqrt{\dfrac{\text{var}_T}{n_T} + \dfrac{\text{var}_C}{n_C}}}$$

Once the t-value is computed, a Student's t distribution table is needed to compare the t-test statistic with the threshold value for a given confidence level. This confidence level is often expressed as a risk, or alpha level, which is usually 0.05. Another important value is the number of degrees of freedom (*df*) for the test. In the t-test, *df* is the sum of the populations in both groups less two. Using the t-value, the alpha level, and *df*, it is possible to look up the t-value in a standard table to determine whether the t-value is large enough to be significant. If it is, one can conclude (to a confidence defined by the alpha level) that the difference between the means for the two groups is statistically significant.

Example: The national average household income, which is based on a random sample of 500 households, is $43,000 with a standard deviation of $12,000. In a particular region, a 25-household sample indicates that the average household income is $39,000 with a standard deviation of $15,000. Determine if the discrepancy between average incomes is statistically significant.

Define the null and alternate hypotheses as follows:

H_0: There is no significant difference between the average incomes.

H_a: There is a significant difference between the average incomes.

Use the Student's t-test to calculate a test statistic. Assume an alpha level of 0.05. Also, convert standard deviations to variances by squaring.

$$t = \frac{\overline{X}_T - \overline{X}_C}{\sqrt{\dfrac{\text{var}_T}{n_T} + \dfrac{\text{var}_C}{n_C}}} = \frac{\$39,000 - \$43,000}{\sqrt{\dfrac{(\$15,000)^2}{25} + \dfrac{(\$12,000)^2}{500}}}$$

$$t = \left| -\frac{4,000}{\sqrt{9,000,000 + 288,000}} \right| \approx 1.31$$

The number of degrees of freedom in this case is 500 + 25 − 2 = 523. In many cases, the table of values for the Student's t distribution will not list this high a number, so ∞ is usually close enough. The critical t-value for an alpha value of 0.05 is 1.65. Since 1.31 < 1.65, there is not sufficient reason to reject the null hypothesis. Thus, it can be concluded to a confidence of 95% that there is no statistically significant difference between the regional average income and the national average income.

14D. Make inferences about a population using binomial, normal, and geometric distributions

Some fundamental parameters of probability distributions are the **expected value**, variance, and standard deviation. The expected value $E(X)$, given a random variable X and an associated probability distribution $f(x)$ is the following for continuous and discrete distributions, respectively:

$$E(X) = \int_{-\infty}^{\infty} xf(x)\, dx$$

$$E(X) = \sum_i x_i f(x_i)$$

The expected (or expectation) value for a random variable X is also sometimes written as $<X>$. The expected value can be applied to random variables such as the mean μ (written as $E(X)$ or $<X>$), the variance (written as $E((X - \mu)^2)$ or $<(X - \mu)^2>$), or any other parameter.

The variance and standard deviation of a probability distribution are defined in the same manner as those in **Competency 012** for statistics.

Additional concepts and applications of various probability distributions are discussed at length in **Competency 013**. Example problems involving calculating population parameters are also provided therein. By applying concepts such as expectation values to these distributions, inferences about the population (such as mean, variance, and skewness) can be made.

14E. Demonstrate an understanding of the use of techniques such as scatter plots, regression lines, correlation coefficients, and residual analysis to explore bivariate data and to make and evaluate predictions

Bivariate data involves information that corresponds to two different variables. Methods of displaying bivariate data are discussed above (such as the scatter plot).

Regression for bivariate data allows description of data and offers the ability to interpolate (and, in some cases, extrapolate) additional data. It is often helpful to use regression to construct a more general trend or distribution based on sample data. To select an appropriate model for the regression, a representative set of data must be examined. It is often helpful, in this case, to plot the data and review it visually on a graph. In this manner, it is relatively simple to select a general class of functions (linear, quadratic, exponential, etc.) that might be used to model the data. There are two basic aspects of regression: selection of an appropriate curve that best fits the data and quantification of the "goodness of fit" of that curve. For instance, if a line can be constructed that passes through every data point of a distribution, then that line is a perfect fit to the data (and, obviously, linear regression is an appropriate choice for the model). If the distribution of data points seems to bear no particular resemblance to the line, then linear regression is probably not a wise choice, and a quantification of the goodness of fit should reflect this fact.

An important consideration prior to performing regression is the presence of **outliers**. An outlier is a piece of data that does not seem to fit with the general trend of the balance of the data. Outliers can result from particular cases that run contrary to a general trend (for instance, the presence of an extremely tall person or extremely short person in a crowd of otherwise average people), or they can result from an error in measurement. Often, it is appropriate to remove outliers from data when performing regression, although the choice to do so requires careful consideration and (sometimes) statistical testing.

The Method of Least Squares

Given a set of data, a curve approximation can be fitted to the data by using the **method of least squares**. The best-fit curve, defined by the function $f(x)$, is assumed to approximate a set of data with coordinates (x_i, y_i) by minimizing the sum of squared differences between the curve and the data. Mathematically, the sum of these squared differences (errors) can be written as follows for a data set with n points.

$$S = \sum_{i=1}^{n} \left[f(x_i) - y_i \right]^2$$

Thus, the best-fit curve approximation to a set of data (x_i, y_i) is $f(x)$ such that S is minimized.

Shown below is a set of data and a linear function that approximates it. The vertical distances between the data points and the line are the errors that are squared and summed to find S.

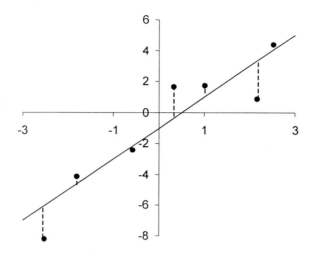

Linear least squares regression

If the curve $f(x)$ that is used to approximate a set of data by minimizing the sum of squared errors (or **residuals**), S, then $f(x)$ is called a **least squares regression line**. The process of determining $f(x)$ is called **linear least squares regression**. In this case, $f(x)$ has the following form:

$$f(x) = ax + b$$

Given a set of data $\{(x_1, y_1), (x_2, y_2), (x_3, y_3), \ldots, (x_n, y_n)\}$, the sum S for linear regression is the following.

$$S = \sum_{i=1}^{n} [ax_i + b - y_i]^2$$

To find $f(x)$, it is necessary to find a and b. This can be done by minimizing S. Since S is a function of both a and b, S must be minimized through the use of partial derivatives. (A partial derivative is exactly the same as a full derivative, except that all variables other than the one being differentiated are treated as constants. Partial derivatives often use the symbol ∂ in place of d.)

Therefore, find the partial derivative with respect to a and the partial derivative with respect to b.

$$\frac{\partial S}{\partial a} = \frac{\partial}{\partial a} \sum_{i=1}^{n} [ax_i + b - y_i]^2 \qquad \frac{\partial S}{\partial b} = \frac{\partial}{\partial b} \sum_{i=1}^{n} [ax_i + b - y_i]^2$$

$$\frac{\partial S}{\partial a} = \sum_{i=1}^{n} 2x_i [ax_i + b - y_i] \qquad \frac{\partial S}{\partial b} = \sum_{i=1}^{n} 2[ax_i + b - y_i]$$

Set these equal to zero. This yields a system of equations that can be solved to find a and b. Although the algebra is somewhat involved, it is not conceptually difficult. The results are given

$$a = \frac{n\sum\limits_{i=1}^{n} x_i y_i - \sum\limits_{i=1}^{n} x_i \sum\limits_{i=1}^{n} y_i}{n\sum\limits_{i=1}^{n} x_i^2 - \left[\sum\limits_{i=1}^{n} x_i\right]^2}$$

Note that the average x value for the data (which is the sum of all x values divided by n) and the average y value for the data (which is the sum of all y values divided by n) can be used to simplify the expression. The average x value is defined as $\overline{x}$ and the average y value is defined as $\overline{y}$.

$$a = \frac{\sum\limits_{i=1}^{n} x_i y_i - n\overline{xy}}{\sum\limits_{i=1}^{n} x_i^2 - n\overline{x}^2}$$

Since the expression for b is complicated, it suffices to the above expression for b in terms of a.

$$b = \frac{1}{n}\left(\sum_{i=1}^{n} y_i - a\sum_{i=1}^{n} x_i\right)$$
$$b = \overline{y} - a\overline{x}$$

Thus, given a set of data, the linear least squares regression line can be found by calculating a and b as shown above.

The **correlation coefficient**, r, can be used as a measure of the quality of $f(x)$ as a fit to the data set. The value of r ranges from zero (for a poor fit) to one (for a good fit). The correlation coefficient formula is given below.

$$r^2 = \frac{\left[\displaystyle\sum_{i=1}^{n} x_i y_i - \frac{1}{n}\sum_{i=1}^{n} x_i \sum_{i=1}^{n} y_i\right]^2}{\left[\displaystyle\sum_{i=1}^{n} x_i^2 - \frac{1}{n}\left(\sum_{i=1}^{n} x_i\right)^2\right]\left[\displaystyle\sum_{i=1}^{n} y_i^2 - \frac{1}{n}\left(\sum_{i=1}^{n} y_i\right)^2\right]}$$

$$r^2 = \frac{\left(\displaystyle\sum_{i=1}^{n} x_i y_i - n\overline{xy}\right)^2}{\left(\displaystyle\sum_{i=1}^{n} x_i^2 - n\overline{x}^2\right)\left(\displaystyle\sum_{i=1}^{n} y_i^2 - n\overline{y}^2\right)}$$

Example: A company has collected data comparing the age of its employees to their respective income (in thousands of dollars). Find the line that best fits the data (using a least squares approach). Also calculate the correlation coefficient for the fit. The data is given below in the form of (age, income).

$$\{(35,42),(27,23),(54,43),(58,64),(39,51),(31,40)\}$$

The data are plotted in the graph below.

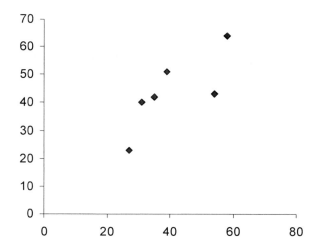

Note that there are six pieces of data. It is helpful to first calculate the following sums:

$$\sum_{i=1}^{6} x_i = 35 + 27 + 54 + 58 + 39 + 31 = 244$$

$$\sum_{i=1}^{6} y_i = 42 + 23 + 43 + 64 + 51 + 40 = 263$$

$$\sum_{i=1}^{6} x_i y_i = 35(42) + 27(23) + 54(43) + 58(64) + 39(51) + 31(40)$$
$$= 11354$$

$$\sum_{i=1}^{6} x_i^2 = 35^2 + 27^2 + 54^2 + 58^2 + 39^2 + 31^2 = 10716$$

$$\sum_{i=1}^{6} y_i^2 = 42^2 + 23^2 + 43^2 + 64^2 + 51^2 + 40^2 = 12439$$

Based on these values, the average x and y values are given below.

$$\bar{x} = \frac{244}{6} \approx 40.67$$

$$\bar{y} = \frac{263}{6} \approx 43.83$$

To find the equation of the least squares regression line, calculate the values of a and b.

$$a = \frac{\sum_{i=1}^{n} x_i y_i - n\bar{x}\bar{y}}{\sum_{i=1}^{n} x_i^2 - n\bar{x}^2} = \frac{11354 - 6(40.67)(43.83)}{10716 - 6(40.67)^2} \approx 0.832$$

$$b = \bar{y} - a\bar{x} = 43.83 - 0.832(40.67) = 9.993$$

Thus, the equation of the least squares regression line is

$$f(x) = 0.832x + 9.993$$

This result can be displayed on the data graph to ensure that there are no egregious errors in the result.

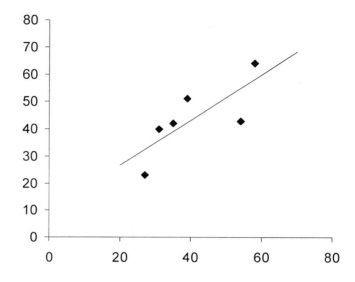

The regression line in the graph above appears to do a good job of approximating the trend of the data. To quantify how well the line fits the data, calculate the correlation coefficient using the formula given above.

$$r^2 = \frac{\left(11354 - 6(40.67)(43.83)\right)^2}{\left(10716 - 6(40.67)^2\right)\left(12439 - 6(43.83)^2\right)}$$

$$r^2 = \frac{\left(658.603\right)^2}{\left(791.707\right)\left(912.587\right)} = 0.600$$

$$r = 0.775$$

Thus, the fit to the data is reasonably good.

DOMAIN V. MATHEMATICAL PROCESSES AND PERSPECTIVES

Competency 015   **The teacher understands mathematical reasoning and problem solving.**

This competency discusses the application of different aspects of reasoning to mathematics. Concepts of proof, deduction and induction, correct mathematical inference, formal and informal reasoning, problem-solving strategies, and validity of mathematical models are presented.

15A.   **Demonstrate an understanding of proof, including indirect proof, in mathematics**

A **proof** is an argument that demonstrates the truth (or falsity) of a proposition. Mathematical proofs begin with certain axioms or known propositions and, by some line of reasoning, deduce a particular conclusion. (For more on deduction and induction, see the next skill section.)

Because not all concepts in mathematics can be proven or otherwise defined (if this were the case, then either circular definitions/proofs would be required—but these are not informative—or an infinite regression of definitions/proofs would be required—but these are impossible), mathematical proofs necessarily start from certain unproven or undefined concepts. In geometry, for instance, the concept of a point is undefined.

Mathematical proof thus attempts to reason in a consistent and orderly way from known premises (as long as they are either defined to be true or are proven to be true) to non-trivial conclusions. This process may involve positively demonstrating a proposition through **direct proof**, which involves showing that the proposition is true, or it may involve **indirect proof**, which involves showing that the negation (opposite) of the proposition is false. Both approaches are valid, but one or the other may be simpler. Because some propositions can be shown to be false through a single counter example, indirect proof is sometimes the simplest method of proof. Indirect proof may also involve using the opposite of the proposition being proved to demonstrate that a contradiction is reached. In such a case, assuming that all other premises are true, then the opposite of the proposition being proved must be false. Consider the following example.

<u>Example:</u> Prove that there are no even prime numbers other than the number 2.

A direct proof of this proposition may be possible, but an indirect proof is much simpler. Assume that the opposite is true: there is an even prime number other than 2. Let this number be called x (an integer). Since x is even, then the following must be true, where y is an integer.

$$\frac{x}{2} = y$$

But if x is evenly divisible by 2, it cannot be a prime number. Thus, a contradiction is reached with the originally assumed proposition that x is prime. This then proves that there are no even prime numbers other than 2.

15B. Apply correct mathematical reasoning to derive valid conclusions from a set of premises

Given a set of premises, deductive reasoning can be used to reach valid conclusions. The key to correct reasoning in this regard is an understanding of the fundamental concepts of the particular area of interest. In number theory, for instance, it is necessary to have a grasp of the properties of real numbers if some conclusion about the set of real numbers (or a subset thereof) is being sought.

In addition to specific knowledge about the particular area about which conclusions are being sought, general knowledge of the process of correct mathematical reasoning is required. The use of deduction in the process of mathematical reasoning is discussed in the previous skill section.

Derivation of valid conclusions first requires consistent application of known rules and principles. Use of unproven or controversial approaches can result in questionable results (unless that approach is also justified). Consistency, even with seemingly strange premises, can lead to interesting conclusions. For instance, although Euclidean geometry requires that the sum of the interior angles of any triangle is 180°, spherical geometry allows other sums (a triangle in spherical geometry could even have three right angles). Thus, even though spherical geometry dispenses with certain results that are seldom questioned, consistency in this context leads to interesting and useful results.

Deriving a valid conclusion requires justification for each step in the reasoning process. Although such justifications need not always be explicitly expressed, making note of them at least mentally helps to avoid reasoning errors.

15C. **Demonstrate an understanding of the use of inductive reasoning to make conjectures and deductive methods to evaluate the validity of conjectures**

Two forms of reasoning are inductive and deductive. **Inductive reasoning** involves making inference from specific facts to general principles; **deductive reasoning** involves making inference from general principles to specific facts. As such, inductive reasoning is generally weaker than deductive reasoning. (Inductive reasoning—or induction—should not be confused with mathematical induction, which is not an example of inductive reasoning, strictly speaking.)

Inductive Reasoning

Inductive reasoning generally involves finding a representative set of examples that support the general application of a broader principle. In a common context, an example of inductive reasoning would be inferring from the fact that only black crows have ever been spotted to the general statement that all crows are black. This inference has a foundation in numerous observations, and it thereby gains significant weight. Nevertheless, it is feasible that somewhere a white (or other colored) crow does exist but simply hasn't yet been spotted. Thus, inductive inferences can never acquire 100% certainty, regardless of the amount of information in support of them.

Regardless of the uncertainty associated with induction, inductive inferences can be helpful for building a theory or for making a conjecture about some aspect of life, mathematics, or any other area. The physical sciences are a particular example where induction is commonly used to develop theories about the universe. Although these theories may be founded on a large body of empirical and mathematical evidence, a single counterexample could topple their status. Thus, again, inductive reasoning can be helpful, but it is much weaker than deductive reasoning.

Inductive reasoning, because it is weaker than deduction, is also less rigorous in its application of specific rules for the process of arriving at conclusions. For instance, there is no rule concerning how much evidence constitutes a sufficient reason to inductively accept a particular hypothesis. (Thus, there is no minimum number of sightings of black crows that is required prior to making an inference that all crows are black.) The particular area in which inductive reasoning is applied and the amount of potential evidence that could reasonably be gathered are factors that help determine what constitutes an acceptable inductive inference.

In a mathematical context, induction can serve to make conjectures for which a proof (or a proof of the contrary) can then be sought. For instance, Fermat's Last Theorem states that there are no integer solutions x, y, and z to the expression $x^n + y^n = z^n$ for $n > 2$. Although this theorem was suspected to be true (largely by induction from numerous test cases) for hundreds of years, only recently was a deductive proof discovered. Thus, induction can serve as a less rigorous method of making tentative conclusions pending a formal proof.

Deductive Reasoning

Deductive reasoning is a method of reasoning that is stronger and more rigorous than inductive reasoning. Deductive arguments reason from a set of premises to a conclusion and are classified as invalid, valid, and sound. An **invalid argument** is one in which the conclusion does not necessarily follow from the premises. A **valid argument** is one in which the conclusion necessarily follows from the premises. A **sound argument** is a valid argument for which all the premises are true. Thus, the following argument is valid but not sound:

> Premise 1: All dogs are black.
> Premise 2: Rover is a dog.
> Conclusion: Rover is black.

Were premises 1 and 2 both true, the conclusion would necessarily be true as well. Premise 1 is false, however, so the argument is valid but not sound. On the other hand, the following argument is both valid *and* sound.

> Premise 1: All integers are real numbers.
> Premise 2: 1 is an integer.
> Conclusion: 1 is a real number.

Both premises 1 and 2 are true, and the conclusion follows from the premises. Specific examples of deductive logical steps that can be taken in developing or evaluating an argument include modus ponens ("if A, then B" and "A is true" necessarily implies "B is true") and modus tollens ("if A, then B" and "B is false" necessarily implies "A is false").

Because deductive reasoning is more rigorous and the rules clearer, the process of arriving at an acceptable conclusion from a given set of premises (or the process of evaluating a deductive argument) is likewise clearer. Demonstrating the truth of the premises, however, may still be a complicated process. The premises may even require inductive reasoning to demonstrate their truth (at least tentatively). Thus, whether a deductive argument is sound can still be a matter that rests on the strength of a particular instance of inductive reasoning.

15D. Apply knowledge of the use of formal and informal reasoning to explore, investigate, and justify mathematical ideas

Formal reasoning, which includes deductive reasoning, follows a structured and orderly approach according to various rules of inference. **Informal reasoning**, which includes inductive reasoning, is less structured and tends not to be as rigorous as formal reasoning. Both of these types of reasoning, however, can be used to justify mathematical ideas.

Formal reasoning is applied for rigorous proofs and deriving conclusions in a way that provides certainty of the results. Informal reasoning is applied to situations where it is necessary to lend evidence to a conjecture or to build a strong (but not necessarily conclusive) case for some conclusion. Because it is less rigorous, informal reasoning tends to provide less certainty, but informal reasoning can be very helpful for finding potential solutions or possible avenues of approach for otherwise intractable problems.

The other skill sections in this competency discuss various particular aspects and methods of formal and informal reasoning and their application to mathematics.

15E. **Recognize that a mathematical problem can be solved in a variety of ways and select an appropriate strategy for a given problem**

The process of problem solving in mathematics is similar to that of other areas. One of the first steps is to identify what is known about the problem. Each problem for which a solution can be found should provide enough information to form a starting point from which a valid sequence of reasoning leads to the desired conclusion: a solution to the problem. Between identification of known information and identification of a solution to the problem is a somewhat gray area that, depending on the problem, could potentially involve myriad different approaches. Two potential approaches that do not involve a "direct" solution method are discussed below.

The **guess-and-check** strategy calls for making an initial guess of the solution, checking the answer, and using the outcome of this check to inform the next guess. With each successive guess, one should get closer to the correct answer. Constructing a table from the guesses can help organize the data.

Example: There are 100 coins in a jar: 10 are dimes, and the rest are pennies and nickels. If there are twice as many pennies as nickels, how many pennies and nickels are in the jar?

Based on the given information, there are 90 total nickels and pennies in the jar (100 coins – 10 dimes = 90 nickels and pennies). Also, there are twice as many pennies as nickels. Using this information, guess results that fulfill the criteria and then adjust the guess in accordance with the result. Continue this iterative process until the correct answer is found: 60 pennies and 30 nickels. The table below illustrates this process.

Number of Pennies	Number of Nickels	Total Number of Pennies and Nickels
40	20	60
80	40	120
70	35	105
60	30	90

Another non-direct approach to problem solving is **working backwards**. If the result of a problem is known (for example, in problems that involve proving a particular result), it is sometimes helpful to begin from the conclusion and attempt to work backwards to a particular known starting point. A slight variation of this approach involves both working backwards and working forwards until a common point is reached somewhere in the middle. The following example from trigonometry illustrates this process.

<u>Example:</u> Prove that $\sin^2 \theta = \dfrac{1}{2} - \dfrac{1}{2}\cos 2\theta$.

If the method for proving this result is not clear, one approach is to work backwards and forwards simultaneously. The following two-column approach organizes the process. Judging from the form of the result, it is apparent that the Pythagorean identity is a potential starting point.

$$\sin^2 \theta + \cos^2 \theta = 1 \qquad\qquad \sin^2 \theta = \frac{1}{2} - \frac{1}{2}\cos 2\theta$$

$$\sin^2 \theta = 1 - \cos^2 \theta \qquad\qquad \sin^2 \theta = \frac{1}{2} - \frac{1}{2}\left(2\cos^2 \theta - 1\right)$$

$$\sin^2 \theta = \frac{1}{2} - \cos^2 \theta + \frac{1}{2}$$

$$\sin^2 \theta = 1 - \cos^2 \theta$$

Thus, a proof is apparent based on the combination of the reasoning in these two columns.

Selection of an appropriate problem-solving strategy depends largely on the type of problem being solved and the particular area of mathematics with which the problem deals. For instance, problems that involve proving a specific result often require different approaches than do problems that involve finding a numerical result.

15F. Evaluate the reasonableness of a solution to a given problem

When solving any problem, it is helpful to evaluate the **reasonableness** of the solution. Often, errors in the solution lead to final results that do not make any sense in the context of the problem. Thus, checking the reasonableness of the solution can be a fast way to help determine if an error was made at some point in the process. Although such checks help to raise confidence in a solution, they do not necessarily guarantee that a solution is correct. For instance, an error can result in a relatively small deviation in a numerical result; although the answer may still seem reasonable, it could still be incorrect. Thus, the reasonableness of a solution is a necessary but not sufficient check of its correctness.

Two characteristics of a numerical answer that can be quickly evaluated are sign and magnitude. If a problem calls for determining the length of a side of some geometric figure, for example, then a negative number should indicate an error at some point in the solution. Similarly, a result that is magnitudes larger that would seem appropriate to the other aspects of the problem (such as the lengths of other measurements) could also indicate an error.

Additionally, the problem may provide information that limits the answer to a certain range. For example, if a problem asks for the average speed of an automobile over some distance and range of speeds, it is clear that the average speed should not exceed the maximum speed, nor should it be less than the minimum speed. Again, although this type of evaluation does not necessarily help to judge answers that fall within this range, it does help rule out results containing particularly egregious errors. On the other hand, if a speed distribution is shown that is weighted heavily toward faster speeds than slower speeds, it would then be reasonable to assume that the correct solution should be at the higher end of the speed range of the car. Similar types of qualitative evaluation or rough estimation for judging the reasonableness of a solution can be applied to other problems as well.

15G. Apply content knowledge to develop a mathematical model of a real-world situation and analyze and evaluate how well the model represents the situation

Mathematical models of real-world situations are just that: models. As a result, any model is likely to contain some deviation from observation, since it is seldom (if ever) that a model is able to take into account all the relevant variables. For instance, an attempt to model the probability of a so-called fair coin is not always as simple as it may seem. Imperfections or weight imbalances in the coin can cause deviations in the probability distribution, as can the method of flipping the coin and other factors such as air currents and even electric or magnetic fields (whose effect on the coin depend on the materials contained in the coin). On the other hand, such factors may have such a small effect on the model for a particular situation that they are negligible. It is thus often necessary to determine which variables or factors must be considered and which can be ignored.

Developing mathematical models requires a solid understanding of the theory associated with the mathematical tools being used as well as the ability to adapt those tools to use in modeling a particular situation. Throughout this guide, the fundamental concepts of various fields in mathematics are reviewed; proper application of these concepts allows the mathematician (or teacher of mathematics) to develop models of real-world phenomena.

Perhaps the surest way to evaluate how well a model represents a real-world situation is to compare the description provided by the model (whether predictions or other information) and compare it to observations of the phenomenon being modeled. Although this is an important first step in validating a model, it is not the only step. The model may correctly describe certain phenomena, but it may also be an inordinately complicated model. (For instance, epicycles may to some extent correctly predict the motion of planets, but much simpler models do the same task.)

In addition to correct results and simplicity, the accuracy of a model can be measured to some extent by its applicability beyond the situation of immediate interest. For instance, Newtonian mechanics in physics is sufficient to explain a wide variety of common and observable phenomena, but it is apparently inadequate for some extreme cases, and it furthermore does not apparently describe the behavior of matter at the atomic and subatomic levels.

Another consideration is of a philosophical nature: does the mathematics feasibly correspond to the observable reality that it describes. For instance, imaginary numbers are a crucial ingredient in a variety of models of phenomena in science and engineering; nevertheless, the correspondence of the imaginary number i to reality is unclear. Whether or not a particular model actually has any meaningful correspondence with reality, regardless of whether it produces correct results, is almost always a matter for debate.

Thus, evaluating a mathematical model involves multiple levels of consideration, some of which may be considered more or less relevant depending on the purpose of the model. (For example, if the model is simply intended to provide a fast prediction of some physical quantity, the philosophical considerations may be unimportant.) An appropriate evaluation requires weighing a number of factors and giving them the suitable influence in the evaluation.

15H. Demonstrate an understanding of estimation and evaluate its appropriate uses

Estimation is discussed in detail in **Competency 003.**

Competency 016 **The teacher understands mathematical connections within and outside of mathematics and how to communicate mathematical ideas and concepts.**

This section discusses various representations of mathematical ideas and concepts as well as the application of mathematics to other fields. In addition, the proper use of mathematical terminology is briefly reviewed. Many of the themes presented in this section are illustrated throughout the guide, rather than being discussed here at length.

16A. **Recognize and use multiple representations of a mathematical concept (e.g., a point and its coordinates, the area of circle as a quadratic function in r, probability as the ratio of two areas)**

The recognition and use of multiple representations of mathematical concepts can be useful skills on a number of levels. From a pedagogical perspective, the use of several different representations of a concept can help provide perspective that illuminates the concept, and it can be a way to present the information to different students who may each have slightly different conceptual strengths or approaches to learning mathematics. From a practical perspective, solving problems can often be facilitated by using slightly different representations of the information presented in the problem statement.

Although there are innumerable instances of mathematical concepts that can be expressed using a number of different representations, the following examples suffice to illustrate this idea. Throughout this guide, additional examples can be found, especially as tools and concepts from multiple areas of mathematics are applied to certain problems.

The concept of a point, for instance, is interchangeable with a set of coordinates. In certain cases where a coordinate system is helpful in solving a problem or explicating a concept, the use of coordinates to represent a point is the best representation. In other cases, the use of a system of coordinates may be an unneeded factor that would simply complicate the problem.

In addition, a plane region can be viewed as a geometric concept or as a definite integral of a function in a coordinate plane. In either case, the same concept is being presented, but one or the other of the representations might be better in the context of a particular problem or task.

16B. **Use mathematics to model and solve problems in other disciplines, such as art, music, science, social science, and business**

Artists, musicians, scientists, social scientists, and those in business use mathematical modeling to solve problems in their disciplines. These disciplines rely on the tools and symbols of mathematics to model natural events and manipulate data. Mathematics is a key aspect of visual art.

Artists use the geometric properties of shapes, ratios, and proportions in creating paintings and sculptures. For example, mathematics is essential to the concept of perspective. Artists must determine the appropriate lengths and heights of objects to portray three-dimensional distance in two dimensions.

Mathematics is also an important part of music. Many musical terms have mathematical connections. For example, the musical octave contains twelve notes and spans a factor of two in frequency. In other words, the frequency—the speed of vibration that determines tone and sound quality—doubles from the first note in an octave to the last. Thus, starting from any note we can determine the frequency of any other note using the following formula.

$$\text{Freq} = \text{note} \times 2^{N/12}$$

Here, N is the number of notes from the starting point and note is the frequency of the starting note. Mathematical understanding of frequency plays an important role in the tuning of musical instruments.

In addition to the visual and auditory arts, mathematics is an integral part of most scientific disciplines. The uses of mathematics in science are almost endless, and the following are but a few examples of how scientists use mathematics. Physical scientists use vectors, functions, derivatives, and integrals to describe and model the movement of objects. Biologists and ecologists use mathematics to model ecosystems and study DNA. Also, chemists use mathematics to study the interaction of molecules and to determine proper amounts and proportions of reactants.

Many social science disciplines use mathematics to model and solve problems. Economists, for example, use functions, graphs, and matrices to model the activities of producers, consumers, and firms. Political scientists use mathematics to model the behavior and opinions of the electorate. In addition, sociologists use mathematical functions to model the behavior of humans and human populations.

Finally, mathematical problem solving and modeling is essential to business planning and execution. For example, businesses rely on mathematical projections to plan business strategy. Additionally, stock market analysis and accounting rely on mathematical concepts.

16C. Express mathematical statements using developmentally appropriate language, standard English, mathematical language, and symbolic mathematics

Mathematics is, in some ways, a formalization of language that concerns such concepts as quantity and organization. Mathematics often involves symbolic representations, which can help alleviate the ambiguities found in common language. Naturally, then, communication of mathematical ideas requires conversion back and forth from verbal and symbolic forms is a necessary skill. These two forms can often help to elucidate one another when an attempt is made to understand an idea that they represent.

Mathematical ideas and expressions may sometimes be simple to translate into language; for instance, basic arithmetic operations are usually fairly easy to express in everyday language (although complicated expressions may be less so). In some cases, common language more easily expresses certain ideas than does symbolic language (and sometimes vice versa). Much of the translation process is learned through practicing expression of mathematical ideas in verbal (or written) form and by translating verbal or written expressions into a symbolic form.

The following examples are just a few illustrations of the translation process. The material throughout this guide attempts to present mathematical ideas both in symbolic and written forms. Thus, practicing by carefully following the text and example problems and by attempting to articulate the various concepts both in English and in mathematical symbols should help the student (and teacher) of mathematics gain mastery of this skill.

Example: Find a symbolic expression for the area inside an elliptical region with a minor axis of length *a* and a major axis of length *b*.

Although this written expression of can simply be summed up in the expression given in the problem, the symbolic form is significantly more complicated. First, find the symbolic expression *f*(*x*) for an ellipse in a coordinate plane (assume the major axis is coincident with the *x*-axis):

$$f(x) = \pm \frac{a}{2}\left(1 - \frac{4x^2}{b^2}\right)^{1/2}$$

The area *A* inside this region can be expressed using integral notation:

$$A = \int_{-b}^{b} \frac{a}{2}\left(1 - \frac{4x^2}{b^2}\right)^{1/2} dx$$

This integral form is one particular symbolic expression. Simpler (in some sense) forms could also be found—for instance, by evaluating the integral (although such results are not included here).

Example: Express the following in written language form: {..., −2, −1, 0, 1, 2,...}.

This symbolic expression, in written language form, is simply "the set of integers."

16D. Communicate mathematical ideas using a variety of representations (e.g., numeric, verbal, graphic, pictorial, symbolic, concrete)

Throughout this guide, mathematical operations and situations are represented through words, algebraic symbols, geometric diagrams and graphs. A few commonly used representations are discussed below.

The basic mathematical operations include addition, subtraction, multiplication and division. In word problems, these are represented by the following typical expressions.

Operation	Descriptive Words
Addition	"plus", "combine", "sum", "total", "put together"
Subtraction	"minus", "less", "take away", "difference"
Multiplication	"product", "times", "groups of"
Division	"quotient", "into", "split into equal groups",

Some verbal and symbolic representations of basic mathematical operations include the following:

7 added to a number	$n + 7$
a number decreased by 8	$n - 8$
12 times a number divided by 7	$12n \div 7$
28 less than a number	$n - 28$
the ratio of a number to 55	$\dfrac{n}{55}$
4 times the sum of a number and 21	$4(n + 21)$

Multiplication can be shown using arrays. For instance, 3×4 can be expressed as 3 rows of 4 each

In a similar manner, addition and subtraction can be demonstrated with symbols.

$$\psi \, \psi \, \psi \, \xi \, \xi \, \xi \, \xi$$
$$3 + 4 = 7$$
$$7 - 3 = 4$$

Fractions can be represented using pattern blocks, fraction bars, or paper folding.

Diagrams of arithmetic operations can present mathematical data in visual form. For example, a number line can be used to add and subtract, as illustrated below.

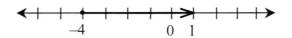

Five added to negative four on the number line or −4 + 5 = 1.

Pictorial representations can also be used to explain the arithmetic processes.

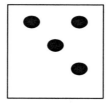 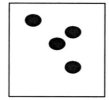

The diagram above shows two groups of four equal eight, or 2 x 4 = 8. The next diagram illustrates addition of two objects to three objects, resulting in five objects.

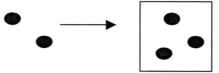

Concrete examples are real world applications of mathematical concepts. For example, measuring the shadow produced by a tree or building is a real-world application of trigonometric functions, acceleration or velocity of a car is an application of derivatives, and finding the volume or area of a swimming pool is a real-world application of geometric principles.

Pictorial illustrations of mathematic concepts help clarify difficult ideas and simplify problem solving. The following example illustrates the use of pictures.

Rectangle R represents the 300 students in School A. Circle P represents the 150 students that participated in band. Circle Q represents the 170 students that participated in a sport. 70 students participated in both band and a sport.

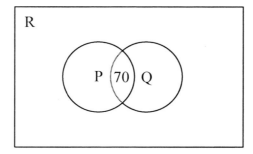

Symbolic representation is the basic language of mathematics. Converting data to symbols allows for easy manipulation and problem solving. Students should have the ability to recognize what the symbolic notation represents and convert information into symbolic form. For example, from the graph of a line, students should have the ability to determine the slope and intercepts and derive the line's equation from the observed data. Another possible application of symbolic representation is the formulation of algebraic expressions and relations from data presented in word-problem form.

16E. Demonstrate an understanding of the use of visual media such as graphs, tables, diagrams, and animations to communicate mathematical information

Although symbolic and verbal presentations of mathematical concepts and data can be both useful and informative, they are not always the most lucid representations of that information. The use of visual media can be helpful in numerous cases. For instance, graphs and tables of data can in many cases provide a clearer representation of that data than can, for instance, a symbolic expression (from some form of regression, for example). Diagrams can also be extremely helpful, especially in problem-solving contexts. One of the chief rules of solving a problem is to draw a diagram (where appropriate) illustrating the problem; this approach helps organize information and it provides a perspective that often makes the information more accessible than it would be from words and mathematical expressions alone. In a similar fashion, animations can also be helpful. Although animations generally require more technology (typically a computer) to construct than do diagrams, they provide an additional dimension to the visual presentation.

Throughout this guide, the concepts and examples that are presented often include graphs, tables, and diagrams to illustrate the information being presented.

16F. The beginning teacher uses the language of mathematics as a precise means of expressing mathematical ideas

The above section dealing with various mathematical representations briefly covers mathematical terminology. Understanding jargon in any discipline, whether mathematics or another field, typically requires study of that particular discipline. Mathematics is a broad field covering a range of subareas, and each has its own particular terms (although there may be a large overlap of terminology with that of other areas of mathematics). The best way for a teacher to learn to use appropriate mathematical terminology is to have a solid understanding of both the fundamental and more advanced concepts of the field he is teaching. Throughout this guide, an attempt is made to present mathematical concepts both symbolically and in a written form that makes use of appropriate terminology. Thus, a review of the material should help reinforce knowledge and use of these terms.

16G. Understand the structural properties common to the mathematical disciplines

The various mathematical disciplines share certain structural properties that can be identified and used to help gain a greater understanding of mathematics in general. Some common threads that run through all mathematical disciplines include the use of deductive inference when applying mathematical tools and the use of numbers, symbols, or other means to quantify or organize data. These and other structural properties can be seen throughout this guide.

DOMAIN VI. MATHEMATICAL LEARNING, INSTRUCTION, AND ASSESSMENT

Competency 017   **The teacher understands how children learn and develop mathematical skills, procedures, and concepts.**

This competency discusses theories and principles of mathematics instruction and their use, along with various tools and strategies, in promoting more effective math learning for students with a variety of backgrounds and learning styles.

17A. Apply theories and principles of learning mathematics to plan appropriate instructional activities for all students

Teachers can use theories of learning to plan curriculum and instructional activities. Research indicates that students learn math more easily in an applied, project-based setting. In addition, prior knowledge, learning, and self-taught understanding are important factors that dictate a student's ability to learn and preferred method of learning.

Many educators believe that the best method of teaching math is **situated learning**. Proponents of situated learning argue that learning is largely a function of the activity, context, and environment in which learning occurs. According to situated learning theory, students learn more easily from instruction involving relevant, real-world situations and applications rather than abstract thoughts and ideas. Research or project-based learning is a product of situated learning theory. Open-ended research tasks and projects promote learning by engaging students on multiple levels. Such tasks require the use of multiple skills and reasoning strategies and help keep students focused and attentive. Additionally, projects promote active learning by encouraging the sharing of thoughts and ideas and teacher-student and student-student interaction.

17B. Understand how students differ in their approaches to learning mathematics with regard to diversity

The cultural and ethnic background of a student greatly affects his or her approach to learning mathematics. In addition, factors such as gender, socioeconomic status, and learning disabilities can affect student learning styles. Teachers must have the ability to tailor their teaching style, methods, and curriculum to the varying learning styles present in a diverse classroom.

Many researchers have studied diversity issues in teaching math. A few references are given below. High expectations and a high level of peer interaction through group study or peer tutoring has been found to be helpful. A relatively informal atmosphere that encourages questioning and guides students to find their own solutions to problems is conducive to math learning as well.

http://math.unipa.it/~grim/21_project/21_Charlotte_LongPaperEdit.pdf

http://www.unige.ch/math/EnsMath/Rome2008/WG3/Papers/BOALER.pdf

http://mathforum.org/~sarah/Discussion.Sessions/biblio.attitudes.html

17C. Use students' prior mathematical knowledge to build conceptual links to new knowledge and plans instruction that builds on students' strengths and addresses students' needs

A popular theory of math learning is **constructivism**. Constructivists argue that prior knowledge greatly influences the learning of math and learning is cumulative and vertically structured. Instruction must build on the innate knowledge of students and address any common misconceptions. Thus, it is important for teachers to ensure that students possess the prerequisite knowledge and ideas required to learn a particular topic. Even without an appeal to constructivism, it is obvious that a student who does not understand the concept of percentage will not be able to do a problem involving interest rates.

Teachers can gain insight into the prior knowledge of students by beginning each lesson with open-ended questions that allow students to share their thoughts and ideas on the subject or topic. A short pre-test covering the prerequisite topics can also be useful as an assessment tool.

In order to identify the prerequisite skills needed to solve a particular kind of problem, the broad concepts that underlie the problem must first be identified. For each concept, one can then list the specific skills needed to perform the related mathematical operations. This kind of hierarchical analysis may be summarized in a tree diagram as shown below.

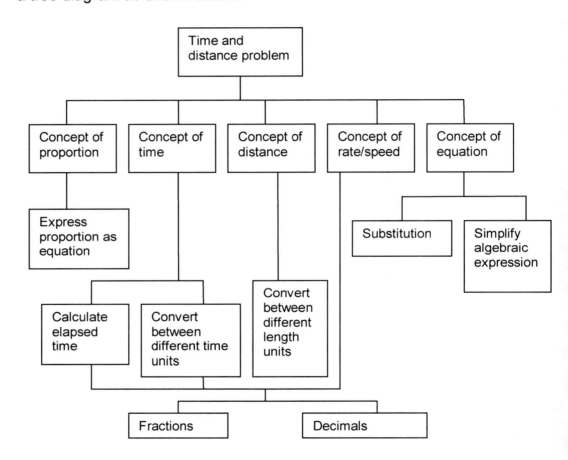

The above analysis can of course be done in different ways. The essential idea is to identify all the pieces that go into learning a topic.

Once the gaps and weaknesses in the student's prerequisite knowledge are identified, the teacher will need to review those topics before teaching the new content. This can be done through discussion, written exercises as well as through hands-on activities.

17D. Understand how learning may be assisted through the use of mathematics manipulatives and technological tools

The use of supplementary materials in the classroom can greatly enhance the learning experience by stimulating student interest and satisfying different learning styles. Manipulatives, models, and technology are examples of tools available to teachers.

Manipulatives are materials that students can physically handle and move. Manipulatives allow students to understand mathematic concepts by allowing them to see concrete examples of abstract processes. Manipulatives are attractive to students because they appeal to the students' visual and tactile senses. Available for all levels of math, manipulatives are useful tools for reinforcing operations and concepts. They are not, however, a substitute for the development of sound computational skills.

Models are another means of representing mathematical concepts by relating the concepts to real-world situations. Teachers must choose wisely when devising and selecting models because, to be effective, models must be applied properly. For example, a building with floors above and below ground is a good model for introducing the concept of negative numbers. It would be difficult, however, to use the building model in teaching subtraction of negative numbers.

Finally, there are many forms of **technology** available to math teachers. For example, students can test their understanding of math concepts by working on specific computer programs and websites. Graphing calculators can help students visualize the graphs of functions. Teachers can also enhance their lectures and classroom presentations by creating multimedia presentations.

See **Essential Tips for Every Math Teacher at** the end of this guide for ideas about using manipulatives, software, and other educational aids.

17E. Understand how to motivate students and actively engage them in the learning process by using a variety of interesting, challenging, and worthwhile mathematical tasks in individual, small-group, and large-group settings

For specific teaching ideas see **Essential Tips for Every Math Teacher** at the end of this guide.

17F. Understand how to provide instruction along a continuum from concrete to abstract

According to Piaget, there are four primary cognitive structures or development stages: sensorimotor, preoperations, concrete operations, and formal operations. In the sensorimotor stage (0-2 years), intelligence takes the form of motor actions. In the preoperation stage (3-7 years), intelligence is intuitive in nature. Intelligence in the concrete operational stage (8-11 years) is logical but depends upon concrete referents. In the final stage of formal operations (12-15 years), thinking involves abstractions.

Even though middle school students are typically ready to approach mathematics in abstract ways, some of them still require concrete referents such as manipulatives. It is useful to keep in mind that the developmental stages of individuals vary. In addition, different people have different learning styles, some tending more towards the visual and others relatively verbal. Research has shown that learning is most effective when information is presented through multiple modalities or representations. Most mathematics textbooks now use this multi-modal approach.

Also see **Skill 18D.**

17G. Recognize the implications of current trends and research in mathematics and mathematics education

The challenges involved in the teaching of math are well recognized in academia and have spawned many research projects aimed at improving the quality of mathematics education. Teachers have access to many resources that can help to keep them informed about current research and provide them tools to implement new ideas in their teaching. These include the websites of the National Council of Teachers of Mathematics (NCTM) and other organizations. See the introduction to **Essential Tips for Every Math Teacher** at the end of this guide for links to professional development resources for math teachers.

Competency 018   The teacher understands how to plan, organize, and implement instruction using knowledge of students, subject matter, and statewide curriculum (Texas Essential Knowledge and Skills [TEKS]) to teach all students to use mathematics.

This competency discusses specific methods, tools, and techniques used in mathematics instruction with particular reference to the statewide Texas curriculum TEKS. The interconnected nature of mathematics, the need to transition from concrete to symbolic to abstract representation, the value of questioning as a teaching strategy, the use of technology and the connections between mathematics and different types of careers are considered.

18A.   Demonstrate an understanding of a variety of instructional methods, tools, and tasks that promote students' ability to do mathematics described in the TEKS

The Texas Essential Knowledge and Skills (TEKS) (http://ritter.tea.state.tx.us/teks/) are a comprehensive list of standards for subject matter learning. TEKS provide teachers with a framework for curriculum design and instructional method selection. The different skills described in TEKS require different teaching strategies and techniques.

The primary goals of middle school math instruction, as defined by TEKS, are the building of a strong foundation in mathematical concepts and the development of problem-solving and analytical skills. Direct teaching methods, including lecture and demonstration, are particularly effective in teaching basic mathematical concepts. To stimulate interest, accommodate different learning styles and enhance understanding, teachers should incorporate manipulatives and technology into their lectures and demonstrations. Indirect teaching methods, including cooperative learning, discussion and projects, promote the development of problem solving skills. Cooperative learning and discussion allow students to share ideas and strategies with their peers. In addition, projects require students to apply knowledge and develop and implement problem-solving strategies.

18B. **Understand planning strategies for developing mathematical instruction as a discipline of interconnected concepts and procedures**

Recognition and understanding of the relationships between concepts and topics is important to mathematical problem solving and the explanation of more complex processes. It becomes much easier for a student to retain information when it is presented from different viewpoints and linked to other familiar concepts. Ideally, a teacher will not present the information straight away but will let students think for themselves and discover the connections on their own with guidance from the teacher. Some examples of connections between familiar mathematical concepts are discussed below.

Multiplication is simply repeated addition. This relationship explains the concept of variable addition.

We can show that the expression 4x + 3x = 7x is true by rewriting 4 times x and 3 times x as repeated addition, yielding the expression (x + x + x + x) + (x + x + x). Thus, because of the relationship between multiplication and addition, variable addition is accomplished by coefficient addition.

Addition and subtraction are really the same operation acting in opposite directions on the number line. Understanding this concept helps students in working with negative numbers which are difficult for many middle-school children to grasp.

The concept of **rate appears in many different guises** in mathematics such as in the speed of a vehicle, interest rate or the price per unit of an item. The concept of rate is also directly connected to the concept of slope of a straight line.

Commonly used formulae such as $a^2 - b^2 = (a+b)(a-b)$ or $(a+b)^2 = a^2 + 2ab + b^2$ are not magical relationships that need to be memorized. They can simply be calculated by performing the familiar **FOIL** operation.

Example: $(a+b)(a-b) = a^2 - ab + ba - b^2 = a^2 - b^2$

In geometry, the perimeters, areas and volumes of different figures are usually presented as separate formulae. It is useful to point out that every **area contains the product of two lengths** (e.g. lw or πr^2) and every **volume contains the product of three lengths** (e.g. l^3, $\pi r^2 h$). This helps students understand the meaning of square and cubic units.

The relationships between points, lines and planes become easier to visualize if one understands that **a point is to a line as a line is to a plane**. Just as two lines intersect in a point, two planes intersect in a line.

Students can discover many more connections in the classroom with the teacher's help. This will not only enhance the quality of their learning but will also make them better and more eager learners.

18C. Develop clear learning goals to plan, deliver, assess, and reevaluate instruction based on the TEKS

The TEKS provide teachers with a comprehensive list of skills that the state requires students to master. Utilizing the learning goals presented in TEKS, teachers can plan instruction to promote student understanding. In addition, teachers can deliver instruction in ways that are appropriate to the specific skill, classroom environment and student population. To assess the effectiveness of instruction, teachers can design tests that evaluate student mastery of specific skills. In grading such tests, teachers should look for patterns in student mistakes and errors that may indicate a deficiency in the instructional plan. In reevaluating instruction, teachers can attempt to use different instructional methods or shift areas of emphasis to meet the needs of the students.

Mathematics TEKS toolkit:
http://www.utdanacenter.org/mathtoolkit/

18D. Understand procedures for developing instruction that establishes transitions between concrete, symbolic, and abstract representations of mathematical knowledge

When introducing a new mathematical concept to students, teachers should utilize the concrete-to-representational-to-abstract sequence of instruction. The first step of the instructional progression is the introduction of a concept modeled with concrete materials. The second step is the translation of concrete models into representational diagrams or pictures. The third and final step is the translation of representational models into abstract models using only numbers and symbols.

Teachers should first use concrete models to introduce a mathematical concept because they are easiest to understand. For example, teachers can allow students to use counting blocks to learn basic arithmetic. Teachers should give students ample time and many opportunities to experiment, practice, and demonstrate mastery with the concrete materials.

The second step in the learning process is the translation of concrete materials to representational models. For example, students may use tally marks or pictures to represent the counting blocks they used in the previous stage. Once again, teachers should give students ample time to master the concept on the representational level.

The final step in the learning process is the translation of representational models into abstract numbers and symbols. For example, students represent the processes carried out in the previous stages using only numbers and arithmetic symbols.

To ease the transition, teachers should associate numbers and symbols with the concrete and representational models throughout the learning progression.

18E. Apply knowledge of a variety of instructional delivery methods, such as individual, structured small-group, and large-group formats

Successful teachers select and implement instructional delivery methods that best fit the needs of a particular classroom format. Individual, small-group and large-group classroom formats require different techniques and methods of instruction.

Individual instruction allows the teacher to interact closely with the student. Teachers may use a variety of methods in an individual setting that are not practical when working with a large number of students. For example, teachers can use manipulatives to illustrate a mathematical concept.

In addition, teachers can observe and evaluate the student's reasoning and problem solving skills through verbal questioning and by checking the student's written work. Finally, individual instruction allows the teacher to work problems with the student, thus familiarizing the student with the problem-solving process.

Small-group formats require the teacher to provide instruction to multiple students at the same time. Because the size of the group is small, instructional methods that encourage student interaction and cooperative learning are particularly effective. For example, group projects, discussion, and question-and-answer sessions promote cooperative learning and maintain student interest. In addition, working problems as a group or in pairs can help students learn problem-solving strategies from each other.

Large-group formats require instructional methods that can effectively deliver information to a large number of students. Lecture is a common instructional method for large groups. In addition, demonstrating methods of problem solving and allowing students to ask questions about homework and test problems is an effective strategy for teaching large-groups.

18F. Understand how to create a learning environment that provides all students, including English Language Learners, with opportunities to develop and improve mathematical skills and procedures

Teachers and school officials must understand the special needs of English Language Learners. Mathematic assessments may understate the abilities of English Language Learners because poor test scores may stem from difficulty in reading comprehension, not a lack of understanding of mathematic principles. Uncharacteristically poor performance on word problems by English Language Learners is a sign that reading comprehension, not mathematic understanding, is the underlying problem.

The TSU Math for English Language Learners Project provides a lot of helpful information on this topic: http://www.tsusmell.org/.

18G. **Demonstrate an understanding of a variety of questioning strategies to encourage mathematical discourse and to help students analyze and evaluate their mathematical thinking**

As the teacher's role in the classroom changes from lecturer to facilitator, the questions need to further stimulate students in various ways.

- Helping students work together
  What do you think about what John said?
  Do you agree? Disagree?
  Can anyone explain that differently?

- Helping students determine for themselves if an answer is correct
  Why do you think that is true?
  How did you get that answer?
  Do you think that is reasonable? Why?

- Helping students learn to reason mathematically
  Will that method always work?
  Can you think of a case where it is not true?
  How can you prove that?
  Is that answer true in all cases?

- Helping student brainstorm and problem solve
  Is there a pattern?
  What else can you do?
  Can you predict the answer?
  What if...?

- Helping students connect mathematical ideas
  What did we learn before that is like this?
  Can you give an example?
  What math did you see on television last night? in the newspaper?

18H. **Understand how technological tools and manipulatives can be used appropriately to assist students in developing, comprehending, and applying mathematical concepts**

See **Skill 17D**.

18l. Understand how to relate mathematics to students' lives and a variety of careers and professions

Teachers can increase student interest in math and promote learning and understanding by relating mathematical concepts to the lives of students. Instead of using only abstract presentations and examples, teachers should relate concepts to real-world situations to shift the emphasis from memorization and abstract application to understanding and applied problem solving. In addition, relating math to careers and professions helps illustrate the relevance of math and aids in the career exploration process.

Artists, musicians, scientists, social scientists, and business people use mathematical modeling to solve problems in their disciplines. These disciplines rely on the tools and symbols of mathematics to model natural events and manipulate data. Mathematics is a key aspect of visual art.

Artists use the geometric properties of shapes, ratios, and proportions in creating paintings and sculptures. For example, mathematics is essential to the concept of perspective. Artists must determine the appropriate lengths and heights of objects to portray three-dimensional distance in two dimensions.

Mathematics is also an important part of music. Many musical terms have mathematical connections. For example, the musical octave contains twelve notes and spans a factor of two in frequency. In other words, the frequency, the speed of vibration that determines tone and sound quality, doubles from the first note in an octave to the last. Thus, starting from any note we can determine the frequency of any other note with the following formula.

$$\text{Freq} = \text{note} \times 2^{N/12}$$

Where N is the number of notes from the starting point and note is the frequency of the starting note. Mathematical understanding of frequency plays an important role in the tuning of musical instruments.

In addition to the visual and auditory arts, mathematics is an integral part of most scientific disciplines. The uses of mathematics in science are almost endless. The following are but a few examples of how scientists use mathematics. Physical scientists use vectors, functions, derivatives, and integrals to describe and model the movement of objects. Biologists and ecologists use mathematics to model ecosystems and study DNA. Finally, chemists use mathematics to study the interaction of molecules and to determine proper amounts and proportions of reactants.

Many social science disciplines use mathematics to model and solve problems. Economists, for example, use functions, graphs, and matrices to model the activities of producers, consumers, and firms. Political scientists use mathematics to model the behavior and opinions of the electorate. Finally, sociologists use mathematical functions to model the behavior of humans and human populations.

Finally, mathematical problem solving and modeling is essential to business planning and execution. For example, businesses rely on mathematical projections to plan business strategy. Additionally, stock market analysis and accounting rely on mathematical concepts.

Competency 019   The teacher understands assessment and uses a variety of formal and informal assessment techniques to monitor and guide mathematics instruction and to evaluate student progress.

The focus of this competency is on the assessment of mathematical learning. In addition to the purpose and characteristics of different types of assessments, this competency discusses how assessments can be selected, developed and evaluated and how instruction can be related to the assessment process and results.

19A.   Demonstrate an understanding of the purpose, characteristics, and uses of various assessments in mathematics, including formative and summative assessments

The primary purpose of student assessment is to evaluate the effectiveness of the curriculum and instruction by measuring student performance. Teachers and school officials use the results of student assessments to monitor student progress and modify and design curriculum to meet the needs of the students. Teachers and school officials carefully assess the results of tests to determine the parts of the curriculum that need altering. For example, the results of a test may indicate that the majority of the students in a class struggle with problems involving logarithmic functions. In response to such findings, the teacher would evaluate the method of logarithmic function instruction and make the necessary changes to increase student understanding.

Student assessment is an important part of the educational process. High quality assessment methods are necessary for the development and maintenance of a successful learning environment. Teachers must develop and implement assessment procedures that accurately evaluate student progress, test content areas of greatest importance, and enhance and improve learning. To enhance learning and accurately evaluate student progress, teachers should use a variety of assessment tasks to gain a better understanding a student's strengths and weaknesses. Finally, teachers should implement scoring patterns that fairly and accurately evaluate student performance.

A special type of student assessment, state **standardized testing**, is an important tool for curriculum design and modification. Most states have stated curriculum standards that mandate what students should know. Teachers can use the standards to focus their instruction and curriculum planning. State tests evaluate and report student performance on the specific curriculum standards.

Thus, teachers can easily determine the areas that require greater attention.

Teachers should use a variety of assessment procedures to evaluate student knowledge and understanding. In addition to the traditional methods of performance assessment like multiple choice, true/false, and matching tests, there are many other methods of student assessment available to teachers. Alternative assessment is any type of assessment in which students create a response rather than choose an answer. It is sometimes know as **formative assessment**, due to the emphasis placed on feedback and the flow of communication between teacher and student. It is the opposite of **summative assessment**, which occurs periodically and consists of temporary interaction between teacher and student.

Short response and **essay** questions are alternative methods of performance assessment. In responding to such questions, students must utilize verbal, graphical, and mathematical skills to construct answers to problems. These multi-faceted responses allow the teacher to examine more closely a student's problem solving and reasoning skills.

Student **portfolios** are another method of alternative assessment. In creating a portfolio, students collect samples and drafts of their work, self-assessments, and teacher evaluations over a period of time. Such a collection allows students, parents, and teachers to evaluate student progress and achievements. In addition, portfolios provide insight into a student's thought process and learning style.

Projects, **demonstrations**, and **oral presentations** are means of alternative assessment that require students to use different skills than those used on traditional tests. Such assessments require higher order thinking, creativity, and the integration of reasoning and communication skills. The use of predetermined rubrics, with specific criteria for performance assessment, is the accepted method of evaluation for projects, demonstrations, and presentations.

One type of alternative assessment is **bundled testing**. Bundled testing is the grouping of different question formats for the same skill or competency. For example, a bundled test of exponential functions may include multiple choice questions, short response questions, word problems, and essay questions. The variety of questions tests different levels of reasoning and expression.

Scoring methods are an important, and often overlooked, part of effective assessment. Teachers can use a simple three-point scale for evaluating student responses. No answer or an inappropriate answer that shows no understanding scores zero points. A partial response showing a lack of understanding, a lack of explanation, or major computational errors scores one point. A somewhat satisfactory answer that answers most of the question correctly but contains simple computational errors or minor flaws in reasoning receives two points. Finally, a satisfactory response displaying full understanding, adequate explanation, and appropriate reasoning receives three points. When evaluating student responses, teachers should look for common error patterns and mistakes in computation. Teachers should also incorporate questions and scoring procedures that address common error patterns and misconceptions into their methods of assessment.

19B. Understand how to select and develop assessments that are consistent with what is taught and how it is taught

In order to assess whether a student has truly grasped the content of the curriculum taught, teachers must ensure that tests not only evaluate isolated skills but important mathematical concepts as well as thinking processes. The assessment should enhance learning and serve as a tool that identifies areas of misunderstanding. The teacher must also take into account the learning styles of the students being assessed and how the material was approached in the classroom.

Before selecting a particular assessment method, a teacher should develop a list of criteria that reflect the goals of the assessment. The following website provides a variety of resources that may be helpful in planning, developing, and evaluating assessments:
http://mathforum.org/mathed/assessment.html

19C. Demonstrate an understanding of how to develop a variety of assessments and scoring procedures consisting of worthwhile tasks that assess mathematical understanding, common misconceptions, and error patterns

All too often assessments test topics in isolation and lower level procedural skills within each topic. Higher level skills such as reasoning, problem solving, communicating, and connecting ideas are ignored as a result. In order to develop effective assessments that balance conceptual understanding, procedural knowledge, and problem solving and focus on unearthing common misconceptions and error patterns, a predetermined assessment framework is needed as a guide for developing new assessments.

A good assessment framework must specify details such as goals of the assessment, background knowledge expected, type of guidance and instructions to be given as part of the assessment and so on. A framework of this type is often built on an existing curriculum framework. Although each individual assessment may not do so, assessments over the duration of a class as a whole must reflect all facets of framework.

Worthwhile assessment tasks intended to test higher level skills must use connections between different areas of mathematics as well as real world settings. Since the goal is to assess how a student thinks and not whether a student is familiar with a particular type of problem, non-routine problems must be used. One must ensure, however, that the student has been taught all the prerequisite skills, has experience solving novel problems, and that the task is explained clearly with all assumptions explicitly laid out. Tasks must also be structured so that students have the opportunity to show what they know even if they are unable to complete the whole problem.

The New Standards Project provides an assessment system that goes beyond standardized testing: http://www.nctm.org/news/release.aspx?id=770.

19D. **Understand how to evaluate a variety of assessment methods and materials for reliability, validity, absence of bias, clarity of language, and appropriateness of mathematical level**

In the preceding skills we have discussed the goals and characteristics of effective and equitable assessments. These can form the basis for developing a list of specific criteria that all assessments must be checked against. The criteria should include questions about different aspects of the assessment such as mathematical content, task content, mode of representation, cognitive processes being tested, relevance to curriculum. The primary goal of an assessment should be to support learning and not to filter out students.

The following chapter from the book "Measuring What Counts: A Conceptual Guide for Mathematics Assessment" provides a lot of insight into the process of evaluating assessments:
http://www.nap.edu/openbook.php?record_id=2235&page=117

19E. **Understand the relationship between assessment and instruction and know how to evaluate assessment results to design, monitor, and modify instruction to improve mathematical learning for all students, including English Language Learners**

One way to use assessments to improve instruction is to integrate them into the teaching process. In iterative assessments, students receive feedback from the teacher at different stages while the task in progress. Thus the assessment is used as a learning tool.

Even when the assessment is more traditional, the following criteria can help to ensure that it supports learning:
- Reports must provide feedback with regard to different aspects of learning and not just numerical scores
- Reports must be timely so the students have an opportunity to use the feedback
- Scoring rubrics must be specific and address different learning goals
- Students must be given the opportunity to explain their thinking

The following chapters from the book "Measuring What Counts: A Conceptual Guide for Mathematics Assessment" address the use of assessment in improving instruction:
http://www.nap.edu/openbook.php?record_id=2235&page=67
http://www.nap.edu/openbook.php?record_id=2235&page=91

ESSENTIAL TIPS FOR EVERY MATH TEACHER

Pedagogical principles and teaching methods are important for all teachers. They are particularly critical, though, for math teaching since math teachers not only face the difficulty of communicating the subject matter to students but also that of surmounting an all-pervasive cultural fear of mathematics. Math teachers need to take particular care to foster learning in a non-threatening environment that is at the same time genuinely stimulating and challenging.

The National Council of Teachers of Mathematics (NCTM) (http://www.nctm.org/) Principles and Standards emphasizes the teacher's obligation to support all students not only in developing basic mathematics knowledge and skills but also in their ability to understand and reason mathematically to solve problems relevant to today's world. The use of technology in the classroom is strongly advocated.

Resources for middle school teachers are available on the NCTM website at http://www.nctm.org/resources/middle.aspx.

The Mathematics Pathway (http://msteacher.org/math.aspx) on the National Science Digital Library (NSDL) Middle School Portal provides a very comprehensive and rich treasure trove of helpful material linking to various resources on the web including articles as well as interactive instructional modules on various topics.

The Drexel University Math Forum website provides the opportunity to interact with mentors and other math educators online. Some of the material on this website requires paid subscription but there are openly available archives as well. An overview of what the site provides is available at http://mathforum.org/about.forum.html. You may find the "Teacher2Teacher" service particularly useful; you can ask questions or browse the archives for a wealth of nitty-gritty everyday teaching information, suggestions and links to teaching tools.

This website for sixth grade contains animated lessons, discussions of strategies and a glossary of terms using few words and plenty of illustrations. http://students.resa.net/stoutcomputerclass/1math.htm

Other instructional and professional development resources:
http://archives.math.utk.edu/k12.html
http://www.learnalberta.ca/Launch.aspx?content=/content/mesg/html/math6web/math6shell.html
http://mmap.wested.org/webmath/

Pedagogical Principles

Maintain a supportive, non-threatening environment

Many students unfortunately perceive mathematics as a threat. This becomes a particular critical issue at the middle school level where they learn algebra for the first time and are required to think in new ways. Since fear "freezes" the brain and makes thinking really difficult, a student's belief that he is no good at math becomes a self-fulfilling prophecy. A teacher's primary task in this situation is to foster a learning environment where every student feels that he or she can learn to think mathematically. Here are some ways to go about this:

Accept all comments and questions: Acknowledge all questions and comments that students make. If what the student says is inaccurate or irrelevant to the topic in hand, point that out gently but also show your understanding of the thought process that led to the comment. This will encourage students to speak up in class and enhance their learning.

Set aside time for group work: Assign activities to groups of students comprised of mixed ability levels. It is often easier for students to put forward their own thoughts as part of a friendly group discussion than when they are sitting alone at their desks with a worksheet. The more proficient students can help the less able ones and at the same time clarify their own thinking. You will essentially be using the advanced students in the class as a resource in a manner that also contributes to their own development. The struggling students will feel supported by their peers and not isolated from them.

Encourage classroom discussion of math topics: For instance, let the whole class share different ways in which they approach a certain problem. It will give you insight into your students' ways of thinking and make it easier to help them. It will allow even those who just listen to understand and correct errors in their thinking without being put on the spot.

Engage and challenge students

Maintaining a non-threatening environment should not mean dumbing down the math content in the classroom. The right level of challenge and relevance to their daily lives can help to keep students interested and learning. Here are some ideas:

Show connections to the real world: Use real life examples of math problems in your teaching. Some suggestions are given in the next section. Explain the importance of math literacy in society and the pitfalls of not being mathematically aware. An excellent reference is "The 10 Things All Future Mathematicians and Scientists Must Know" by Edward Zaccaro. The title of the book is misleading since it deals with things that every educated person, not just mathematicians and scientists, should know.

Use technology: Make use of calculators and computers including various online, interactive resources in your teaching. The natural affinity today's children have for these devices will definitely help them to engage more deeply in their math learning.

Demonstrate "messy" math: Children often have the mistaken belief that every math problem can be solved by following a particular set of rules; they either know the rules or they don't. In real life, however, math problems can be approached in different ways and often one has to negotiate several blind alleys before getting to the real solution. Children instinctively realize this while doing puzzles or playing games. They just don't associate this kind of thinking with classroom math. The most important insight any math teacher can convey to students is the realization that even if they don't know how to do a problem at first, they can think about it and figure it out as long as they are willing to stay with the problem and make mistakes in the process. An obvious way to do this, of course, is to introduce mathematical puzzles and games in the classroom. The best way, however, is for teachers themselves to take risks occasionally with unfamiliar problems and demonstrate to the class how one can work one's way out of a clueless state.

Show the reasoning behind rules: Even when it is not a required part of the curriculum, explain, whenever possible, how a mathematical rule is derived or how it is connected to other rules. For instance, in explaining the rule for finding the area of a trapezoid, show how one can get to it by thinking of the trapezoid as two triangles. This will reinforce the students' sense of mathematics as something that can be logically arrived at and not something for which they have to remember innumerable rules. Another way to reinforce this idea is to do the same problem using different approaches.

Be willing to take occasional side trips: Be flexible at times and go off topic in order to explore more deeply any questions or comments from the students. Grab a teaching opportunity even if it is irrelevant to the topic under discussion.

Help every student gain a firm grasp of fundamentals
While discussion, reasoning and divergent thinking is to be encouraged, it can only be done on a firm scaffolding of basic math knowledge. A firm grasp of math principles, for most people, does require rote exercises and doing more and more of the same problems. Just as practicing scales is essential for musical creativity, math creativity can only be built on a foundation strengthened by drilling and repetition. Many educators see independent reasoning and traditional rule-based drilling as opposing approaches. An effective teacher, however, must maintain a balance between the two and ensure that students have the basic tools they need to think independently.

<u>Make sure all students actually know basic math rules and concepts</u>: Test students regularly for basic math knowledge and provide reinforcement with additional practice wherever necessary.

<u>Keep reviewing old material</u>: Don't underestimate your students' ability to forget what they haven't seen in a while. Link new topics whenever possible with things your students have learned before and take the opportunity to review previous learning. Most math textbooks nowadays have a spiral review section created with this end in mind.

<u>Keep mental math muscles strong:</u> The calculator, without question, is a very valuable learning tool. Many students, unfortunately, use it as a crutch to the point that they lose the natural feel for numbers and ability to estimate that people develop through mental calculations. As a result, they are often unable to tell when they punch a wrong button and get a totally unreasonable answer. Take your students through frequent mental calculation exercises; you can easily integrate it into class discussions. Teach them useful strategies for making mental estimates.

Specific Teaching Methods

Some commonly used teaching techniques and tools are described below along with links to further information. The links provided in the first part of this chapter also provide a wealth of instructional ideas and material.

A very useful resource is the book "Family Math: The Middle School Years" from the Lawrence Hall of Science, University of California at Berkeley. Although this book was developed for use by families, teachers in school can choose from the many simple activities and games used to reinforce two significant middle school skills, algebraic reasoning and number sense. A further advantage is that all the activities are based on NCTM standards and each activity lists the specific math concepts that are covered.

Here are some tools you can use to make your teaching more effective:

Classroom openers
To start off your class with stimulated, interested and focused students, provide a short opening activity everyday. You can make use of thought-provoking questions, puzzles or tricks. Also use relevant puzzles or tricks to illustrate specific topics at any point in your class. The following website provides some ideas:
http://mathforum.org/k12/k12puzzles/

Real life examples

Connect math to other aspects of your students' lives by using examples and data from the real world whenever possible. It will not only keep them engaged, it will also help answer the perennial question "Why do we have to learn math?" Online resources to get you started:

1. Using weather concepts to teach math:
    http://www.nssl.noaa.gov/edu/ideas/

2. Election math in the classroom:
    http://mathforum.org/t2t/faq/election.html

3. Math worksheets related to the Iditarod, an annual Alaskan sled dog race:
    http://www.educationworld.com/a_lesson/lesson/lesson302.shtml

4. Personal finance examples:
    http://www.publicdebt.treas.gov/mar/marmoneymath.htm

5. Graphing with real data:
    http://www.middleweb.com/Graphing.html

Manipulatives

Manipulatives can help all students learn; particularly those oriented more towards visual and kinesthetic learning. Here are some ideas for the use of manipulatives in the classroom:

1. Use tiles, pattern blocks or geoboards to demonstrate geometry concepts such as shapes, area and perimeter. In the example shown below, 12 tiles are used to form different rectangles.

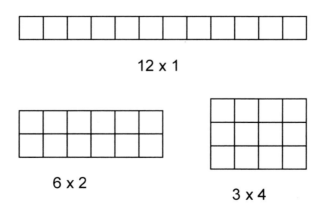

12 x 1

6 x 2

3 x 4

2. Stacks of blocks representing numbers are useful for teaching basic statistics concepts such as mean, median and mode. Rearranging the blocks to make each stack the same height would demonstrate the mean or average value of the data set. The example below shows a data set represented by stacks of blocks. Rearranging the blocks to make the height of each stack equal to three shows that this is the mean value.

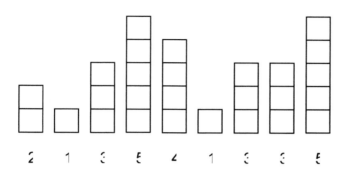

3. Tiles, blocks, or other countable manipulatives such as beans can also be used to demonstrate numbers in different bases. Each stack will represent a place with the number of blocks in the stack showing the place value.

4. Playing cards can be used for a discussion of probability.

5. Addition and subtraction of integers, positive and negative, is a major stumbling block for many middle school students. Two sets of tiles, marked with pluses and minuses respectively, can be used to demonstrate these concepts visually with each "plus" tile canceling a "minus" tile.

$$+4-5=-1$$

$$-3-4=-7$$

6. Percentages may be visualized using two parallel number lines, one showing the actual numbers, the other showing the percentages.

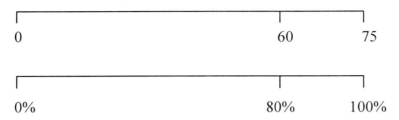

A practical demonstration of percent changes can be made by photocopying a figure using different copier magnifications.

7. Algeblocks are blocks designed specifically for the teaching of algebra with manipulatives:
http://www.etacuisenaire.com/algeblocks/algeblocks.jsp

Software
Many of the online references in this section link to software for learning. A good site that provides easy to use virtual manipulatives as well as accompanying worksheets in some cases is the following:
http://boston.k12.ma.us/teach/technology/select/index.html

Spreadsheets can be very effective math learning tools. Here are some ideas for using spreadsheets in the classroom:
http://www.angelfire.com/wi2/spreadsheet/necc.html

Word problem strategies
Word problems, a challenge for many students even in elementary school, become more complicated and sometimes intimidating in the middle grades. Here are some ideas students can use to tackle them:

1. Identify significant words and numbers in the problem. Highlight or underline them. If necessary, write them in the form of a table.

2. Draw diagrams to clarify the problem. Put down the main items or events and numbers on the diagram and show the relationships between them.

3. Rewrite the problem using fewer and simpler words. One way is to have a standard format for this as shown in the example below.
Problem: Calculate the cost of 3 pencils given that 5 pencils cost 25 cents.
Rewrite as:
Cost of 5 pencils = 25 cents
Cost of 1 pencil = 25/5 = 5 cents
Cost of 3 pencils = 5 X 3 = 15 cents

4. If you have no idea how to approach the problem, try the guess and check approach at first. That will give you a sense of the kind of problem you are dealing with.

5. Create similar word problems of your own.

Equation rule

Solving algebraic equations is a challenge for many learners particularly when they think they need to remember many different rules. Emphasize the fact that they only need to keep only one rule in mind whether they are adding, subtracting, multiplying or dividing numbers or variables:

"Do the same thing to both sides"

A balance or teeter-totter metaphor can help to clarify their understanding of equations. You can also use manipulatives to demonstrate.

Mental math practice

Give students regular practice in doing mental math. The following website offers many mental calculation tips and strategies:
http://mathforum.org/k12/mathtips/mathtips.html

Because frequent calculator use tends to deprive students of a sense of numbers, they will often approach a sequence of multiplications and divisions the hard way. For instance, asked to calculate 770 x 36/ 55, they will first multiply 770 and 36 and then do a long division with the 55. They fail to recognize that both 770 and 55 can be divided by 11 and then by 5 to considerably simplify the problem. Give students plenty of practice in multiplying and dividing a sequence of integers and fractions so they are comfortable with canceling top and bottom terms.

Math language

There is an explosion of new math words as students enter the middle grades and start learning algebra and geometry.

This website provides an animated, colorfully illustrated dictionary of math terms:
http://www.amathsdictionaryforkids.com/

The following site is not colorful and animated but contains brief and clear definitions and many more advanced math terms:
http://www.amathsdictionaryforkids.com/

WEB LINKS

ALGEBRA
Algebra in bite-size pieces with quiz at the end
http://library.thinkquest.org/20991/alg/index.html
Algebra II: http://library.thinkquest.org/20991/alg2/index.html

Different levels plus quiz
http://www.math.com/homeworkhelp/Algebra.html

Clicking on the number leads to solution
http://www.math.armstrong.edu/MathTutorial/index.html

Algebraic Structures
Symbols and sets of numbers:
http://www.wtamu.edu/academic/anns/mps/math/mathlab/beg_algebra/beg_alg_tut2_sets.htm

Integers: http://amby.com/educate/math/integer.html
Card game to add and subtract integers: http://www.education-world.com/a_tsl/archives/03-1/lesson001.shtml
Multiplying integers: http://www.aaastudy.com/mul65_x2.htm

Rational/irrational numbers: http://regentsprep.org/regents/math/math-topic.cfm?TopicCode=rational

Several complex number exercise pages:
http://math.about.com/od/complexnumbers/Complex_Numbers.htm

Polynomial Equations and Inequalities
Systems of equations lessons and practice:
http://regentsprep.org/regents/math/math-topic.cfm?TopicCode=syslin
More practice:
http://www.sparknotes.com/math/algebra1/systemsofequations/problems3.rhtml
Word problems system of equations:
http://regentsprep.org/REgents/math/ALGEBRA/AE3/PracWord.htm
Inequalities: http://regentsprep.org/regents/Math/solvin/PSolvIn.htm
Inequality tutorial, examples, problems
http://www.wtamu.edu/academic/anns/mps/math/mathlab/beg_algebra/beg_alg_tut18_ineq.htm
Graphing linear inequalities tutorial
http://www.wtamu.edu/academic/anns/mps/math/mathlab/beg_algebra/beg_alg_tut24_ineq.htm
Quadratic equations tutorial, examples, problems
http://www.wtamu.edu/academic/anns/mps/math/mathlab/col_algebra/col_alg_tut17_quad.htm

Practice factoring: http://regentsprep.org/Regents/math/math-topic.cfm?TopicCode=factor

Synthetic division tutorial:
http://www.wtamu.edu/academic/anns/mps/math/mathlab/col_algebra/col_alg_tut37_syndiv.htm

Synthetic division Examples and problems: http://www.tpub.com/math1/10h.htm

Functions

Function, domain, range intro and practice
http://www.mathwarehouse.com/algebra/relation/math-function.php

Equations with rational expressions tutorial
http://www.wtamu.edu/academic/anns/mps/math/mathlab/col_algebra/col_alg_tut15_rateq.htm

Practice with rational expressions
http://education.yahoo.com/homework_help/math_help/problem_list?id=minialg1_gt_7_1

Practice simplifying radicals
http://www.bhs87.org/math/practice/radicals/radicalpractice.htm

Radical equations – lesson and practice
http://regentsprep.org/REgents/mathb/mathb-topic.cfm?TopicCode=7D3

Logarithmic functions tutorial
http://www.wtamu.edu/academic/anns/mps/math/mathlab/col_algebra/col_alg_tut43_logfun.htm

Linear Algebra

Practice operations with matrices
http://www.castleton.edu/Math/finite/operation_practice.htm

Matrices, introduction and practice
http://www.math.csusb.edu/math110/src/matrices/basics.html

Vector practice tip: http://www.phy.mtu.edu/~suits/PH2100/vecdot.html

GEOMETRY

Geometry
http://library.thinkquest.org/20991/geo/index.html
http://www.math.com/students/homeworkhelp.html#geometry
http://regentsprep.org/Regents/math/geometry/math-GEOMETRY.htm

Parallelism

Parallel lines practice
http://www.algebralab.org/lessons/lesson.aspx?file=Geometry_AnglesParallelLinesTransversals.xml

Plane Euclidean Geometry

Geometry facts and practice http://www.aaaknow.com/geo.htm

Triangles intro and practice
http://www.staff.vu.edu.au/mcaonline/units/geometry/triangles.html
Polygons exterior and interior angles practice
http://regentsprep.org/Regents/Math/math-topic.cfm?TopicCode=poly
Angles in circles practice
http://regentsprep.org/Regents/math/geometry/GP15/PcirclesN2.htm
Congruence of triangles – lessons, practice
http://regentsprep.org/Regents/math/geometry/GP4/indexGP4.htm
Pythagorean theorem and converse
http://regentsprep.org/Regents/math/geometry/GP13/indexGP13.htm
Circle equation practice
http://www.regentsprep.org/Regents/math/algtrig/ATC1/circlepractice.htm
Interactive parabola http://www.mathwarehouse.com/geometry/parabola/
Ellipse practice problems http://www.mathwarehouse.com/ellipse/equation-of-ellipse.php#equationOfEllipse

Three-Dimensional Geometry
3D figures intro and examples
http://www.mathleague.com/help/geometry/3space.htm

Transformational Geometry
Interactive transformational geometry practice on coordinate plane
http://www.shodor.org/interactivate/activities/Transmographer/
Similar triangles practice
http://regentsprep.org/Regents/math/similar/PracSim.htm

http://www.algebralab.org/practice/practice.aspx?file=Geometry_UsingSimilarTriangles.xml

NUMBER THEORY
Natural Numbers
http://online.math.uh.edu/MiddleSchool/Vocabulary/NumberTheoryVocab.pdf
GCF and LCM practice
http://teachers.henrico.k12.va.us/math/ms/C1Files/01NumberSense/1_5/6035prac.htm

PROBABILITY AND STATISTICS
Probability
Probability intro and practice
http://www.mathgoodies.com/lessons/vol6/intro_probability.html
Permutation and combination practice
http://www.regentsprep.org/Regents/math/algtrig/ATS5/PCPrac.htm
Conditional probability problems
http://homepages.ius.edu/MEHRINGE/T102/Supplements/HandoutConditionalProbability.htm

Statistics

Statistics lessons and interactive practice
http://www.aaaknow.com/sta.htm
Range, mean, median, mode exercises
http://www.mathgoodies.com/lessons/vol8/practice_vol8.html
http://regentsprep.org/regents/Math/mean/Pmeasure.htm

Sample Test

DIRECTIONS: Read each item and select the best response.

1. **The diagram below would be least appropriate for illustrating which of the following?**
   (Average Rigor)(Skill 1C)

   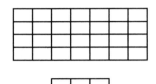

   A) $7 \times 4 + 3$

   B) $31 \div 7$

   C) 28×3

   D) $31 - 3$

2. **2^{-3} is equivalent to**
   (Average Rigor)(Skill 1D)

   A)   0.8

   B)   −0.8

   C)   125

   D)   0.125

3. **What is the number 6 in base three? (Rigorous)(Skill 1A)**

   A) 0

   B) 20

   C) 21

   D) 1001

4. **Which of the following is an irrational number?**
   (Easy)(Skill 1F)

   A) .362626262...

   B) $4\frac{1}{3}$

   C) $\sqrt{5}$

   D) $-\sqrt{16}$

5. **Which denotes a complex number?**
   (Rigorous)(Skill 1F)

   A)   3.678678678...

   B) $-\sqrt{27}$

   C) $123^{1/2}$

   D) $(-100)^{1/2}$

6. Choose the correct statement: (Rigorous)(Skill 1F)

A) Rational and irrational numbers are both proper subsets of the real numbers.

B) The set of whole numbers is a proper subset of the set of natural numbers.

C) The set of integers is a proper subset of the set of irrational numbers.

D) The set of real numbers is a proper subset of the natural, whole, integers, rational, and irrational numbers.

7. $3^{1/2}(9^{1/3})$ is equivalent to (Rigorous)(Skill 2F)

A) $27^{5/6}$

B) $9^{7/12}$

C) $3^{5/6}$

D) $3^{6/7}$

8. How many real numbers lie between −1 and +1 ? (Easy)(Skill 1F)

A) 0

B) 1

C) 17

D) an infinite number

9. Choose the set in which the members are not equivalent. (Average Rigor)(Skill 1D)

A) 1/2, 0.5, 50%

B) 10/5, 2.0, 200%

C) 3/8, 0.385, 38.5%

D) 7/10, 0.7, 70%

10. Change $.\overline{63}$ into a fraction in simplest form. (Average Rigor)(Skill 1E)

A) $\dfrac{63}{100}$

B) $\dfrac{7}{11}$

C) $6\dfrac{3}{10}$

D) $\dfrac{2}{3}$

11. Which is not true? (Average Rigor)(Skill 1F)

A) All irrational numbers are real numbers

B) All integers are rational

C) Zero is a natural number

D) All whole numbers are integers

12. Write the number 81 in exponent form. (Average Rigor) (Skill 1D)

   A) 3^4

   B) 2^5

   C) 3^3

   D) 3^5

13. Write 4.65 x10^{-6} in standard form. (Easy Rigor) (Skill 1E)

   A) 465,000

   B) 4,650,000

   C) 0.0000465

   D) 0.00000465

14. Express .0000456 in scientific notation. (Average)(Skill 1E)

   A) $4.56x10^{-4}$

   B) $45.6x10^{-6}$

   C) $4.56x10^{-6}$

   D) $4.56x10^{-5}$

15. Mr. Brown feeds his cat premium cat food which costs $40 per month. Approximately how much will it cost to feed her for one year? (Easy)(Skill 2A)

   A) $500

   B) $400

   C) $80

   D) $4800

16. $(3.8 \times 10^{17}) \times (.5 \times 10^{-12})$ (Average Rigor)(Skill 2F)

   A) 19×10^5

   B) 1.9×10^5

   C) 1.9×10^6

   D) 1.9×10^7

17. A sofa sells for $520. If the retailer makes a 30% profit, what was the wholesale price? (Average Rigor)(Skill 2A)

   A) $400

   B) $676

   C) $490

   D) $364

18. Evaluate: $3^x \times 3^{2y}$ where x is 1 and y is 2. (Average Rigor)(Skill 2F)

A) 243

B) 81

C) 729

D) 9

19. Evaluate $\sqrt{3} - \sqrt{12} + \sqrt{27}$. (Average Rigor) (Skill 2F)

A) $2\sqrt{3}$

B) 2

C) 3

D) $3\sqrt{2}$

20. Sandra has $34.00, Carl has $42.00. How much more does Carl have than Sandra? Which would be the best method for finding the answer? (Easy)(Skill 2B)

A) addition

B) subtraction

C) division

D) both A and B are equally correct

21. What would be the total cost of a suit for $295.99 and a pair of shoes for $69.95 including 6.5% sales tax? (Average Rigor)(Skill 2A)

A) $389.73

B) $398.37

C) $237.86

D) $315.23

22. What is the Greatest Common Factor of 25 and 40? (Average Rigor)(Skill 3A)

A) 10

B) 5

C) 8

D) 1

23. Which number is divisible by 9 (without using a calculator)? (Easy)(Skill 3A)

A) 3459

B) 9459

C) 5379

D) 2792

24. **Find the LCM of 27, 90 and 84. (Easy) (Skill 3A)**

A) 90

B) 3780

C) 204120

D) 1260

25. **A dress costs $435 plus 6 ½ % sales tax. What is the total cost of the dress? (Rigorous)(Skill 3B)**

A) $460.86

B) $470.79

C) $452.65

D) $463.28

26. **Given that n is a positive even integer, 5n + 4 will always be divisible by: (Average Rigor) (Skill 3A)**

A) 4

B) 5

C) 5n

D) 2

27. **Find the time between 9:45:12 am and 1: 33:19 pm. (Rigorous)(Skill 3B)**

A) 4:35:07

B) 3:48:07

C) 2:48:37

D) 3:17:47

28. **Which of the following is always composite if x is odd, y is even, and both x and y are greater than or equal to 2? (Rigorous)(Skill 3A)**

A) $x + y$

B) $3x + 2y$

C) $5xy$

D) $5x + 3y$

29. **A student had 60 days to appeal the results of an exam. If the results were received on March 23, what was the last day that the student could appeal? (Easy Rigor)(Skill 3B)**

A) May 21

B) May 22

C) May 23

D) May 24

30. $\dfrac{3.5 \times 10^{-10}}{0.7 \times 10^{4}}$
    (Rigorous)(Skill 3C)

    A) 0.5×10^{6}

    B) 5.0×10^{-6}

    C) 5.0×10^{-14}

    D) 0.5×10^{-14}

31. Solve: $\sqrt{75} + \sqrt{147} - \sqrt{48}$
    (Rigorous)(Skill 2F)

    A) 174

    B) $12\sqrt{3}$

    C) $8\sqrt{3}$

    D) 74

32. Simplify: $\sqrt{27} + \sqrt{75}$
    (Easy)(Skill 2F)

    A) $8\sqrt{3}$

    B) 34

    C) $34\sqrt{3}$

    D) $15\sqrt{3}$

33. Given that x, y, and z are prime numbers, which of the following is true?
    (Average Rigor)(Skill 3A)

    A) x + y is always prime

    B) xyz is always prime

    C) xy is sometimes prime

    D) x + y is sometimes prime

34. Find the GCF of $2^{2} \cdot 3^{2} \cdot 5$ and $2^{2} \cdot 3 \cdot 7$.
    (Easy Rigor)(Skill 3A)

    A) $2^{5} \cdot 3^{3} \cdot 5 \cdot 7$

    B) $2 \cdot 3 \cdot 5 \cdot 7$

    C) $2^{2} \cdot 3$

    D) $2^{3} \cdot 3^{2} \cdot 5 \cdot 7$

35. Given even numbers x and y, which could be the LCM of x and y? (Average Rigor)(Skill 3A)

    A) $\dfrac{xy}{2}$

    B) 2xy

    C) 4xy

    D) xy

36. $24 - 3 \times 7 + 2 =$
(Average Rigor)(Skill 3E)

   A) 5

   B) 149

   C) −3

   D) 189

37. Joe reads 20 words/min. and Jan reads 80 words/min. How many minutes will it take Joe to read the same number of words that it takes Jan 40 minutes to read?
(Rigorous)(Skill 3E)

   A) 10

   B) 20

   C) 80

   D) 160

38. $7t - 4 \cdot 2t + 3t \cdot 4 \div 2 =$
(Average Rigor)(Skill 4D)

   A) 5t

   B) 0

   C) 31t

   D) 18t

39. Solve for x:
$3x + 5 \geq 8 + 7x$
(Average Rigor)(Skill 4D)

   A) $x \geq -\dfrac{3}{4}$

   B) $x \leq -\dfrac{3}{4}$

   C) $x \geq \dfrac{3}{4}$

   D) $x \leq \dfrac{3}{4}$

40. Solve for x: $6(x + 2) - 5 = 21 - x.$
(Rigorous) (Skill 4D)

   A) 3

   B) 2

   C) 5

   D) 0

41. Solve for x:
$|2x + 3| > 4$
(Rigorous)(Skill 4D)

   A) $-\dfrac{7}{2} > x > \dfrac{1}{2}$

   B) $-\dfrac{1}{2} > x > \dfrac{7}{2}$

   C) $x < \dfrac{7}{2}$ or $x < -\dfrac{1}{2}$

   D) $x < -\dfrac{7}{2}$ or $x > \dfrac{1}{2}$

42. Three less than four times a number is five times the sum of that number and 6. Which equation could be used to solve this problem?
(Average Rigor)(Skill 4C)

A) $3 - 4n = 5(n + 6)$

B) $3 - 4n + 5n = 6$

C) $4n - 3 = 5n + 6$

D) $4n - 3 = 5(n + 6)$

43. Which axiom is incorrectly applied?
(Average Rigor) (Skill 4D)

$3x + 4 = 7$

Step a. $3x + 4 - 4 = 7 - 4$
additive equality

Step b. $3x + 4 - 4 = 3$
commutative axiom of addition

Step c. $3x + 0 = 3$
additive inverse

Step d. $3x = 3$
additive identity

A) step a

B) step b

C) step c

D) step d

44. Graph the solution:
$|x| + 7 < 13$
(Rigorous)(Skill 4E)

A)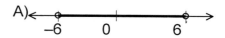

B)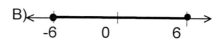

C)

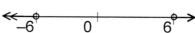

D)

45. Which of the following does not correctly relate an inverse operation?
(Average Rigor) (Skill 4D)

A) $a - b = a + -b$

B) $a \times b = b \div a$

C) $\sqrt{a^2} = a$

D) $a \times \dfrac{1}{a} = 1$

46. Solve for v_0: $d = at(v_t - v_0)$
(Rigorous)(Skill 4D)

A) $v_0 = atd - v_t$

B) $v_0 = d - atv_t$

C) $v_0 = atv_t - d$

D) $v_0 = (atv_t - d)/at$

47. Solve for x: $18 = 4 + |2x|$
(Average Rigor)(Skill 4D)

A) $\{-11, 7\}$

B) $\{-7, 0, 7\}$

C) $\{-7, 7\}$

D) $\{-11, 11\}$

48. Simplify $\dfrac{\dfrac{3}{4}x^2 y^{-3}}{\dfrac{2}{3}xy}$
(Average Rigor)(Skill 4D)

A) $\dfrac{1}{2}xy^{-4}$

B) $\dfrac{1}{2}x^{-1}y^{-4}$

C) $\dfrac{9}{8}xy^{-4}$

D) $\dfrac{9}{8}xy^{-2}$

49. Which of the following is incorrect?
(Rigorous)(Skill 4D)

A) $(x^2 y^3)^2 = x^4 y^6$

B) $m^2 (2n)^3 = 8m^2 n^3$

C) $(m^3 n^4)/(m^2 n^2) = mn^2$

D) $(x + y^2)^2 = x^2 + y^4$

50. What is the solution set for the following equations?
(Skill 4D)
(Rigorous)(Skill 5F)

$3x + 2y = 12$
$12x + 8y = 15$

A) all real numbers

B) x = 4, y = 4

C) x = 2, y = −1

D) $\varnothing$

51. Solve for x by factoring
(Rigorous)(Skill 6A)
$2x^2 - 3x - 2 = 0$.

A) x = (-1,2)

B) x = (0.5,-2)

C) x=(-0.5,2)

D) x=(1,-2)

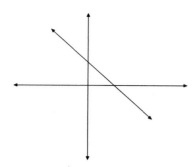

52. Which equation is represented by the above graph?
(Average Rigor) (Skill 5D)

A) $x - y = 3$

B) $x - y = -3$

C) $x + y = 3$

D) $x + y = -3$

53. The length of a picture frame is 2 inches greater than its width. If the area of the frame is 143 square inches, what is its width? (Rigorous)(Skill 6F)

A) 11 inches

B) 13 inches

C) 12 inches

D) 10 inches

54. What is the slope of any line parallel to the line
2x + 4y = 4?
(Rigorous)(Skill 5A)

A) -2

B) -1

C) $-\dfrac{1}{2}$

D) 2

55. If cleaning costs are $32 for 4 hours, how much is it for 10.5 hours? (Easy)(Skill 5E)

A) $112.50

B) $87

C) $84

D) $76.50

56. Solve the following equations: 4x + 3y = 24 and 3x + 2y = 20.
(Rigorous)(Skill 5F)

A) (4/3,3/2)

B) (4,5)

C) (5,5)

D) (12,-8)

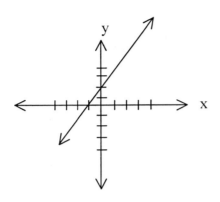

57. What is the equation of the above graph?
(Rigorous)(Skill 5D)

A) $2x + y = 2$

B) $2x - y = -2$

C) $2x - y = 2$

D) $2x + y = -2$

58. Solve for x and y:
x= 3y + 7
7x + 5y = 23
(Moderate Rigor)(Skill 5F)

A) $(-1,4)$

B) $(4, -1)$

C) $(-\dfrac{29}{7}, -\dfrac{26}{7})$

D) $(10, 1)$

59. Solve the system of equations for x, y and z.
(Rigorous)(Skill 5F)

$$3x + 2y - z = 0$$
$$2x + 5y = 8z$$
$$x + 3y + 2z = 7$$

A) $(-1, \ 2, \ 1)$

B) $(1, \ 2, \ -1)$

C) $(-3, \ 4, \ -1)$

D) $(0, \ 1, \ 2)$

60. Which set illustrates a function?
(Easy)(Skill 6B)

A) $\{ (0,1) \ (0,2) \ (0,3) \ (0,4) \}$

B) $\{ (3,9) \ (-3,9) \ (4,16) \ (-4,16) \}$

C) $\{ (1,2) \ (2,3) \ (3,4) \ (1,4) \}$

D) $\{ (2,4) \ (3,6) \ (4,8) \ (4,16) \}$

61. Give the domain for the function over the set of real numbers:

$$y = \frac{3x+2}{2x^2-3}$$

(Rigorous)(Skill 6D)

A) all real numbers

B) all real numbers, $x \neq 0$

C) all real numbers, $x \neq -2$ or 3

D) all real numbers, $x \neq \frac{\pm\sqrt{6}}{2}$

62. If y varies directly as x and x is 2 when y is 6, what is x when y is 18?
(Rigorous) (Skill 5B)

A) 3

B) 6

C) 26

D) 36

63. State the domain of the function $f(x) = \frac{3x-6}{x^2-25}$
(Rigorous) (Skill 6D)

A) $x \neq 2$

B) $x \neq 5, -5$

C) $x \neq 2, -2$

D) $x \neq 5$

64. The volume of water flowing through a pipe varies directly with the square of the radius of the pipe. If the water flows at a rate of 80 liters per minute through a pipe with a radius of 4 cm, at what rate would water flow through a pipe with a radius of 3 cm?
(Average Rigor)(Skill 5B)

A) 45 liters per minute

B) 6.67 liters per minute

C) 60 liters per minute

D) 4.5 liters per minute

65. If y varies inversely as x and x is 4 when y is 6, what is the constant of variation?
(Rigorous)(Skill 6D)

A) 2

B) 12

C) $\frac{3}{2}$

D) 24

66. Find the zeroes of $f(x) = x^3 + x^2 - 14x - 24$
(Rigorous)(Skill 6H)

A) 4, 3, 2

B) 3, −8

C) 7, −2, −1

D) 4, −3, −2

67. The discriminant of a quadratic equation is evaluated and determined to be –3. The equation has (Rigorous)(Skill 6A)

   A) one real root

   B) one complex root

   C) two roots, both real

   D) two roots, both complex

68. Evaluate $x^2 - 3x + 7$ when x = 2. (Easy) (Skill 6A)

   A) 7

   B) 5

   C) 3

   D) 9

69. Which of the following is a factor of $6 + 48m^3$ (Average Rigor)(Skill 6F)

   A) (1 + 2m)

   B) (1 – 8m)

   C) (1 + m – 2m)

   D) (1 – m + 2m)

70. Factor completely:
   8(x – y) + a(y – x)
   (Average Rigor)(Skill 6F)

   A) (8 + a)(y – x)

   B) (8 – a)(y – x)

   C) (a – 8)(y – x)

   D) (a – 8)(y + x)

71. Which of the following is a factor of $k^3 - m^3$?
   (Average Rigor) (Skill 6F)

   A) $k^2 + m^2$

   B) k + m

   C) $k^2 - m^2$

   D) k – m

72. Which graph represents the solution set for $x^2 - 5x > -6$?
   (Rigorous)(Skill 6B)

   A) ⟵┤┼─◯┼┼┼─◯┼┼─⟶
          −2   0   2

   B) ⟵┤◯┼┼┼┼┼─◯⟶
         −3   0   3

   C) ⟵┼┤◯┼┼┼◯┼┼⟶
         −2   0   2

   D) ⟵┤⟵┼┼┼┼◯◯┼┼⟶
         −3   0 2 3

73. Which of the following is a factor of the expression: (Average Rigor) (Skill 6A) $9x^2 + 6x - 35$?

   A) 3x-5

   B) 3x-7

   C) x+3

   D) x-2

74. $f(x) = 3x - 2; \ f^{-1}(x) =$ (Rigorous)(Skill 6E)

   A) $3x + 2$

   B) $\dfrac{x}{6}$

   C) $2x - 3$

   D) $\dfrac{x+2}{3}$

75. Which graph represents the equation of $y = x^2 + 3x$? (Rigorous)(Skill 6B)

   A)   B)

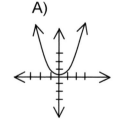   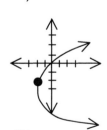

   C)   D)

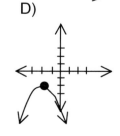

76. Solve for x.

   $3x^2 - 2 + 4(x^2 - 3) = 0$
   (Rigorous)(Skill 6A)

   A) $\{ -\sqrt{2} \ , \ \sqrt{2} \}$

   B) $\{ 2, -2 \}$

   C) $\{ 0, \ \sqrt{3}, \ -\sqrt{3} \}$

   D) $\{ 7, -7 \}$

77. For an acute angle x, sinx = 3/5. What is cotx?(Rigorous) (Skill 8E)

   A) $\dfrac{5}{3}$

   B) $\dfrac{3}{4}$

   C) 1.33

   D) 1

78. Which expression is not equal to sinx? (Average Rigor)(Skill 8E)

   A) $\sqrt{1 - \cos^2 x}$

   B) $\tan x \cos x$

   C) $\dfrac{1}{\csc x}$

   D) $\dfrac{1}{\sec x}$

79. The formula for solving a quadratic equation is: (Rigorous) (Skill 6A)

A) $x = \dfrac{-b \pm \sqrt{b^2 - 4ac}}{2a}$

B) $x = \dfrac{-b \pm \sqrt{b^2 - 4a}}{2a}$

C) $x = \dfrac{b \pm \sqrt{b^2 - 4ac}}{2a}$

D) $x = \dfrac{b \pm \sqrt{b^3 - 4ac}}{2a}$

80. If you have a triangle with these dimensions, solve for x if angle b is 27 degrees. (Rigorous)(Skill 8E)

A) 8.45

B) 7.26

C) 7.78

D) 6.89

81. Find the missing side c: (Average Rigor)(Skill 8E)

A) 11.65

B) 19.5

C) 23

D) 26.2

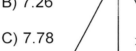

82. Find side c in the following right-angled triangle. (Average rigor)(Skill 8E)

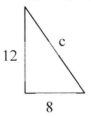

A) 15.56

B) 14.42

C) 16.94

D) 14.60

83. A car is driving north at 74 miles per hour from point A. Another car is driving due east at 65 miles per hour. How far are the cars away from each other after 2 hours? (Rigorous)(Skill 8E)

A) 175.87

B) 232.66

C) 196.99

D) 202.43

84. If three cups of concentrate are needed to make 2 gallons of fruit punch, how many cups are needed to make 5 gallons?
(Easy)(Skill 8A)

A) 6 cups

B) 7 cups

C) 7.5 cups

D) 10 cups

85. The mass of a cookie is closest to:
(Easy Rigor)(Skill 8A)

A) 0.5 kg

B) 0.5 grams

C) 15 grams

D) 1.5 grams

86. A man's waist, measured using a tape with the smallest unit of 1 cm, measures 90 cm. What is the greatest possible error for the measurement?
(Average Rigor)(Skill 8D)

A) ± 1 m

B) ± 8 cm

C) ± 1 cm

D) ± 5 mm

87. 3 km is equivalent to
(Easy)(Skill 8B)

A) 300 cm

B) 300 m

C) 3000 cm

D) 3000 m

88. 4 square yards is equivalent to:
(Average)(Skill 8B)

A) 12 square feet

B) 48 square feet

C) 36 square feet

D) 108 square feet

89. 2.25 teaspoons equals to how many milliliters? (Easy Rigor)(Skill 8B)

A) 11.25 ml

B) 13.25 ml

C) 13 ml

D) 10 ml

90. You have a gallon of water and remove a total of 30 ounces. How many milliliters do you have left?
(Rigorous)(Skill 8B)

    A)   2900 ml

    B)   1100 ml

    C)   980 ml

    D)   1000 ml

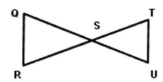

91. Given QS ≅ TS and RS ≅ US, prove △QRS ≅ △TUS.

I) QS ≅ TS	1) Given
2) RS ≅ US	2) Given
3) ∠TSU ≅ ∠QSR	3) ?
4) △TSU ≅ △QSR	4) SAS

Give the reason which justifies step 3.
(Average Rigor) (Skill 9C)

A) Congruent parts of congruent triangles are congruent

B) Reflexive axiom of equality

C) Alternate interior angle Theorem

D) Vertical angle theorem

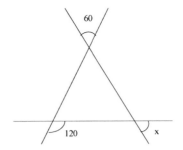

Note: Figure not drawn to scale.

92. In the figure above, what is the value of x?
(Rigorous)(Skill 9A)

A) 50

B) 60

C) 75

D) 80

93. The diagram which illustrates the construction of a perpendicular to the line at a given point on the line.
(Average Rigor) (Skill 9D)

A)

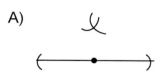

B)

C)

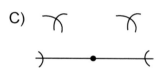

D)

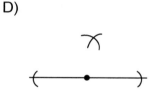

94. Which of the following can be defined?
(Easy)(Skill 9A)

A) point

B) ray

C) line

D) plane

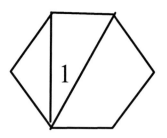

95. Given the regular hexagon above, determine the measure of angle 1.
(Rigorous)(Skill 9E)

A) 30°

B) 60°

C) 120°

D) 45°

96. Line p has a negative slope and passes through the point (0, 0). If line q is perpendicular to line p, which of the following must be true?
(Rigorous)(Skill 11E)

A) Line q has a negative y-intercept.

B) Line q passes through the point (0,0)

C) Line q has a positive slope.

D) Line q has a positive y-intercept.

97. What happens to the volume of a square pyramid when the sides of the base are tripled? (Rigorous)(Skill 10B)

A) The volume is increased by 9

B) The volume is increased by 8

C) The volume is increased by 27

D) The volume is increased by 16

98. What is the length of a fourth of a circle with a diameter of 24 cm? (Average Rigor)(Skill 10A)

A) 18.85

B) 75.4

C) 32.45

D) 20.75

99. If the radius of a right circular cylinder is doubled, how does its volume change? (Rigorous)(Skill 10B)

A) no change

B) also is doubled

C) four times the original

D) pi times the original

100. Determine the volume of a sphere to the nearest cm if the surface area is 113 cm^2. (Rigorous)(Skill 10A)

A) 113 cm^3

B) 339 cm^3

C) 37.7 cm^3

D) 226 cm^3

101. Determine the area of the shaded region of the trapezoid in terms of x and y(the height of $\triangle ABC$). $\overline{DE}$ = 2x & $\overline{DC}$ = 3x. (Rigorous)(Skill 10C)

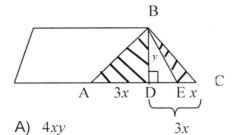

A) $4xy$

B) $2xy$

C) $3x^2y$

D) There is not enough information given.

102. Compute the surface area of the prism. (Average Rigor) (Skill 10A)

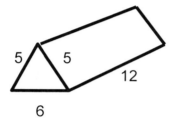

5   5
    12
6

A) 204

B) 216

C) 360

D) 180

103. If the area of the base of a regular square pyramid is tripled, how does its volume change?
(Rigorous)(Skill 10B)

A) double the original

B) triple the original

C) nine times the original

D) no change

104. How does lateral area differ from total surface area in prisms, pyramids, and cones?
(Easy)(Skill 10A)

A) For the lateral area, only use surfaces perpendicular to the base.

B) They are both the same.

C) The lateral area does not include the base.

D) The lateral area is always a factor of pi.

105. If the area of the base of a cone is tripled, the volume will be:
(Average Rigor)(Skill 10B)

A) the same as the original

B) 9 times the original

C) 3 times the original

D) 3π times the original

106. Find the length of a box with surface area of 94 sq. ft. with a width of 3 feet and a depth of 4 feet.
(Rigorous)(Skill 10C)

A) 3 ft.

B) 4 ft.

C) 5 ft

D) 6 ft.

107. **What is the volume of a cylinder of a height 8 cm and a diameter of 4 cm?**

    (Average Rigor)(Skill 10A)

    A) 95.45

    B) 100.5

    C) 110.3

    D) 105.4

108. **What is the surface area of a sphere with a circumference of 46 cm?**

    (Rigorous)(Skill 10A)

    A) 475.6

    B) 546.7

    C) 673.4

    D) 643.5

109. **Given similar polygons with corresponding sides 6 and 8, what is the area of the smaller if the area of the larger is 64?**
    (Average Rigor)(Skill 10B)

    A) 48

    B) 36

C) 144

D) 78

110. **In similar polygons, if the perimeters are in a ratio of x : y, the sides are in a ratio of:**
    (Average Rigor)
    (Skill 10B)

    A) $x : y$

    B) $x^2 : y^2$

    C) $2x : y$

    D) $\frac{1}{2}x : y$

111. **If a circle has an area of 25 cm^2, what is its circumference to the nearest tenth of a centimeter?**
    (Rigorous)(Skill 10A)

    A) 78.5 cm

    B) 17.7 cm

    C) 8.9 cm

    D) 15.7 cm

112. **Compute the area of the shaded region, given a radius of 5 meters. O is the center.**
    (Rigorous)(Skill 10C)

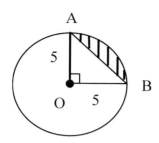

A) 7.13 cm²

B) 7.13 m²

C) 78.5 m²

D) 19.63 m²

A) 136.47 m²

B) 148.48 m²

C) 293.86 m²

D) 178.47 m²

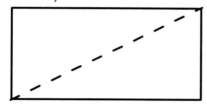

113. The above diagram is most likely used in deriving a formula for which of the following?
(Easy)(Skill 10A)

A) the area of a rectangle

B) the area of a triangle

C) the perimeter of a triangle

D) the surface area of a prism

114. Find the area of the figure pictured below.
(Rigorous)(Skill 10C)

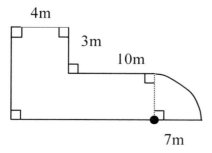

115. Given a 30 meter x 60 meter garden with a circular fountain with a 5 meter radius, calculate the area of the portion of the garden not occupied by the fountain.
(Rigorous)(Skill 10C)

A) 1721 m²

B) 1879 m²

C) 2585 m²

D) 1015 m²

116. Find the area of the shaded region given square ABCD with side AB=10m and circle E.
(Rigorous)(Skill 10C)

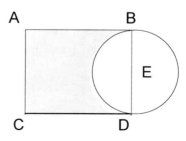

A) 178.5 m²

B) 139.25 m^2

C) 71 m^2

D) 60.75 m^2

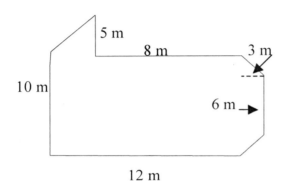

5 m

8 m

3 m

10 m

6 m

12 m

117. Compute the area of the polygon shown above.

(Rigorous)(Skill 10C)

A) 178 m^2

B) 154 m^2

C) 43 m^2

D) 188 m^2

118. Find the area of the figure below.
(Average Rigor)(Skill 10C)

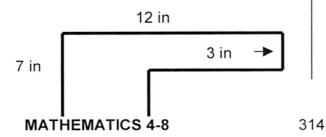

12 in

3 in

7 in

5 in

A) 56 in^2

B) 27 in^2

C) 71 in^2

D) 170 in^2

119. Which one is not one of the transformations that occur in a tessellation? (Easy Rigor)(Skill 11B)

A) translation

B) rotation

C) reflection

D) stellar reflection

120. Find the slope of the line (11, 25) and (4, 4)(Rigorous) (Skill 11E)

A) 3

B) 4

C) 4.5

D) 1.7

B) 6, 11, 16

C) 6, 11, 14

121. Find the center of a circle with a diameter whose endpoints are (4,5) and (-4, -6). (Average Rigor) (Skill 11E)

D) 6.5, 11, 14.5

A) $(-2, \frac{1}{2})$

124. Find the percentile of the score 98. (Average Rigor)(Skill 12F)

B) $(0, -\frac{1}{2})$

33, 35, 38, 49, 59, 70, 89, 93, 98, 99, 104, 108

C) (-1, 0)

A) 59 percentile

D) (0, 1)

B) 98 percentile

122. Find the midpoint of (2,5) and (7,–4). (Average Rigor) (Skill 11E)

A) (9,–1)

C) 75 percentile

B) (5, 9)

C) $(\frac{9}{2}, -\frac{1}{2})$

D) 95 percentile

D) $(\frac{9}{2}, \frac{1}{2})$

125. The tenth percentile is in what stanine? (Easy Rigor)(Skill 12F)

123. What is the first, second and third quartile for the following? (Average Rigor) (Skill 12D)

A) First

5, 5, 5, 6, 7, 9, 9, 10, 11, 12, 13, 13, 14, 15, 16, 17,17

A) 5, 10, 15

B) Second

C) Third

D) Fourth

126. What is the range of the following numbers? (Average Rigor)(Skill 12D)

34, 14, 43, 35, 45, 18, 33, 42

A) 31

B) 32

C) 26

D) 19

127. Find the median of the following set of data:

14 3 7 6 11 20

(Average Rigor)(Skill 12D)

A) 9

B) 8.5

C) 7

D) 11

128. Compute the median for the following data set:

{12, 19, 13, 16, 17, 14}

(Average Rigor)(Skill 12D)

A) 14.5

B) 15.17

C) 15

D) 16

129. Corporate salaries are listed for several employees. Which would be the best measure of central tendency? (Average Rigor) (Skill 12D)

$24,000 $24,000 $26,000

$28,000 $30,000 $120,000

A) mean

B.) median

C) mode

D) no difference

130. Half the students in a class

scored 80% on an exam, most of the rest scored 85% except for one student who scored 10%. Which would be the best measure of central tendency for the test scores? **(Rigorous)(Skill 12D)**

A) mean

B) median

C) mode

D) either the median or the mode because they are equal

131. **A student scored in the 87th percentile on a standardized test. Which would be the best interpretation of his score? (Average Rigor)(Skill 12F)**

A) Only 13% of the students who took the test scored higher.

B) This student should be getting mostly Bs on his report card.

C) This student performed below average on the test.

D) This is the equivalent of missing 13 questions on a 100 question exam.

132. **Which statement is true about George's budget? (Easy)(Skill 12A)**

A) George spends the greatest portion of his income on food.

B) George spends twice as much on utilities as he does on his mortgage.

C) George spends twice as much on utilities as he does on food.

D) George spends the same amount on food and utilities as he does on mortgage.

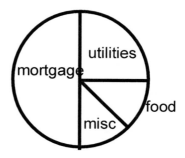

133. **Given a drawer with 5 black socks, 3 blue socks, and 2 red socks, what is the probability that you will draw two black socks in two draws in a dark room? (Average Rigor)(Skill 13B)**

A) $\dfrac{2}{9}$

B) $\dfrac{1}{4}$

C) $\dfrac{17}{18}$

D) $\dfrac{1}{18}$

134. **A sack of candy has 3**

peppermints, 2 butterscotch drops and 3 cinnamon drops. One candy is drawn and replaced, then another candy is drawn; what is the probability that both will be butterscotch?
(Average Rigor)(Skill 13B)

A) $\frac{1}{2}$

B) $\frac{1}{28}$

C) $\frac{1}{4}$

D) $\frac{1}{16}$

135. Given a spinner with the numbers one through eight, what is the probability that you will spin an even number or a number greater than four?
(Easy)(Skill 13B)

A) $\frac{1}{4}$

B) $\frac{1}{2}$

C) $\frac{3}{4}$

D) 1

136. If a horse will probably win three races out of ten, what are the odds that he will win? (Rigorous)(Skill 13B)

A) 3:10

B) 7:10

C) 3:7

D) 7:3

137. A jar contains 3 red marbles, 5 white marbles, 1 green marble and 15 blue marbles. If one marble is picked at random from the jar, what is the probability that it will be red? (Easy)(Skill 13B)

A) $\frac{1}{3}$

B) $\frac{1}{8}$

C) $\frac{3}{8}$

D) $\frac{1}{24}$

138. How many ways are there to choose a potato and two green vegetables from a choice of three potatoes and seven green vegetables? (Rigorous)(Skill 13B)

A) 126

B) 63

C) 21

D) 252

139. A measure of association

    between two variables is
    called: (Easy) (Skill 14E)

    A) Associate

    B) Correlation

    C) Confidence interval

    D) Variation

140. A boat travels 30 miles
    upstream in three hours. It
    makes the return trip in one
    and a half hours. What is the
    speed of the boat in still
    water?
    (Average Rigor)(Skill 15F)

    A) 10 mph

    B) 15 mph

    C) 20 mph

    D) 30 mph

141. Estimate the sum of 1498 +
    1309. (Easy Rigor)(Skill 15H)

    A) 2900

    B) 2850

    C) 2800

    D) 2600

142. Ginny and Nick head back to their respective colleges after being home for the weekend. They leave their house at the same time and drive for 4 hours. Ginny drives due south at the average rate of 60 miles per hour and Nick drives due east at the average rate of 60 miles per hour. What is the straight-line distance between them, in miles, at the end of the 4 hours? (Average Rigor) (Skill 15G)

A) $120\sqrt{2}$

B) 240

C) $240\sqrt{2}$

D) 288

143. Choose the least appropriate set of manipulatives for a sixth grade class. (Easy)(Skill 18A)

A) graphing calculators, compasses, rulers, conic section models

B) two color counters, origami paper, markers, yarn

C) balance, meter stick, colored pencils, beads

D) paper cups, beans, tangrams, geoboards

144. Which is not an acceptable way of getting at student performance in math: (Easy)(Skill 19A)

A) Student Portfolios

B) Formal tests

C) Student Projects

D) Term Paper

145. If 80 students are in sports and 100 students are in band with 20 students in both band and sports, identify that pictorially. (Average Rigor)(Skill 16D)

A)

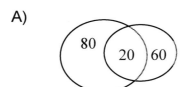

B)

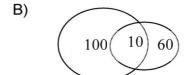

C)

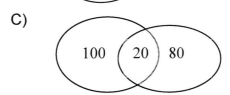

D)

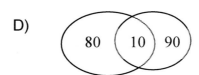

Answer Key

1. C	38. A	75. C	112. B
2. D	39. B	76. A	113. B
3. B	40. B	77. C	114. B
4. C	41. D	78. D	115. A
5. D	42. D	79. A	116. D
6. A	43. B	80. B	117. B
7. B	44. A	81. D	118. A
8. D	45. B	82. B	119. D
9. C	46. D	83. C	120. A
10. B	47. C	84. C	121. B
11. C	48. C	85. C	122. D
12. A	49. D	86. D	123. D
13. D	50. D	87. D	124. C
14. D	51. C	88. C	125. B
15. A	52. C	89. A	126. A
16. B	53. A	90. A	127. A
17. A	54. C	91. D	128. C
18. A	55. C	92. B	129. B
19. A	56. D	93. D	130. B
20. B	57. B	94. B	131. A
21. A	58. B	95. A	132. C
22. B	59. A	96. C	133. A
23. B	60. B	97. A	134. D
24. B	61. D	98. A	135. C
25. D	62. B	99. C	136. C
26. D	63. B	100. A	137. B
27. B	64. A	101. B	138. A
28. C	65. D	102. B	139. B
29. B	66. D	103. B	140. B
30. C	67. D	104. C	141. C
31. C	68. B	105. C	142. C
32. A	69. A	106. C	143. A
33. D	70. C	107. B	144. D
34. C	71. D	108. C	145. A
35. A	72. D	109. B	
36. A	73. A	110. A	
37. D	74. D	111. B	

Rigor Table

Easy 20%	Average Rigor 40%	Rigorous 40%
4,8,13,15,20,23,24,29,32, 34,55,60,68,84,85,87,89, 94,104,113,119,125,132, 135,137,139,141,143,144	1,2,9,10,11,12,14,16,17, 18,19,21,22,26,33,35,36, 38,39,42,43,45,47,52,58 64,69,70,71,73,78,81,82, 86,88,91,93,98,102,105, 107,109,110,118,121,122 123,124,126,127,128,129 131,133,134,140,142,145	3,5,6,7,25,27,28,30,31,37 40,41,44,46,48,49,50,51, 53,54,56,57,59,61,62,63 65,66,67,72,74,75,76,77, 79,80,83,90,92,95,96,97 99,100,101,103,106,108 111,112,114,115,116,117 120,130,136,138

Rationales with Sample Questions

The following represent one way to solve the problems and obtain a correct answer.

There are many other mathematically correct ways of determining the correct answer.

1. **The diagram below would be least appropriate for illustrating which of the following?   (Average Rigor)(Skill 1C)**

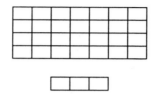

A) $7 \times 4 + 3$

B) $31 \div 7$

C) 28×3

D) $31 - 3$

Answer: C

C is inappropriate. A shows a 7x4 rectangle with 3 additional units. B is the division based on A . D shows how mental subtraction might be visualized leaving a composite difference.

2. **2^{-3} is equivalent to (Average Rigor)(Skill 1D)**

A) 0.8

B) −0.8

C) 125

D) 0.125

Answer: D

Express 2^{-3} as the fraction 1/8, then convert to a decimal.

3.   **What is the number 6 in base three? (Rigorous)(Skill 1A)**

  A) 10

  B) 20

  C) 21

  D) 1001

Answer: B

In base three, the counting numbers are 0,1,2,10,11,12,20,21,22,… so that the number six is 20.

4.   **Which of the following is an irrational number? (Easy)(Skill 1F)**

  A) .362626262...

  B) $4\frac{1}{3}$

  C) $\sqrt{5}$

  D) $-\sqrt{16}$

Answer: C

$\sqrt{5}$ is an irrational number. A is a repeating decimal (decimals that do not repeat are irrational). A and B can both be expressed as fractions. D can be simplified to –4, an integer and rational number.

5.   **Which denotes a complex number? (Rigorous)(Skill 1F)**

  A) 3.678678678…

  B) $-\sqrt{27}$

  C) $123^{1/2}$

  D) $(-100)^{1/2}$

Answer: D

A complex number contains an imaginary part that involves the square root of a negative number. The complex number *i* is defined as the square root of –1.

6. **Choose the correct statement: (Rigorous)(Skill 1F)**

    A) Rational and irrational numbers are both proper subsets of the real numbers.

    B) The set of whole numbers is a proper subset of the set of natural numbers.

    C) The set of integers is a proper subset of the set of irrational numbers.

    D) The set of real numbers is a proper subset of the natural, whole, integers, rational, and irrational numbers.

Answer: A

A proper subset is completely contained in but not equal to the original set.

7. $3^{1/2}(9^{1/3})$ **is equivalent to (Rigorous)(Skill 2F)**

    A) $27^{5/6}$

    B) $9^{7/12}$

    C) $3^{5/6}$

    D) $3^{6/7}$

Answer: B

Getting the bases the same gives us $3^{\frac{1}{2}}3^{\frac{2}{3}}$. Adding exponents gives $3^{\frac{7}{6}}$. Then some additional manipulation of exponents produces $3^{\frac{7}{6}} = 3^{\frac{14}{12}} = \left(3^2\right)^{\frac{7}{12}} = 9^{\frac{7}{12}}$.

8. **How many real numbers lie between –1 and +1 ?**
    (Easy)(Skill 1F)

    A) 0

    B) 1

    C) 17

    D) an infinite number

Answer: D

There are an infinite number of real numbers between any two real numbers.

9. **Choose the set in which the members are <u>not</u> equivalent.**
    (Average Rigor)(Skill 1D)

    A) 1/2, 0.5, 50%

    B) 10/5, 2.0, 200%

    C) 3/8, 0.385, 38.5%

    D) 7/10, 0.7, 70%

Answer: C

3/8 is equivalent to .375 and 37.5%.

10. Change $.\overline{63}$ into a fraction in simplest form. (Average Rigor)(Skill 1E)

  A) $\dfrac{63}{100}$

  B) $\dfrac{7}{11}$

  C) $6\dfrac{3}{10}$

  D) $\dfrac{2}{3}$

Answer: B

Let N = .636363…. Then multiplying both sides of the equation by 100 or 10^2 (because there are 2 repeated numbers), we get 100N = 63.636363… Then subtracting the two equations gives 99N = 63 or N = $\dfrac{63}{99} = \dfrac{7}{11}$.

11. Which is not true? (Average Rigor)(Skill 1F)

  A) All irrational number s are real numbers

  B) All integers are rational

  C) zero is a natural number

  D) All whole numbers are integers

Answer: C

Zero is not a natural number or "counting number".

12. Write the number 81 in exponent form. (Average Rigor)(Skill 1D)

  A) 3^4

  B) 2^5

  C) 3^3

  D) 3^5

Answer: A

81 is 3 x 3 x 3 x3 or 3^4.

13. **Write 4.65 x10⁻⁶ in standard form. (Easy) (Skill 1E)**

A) 465,000

B) 4,650,000

C) 0.0000465

D) 0.00000465

Answer: D

Move the decimal place six places to the left.

14. **Express .0000456 in scientific notation. (Average Rigor)(Skill 1E)**

A) $4.56x10^{-4}$

B) $45.6x10^{-6}$

C) $4.56x10^{-6}$

D) $4.56x10^{-5}$

Answer: D

In scientific notation, the decimal point belongs to the right of the 4, the first significant digit. To get from 4.56×10^{-5} back to 0.0000456, we would move the decimal point 5 places to the left.

15. **Mr. Brown feeds his cat premium cat food which costs $40 per month. Approximately how much will it cost to feed her for one year? (Easy) (Skill 2A)**

A) $500

B) $400

C) $80

D) $4800

Answer: A

12(40) = 480 which is closest to $500.

16. $(3.8 \times 10^{17}) \times (.5 \times 10^{-12})$ (Average Rigor)(Skill 2F)

   A) 19×10^5

   B) 1.9×10^5

   C) 1.9×10^6

   D) 1.9×10^7

Answer: B

Multiply the decimals and add the exponents.

17. **A sofa sells for $520. If the retailer makes a 30% profit, what was the wholesale price? (Average Rigor)(Skill 2A)**

   A) $400

   B) $676

   C) $490

   D) $364

$x + .30x = 520$

Answer: A

Let x be the wholesale price, then x + .30x = 520, 1.30x = 520. Divide both sides by 1.30.

18. **Evaluate $3^x \times 3^{2y}$ where x is 1 and y is 2. (Average Rigor)(Skill 2F)**

   A) 243

   B) 81

   C) 729

   D) 9

Answer A.

Since $a^x \times a^y = a^{(x+y)}$, the answer is $3^{(x+2y)}$ or 3^5 which equals 243.

19. Evaluate $\sqrt{3} - \sqrt{12} + \sqrt{27}$.
    (Average Rigor) (Skill 2F)

    A) $2\sqrt{3}$

    B) 2

    C) 3

    D) $3\sqrt{2}$

Answer: A

$$\sqrt{3} - \sqrt{12} + \sqrt{27} = \sqrt{3} - \sqrt{2^2 \times 3} + \sqrt{3^2 \times 3} = \sqrt{3} - 2\sqrt{3} + 3\sqrt{3} = 2\sqrt{3}$$

20. Sandra has $34.00, Carl has $42.00. How much more does Carl have than Sandra? Which would be the best method for finding the answer? (Easy)(Skill 2B)

    A) addition

    B) subtraction

    C) division

    D) both A and B are equally correct

Answer: B

To find how much more money Carl has than Sandra, it is necessary to subtract Sandra's amount from Carl's amount. This gives $42.00 - $34.00 = $8.00, which is indeed the difference. Answer B is then the correct response.

21. **What would be the total cost of a suit for $295.99 and a pair of shoes for $69.95 including 6.5% sales tax? (Average Rigor)(Skill 2A)**

   A) $389.73

   B) $398.37

   C) $237.86

   D) $315.23

Answer: A

Before the tax, the total comes to $365.94. Then .065(365.94) = 23.79. With the tax added on, the total bill is 365.94 + 23.79 = $389.73. (Quicker way: 1.065(365.94) = 389.73.)

22. **What is the Greatest Common Factor of 25 and 40? (Average Rigor)(Skill 3A)**

   A) 10

   B) 5

   C) 8

   D) 1

Answer: B

In terms of prime factors, $25=5^2$ and $40 =2^3.5$. The greatest common factor is 5.

23. **Which number is divisible by 9 (without using a calculator)? (Moderate Rigor)(Skill 3A)**

   A) 3459

   B) 9459

   C) 5379

   D) 2792

Answer: B

A number is divisible by nine if the sum of its digits is divisible by 9.

24. **Find the LCM of 27, 90 and 84.(Skill 3A)**

    A) 90

    B) 3780

    C) 204120

    D) 1260

Answer: B

To find the LCM of the above numbers, factor each into its prime factors and multiply each common factor the maximum number of times it occurs. Thus 27=3x3x3; 90=2x3x3x5; 84=2x2x3x7; LCM = 2x2x3x3x3x5x7=3780.

25. **A dress costs $435 plus 6 ½ % sales tax. What is the total cost of the dress? (Rigorous)(Skill 3B)**

    A) $460.86

    B) $470.79

    C) $452.65

    D) $463.28

Answer: D
The tax is 0.065 x 435 or $28.28. The total is $463.28

26. **Given that n is a positive even integer, 5n + 4 will always be divisible by: (Average Rigor)(Skill 3A)**

    A) 4

    B) 5

    C) 5n

    D) 2

Answer: D

5n is always even and an even number added to an even number is always even and thus divisible by 2.

27. **Find the time between 9:45:12 am and 1: 33: 19 pm.**
    (Rigorous)(Skill 3B)

    A) 4:35:07

    B) 3:48:07

    C) 2:48:37

    D) 3:17:47

Answer: B

$$
\begin{array}{r}
\text{Subtract } 13{:}33{:}19 \\
- \quad 9{:}45{:}12 \\
\hline
3{:}48{:}07
\end{array}
$$

28. **Which of the following is always composite if x is odd, y is even, and both x and y are greater than or equal to 2? (Rigorous)(Skill 3A)**

    A) $x + y$

    B) $3x + 2y$

    C) $5xy$

    D) $5x + 3y$

Answer: C

A composite number is a number which is not prime. The prime number sequence begins 2,3,5,7,11,13,17,....   To determine which of the expressions is <u>always</u> composite, experiment with different values of x and y, such as x=3 and y=2, or x=5 and y=2. It turns out that 5xy will always be an even number, and therefore, composite.

29. **A student had 60 days to appeal the results of an exam. If the results were received on March 23, what was the last day that the student could appeal? (Average Rigor)(Skill 3B)**

    A) May 21

    B) May 22

    C) May 23

    D) May 24

Answer: B

Recall: 30 days in April and 31 in March. 8 days in March + 30 days in April + 22 days in May brings him to a total of 60 days on May 22.

30. $\dfrac{3.5 \times 10^{-10}}{0.7 \times 10^{4}}$

    (Rigorous)(Skill 3C)

    A) 0.5×10^{6}

    B) 5.0×10^{-6}

    C) 5.0×10^{-14}

    D) 0.5×10^{-14}

Answer: C

Divide the decimals and subtract the exponents.

31. Solve: $\sqrt{75} + \sqrt{147} - \sqrt{48}$
(Rigorous)(Skill 2F)

A) 174

B) $12\sqrt{3}$

C) $8\sqrt{3}$

D) 74

Answer: C

Simplify each radical by factoring out the perfect squares:
$5\sqrt{3} + 7\sqrt{3} - 4\sqrt{3} = 8\sqrt{3}$

32. Simplify: $\sqrt{27} + \sqrt{75}$ (Average Rigor)(Skill 2F)

A) $8\sqrt{3}$

B) 34

C) $34\sqrt{3}$

D) $15\sqrt{3}$

Answer: A

Simplifying radicals gives $\sqrt{27} + \sqrt{75} = 3\sqrt{3} + 5\sqrt{3} = 8\sqrt{3}$. Answer is A.

33. Given that x, y, and z are prime numbers, which of the following is true? (Average Rigor)(Skill 3A)

    A) x + y is always prime

    B) xyz is always prime

    C) xy is sometimes prime

    D) x + y is sometimes prime

Answer: D

x + y is sometimes prime. B and C show the products of two numbers which are always composite. x + y may sometimes be prime but not always (e.g. 3 + 2 = 5 is prime but 3 + 3 = 6 is not).

34. Find the GCF of $2^2 \cdot 3^2 \cdot 5$ and $2^2 \cdot 3 \cdot 7$. (Average Rigor)(Skill 3A)

    A) $2^5 \cdot 3^3 \cdot 5 \cdot 7$

    B) $2 \cdot 3 \cdot 5 \cdot 7$

    C) $2^2 \cdot 3$

    D) $2^3 \cdot 3^2 \cdot 5 \cdot 7$

Answer: C

Choose the highest common exponent for each prime factor.

35. Given even numbers x and y, which could be the LCM of x and y? (Average Rigor)(Skill 3A)

    A) $\dfrac{xy}{2}$

    B) 2xy

    C) 4xy

    D) xy

Answer: A

Although choices B, C and D are common multiples, when both numbers are even, the product can be divided by two to obtain the least common multiple.

36. $24 - 3 \times 7 + 2 =$ (Average Rigor)(Skill 3E)

   A) 5

   B) 149

   C) –3

   D) 189

Answer: A

According to the order of operations, multiplication is performed first, then addition and subtraction from left to right.

37. **Joe reads 20 words/min., and Jan reads 80 words/min. How many minutes will it take Joe to read the same number of words that it takes Jan 40 minutes to read? (Rigorous)(Skill 3E)**

   A) 10

   B) 20

   C) 80

   D) 160

Rate • Speed = total

Answer: D

If Jan reads 80 words/minute, she will read 3200 words in 40 minutes.

$$\frac{3200}{20} = 160$$

At 20 words per minute, it will take Joe 160 minutes to read 3200 words.

38. $7t - 4 \cdot 2t + 3t \cdot 4 \div 2 =$ (Average Rigor)(Skill 4D)

   A) 5t

   B) 0

   C) 31t

   D) 18t

Answer: A

First perform multiplication and division from left to right; 7t −8t + 6t, then add and subtract from left to right.

39. **Solve for x: 3x + 5 ≥ 8 + 7x (Average Rigor)(Skill 4D)**

   A) $x \geq -\dfrac{3}{4}$

   B) $x \leq -\dfrac{3}{4}$

   C) $x \geq \dfrac{3}{4}$

   D) $x \leq \dfrac{3}{4}$

Answer: B

Using additive equality, −3 ≥ 4x. Divide both sides by 4 to obtain −3/4 ≥ x.

40. **Solve for x:** $6(x + 2) - 5 = 21 - x.$
   (Easy Rigor)(Skill 4D)

   A) 3

   B) 2

   C) 5

   D) 0

Answer: B

$6(x + 2) - 5 = 21 - x \Rightarrow 6x + 12 - 5 = 21 - x \Rightarrow 7x = 21 - 7 \Rightarrow 7x = 14 \Rightarrow x = 2$

41. Solve for x: $|2x + 3| > 4$ (Rigorous)(Skill 4D)

A) $-\dfrac{7}{2} > x > \dfrac{1}{2}$

B) $-\dfrac{1}{2} > x > \dfrac{7}{2}$

C) $x < \dfrac{7}{2}$ or $x < -\dfrac{1}{2}$

D) $x < -\dfrac{7}{2}$ or $x > \dfrac{1}{2}$

Answer: D

The quantity within the absolute value symbols must be either > 4 or < -4.
Solve the two inequalities $2x + 3 > 4$ or $2x + 3 < -4$

42. Three less than four times a number is five times the sum of that number and 6. Which equation could be used to solve this problem? (Average Rigor)(Skill 4C)

A) $3 - 4n = 5(n + 6)$

B) $3 - 4n + 5n = 6$

C) $4n - 3 = 5n + 6$

D) $4n - 3 = 5(n + 6)$

Answer: D

Be sure to enclose the sum of the number and 6 in parentheses.

43. Which axiom is incorrectly applied? (Average Rigor)(Skill 4D)

$3x + 4 = 7$

Step a. $3x + 4 - 4 = 7 - 4$
additive equality

Step b. $3x + 4 - 4 = 3$
commutative axiom of addition

Step c. $3x + 0 = 3$
additive inverse

Step d. $3x = 3$
additive identity

A) step a

B) step b

C) step c

D) step d

Answer: B

In simplifying from step a to step b, 3 replaced $7 - 4$, therefore the correct justification would be subtraction or substitution.

44. Graph the solution: $|x| + 7 < 13$ (Rigorous)(Skill 4E)

A)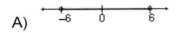

B)

C)

D)

Answer: A

Solve by adding –7 to each side of the inequality. Since the absolute value of x is less than 6, x must be between –6 and 6. The end points are not included so the circles on the graph are hollow.

45. **Which of the following does not correctly relate an inverse operation? (Average Rigor)(Skill 4D)**

A) $a - b = a + -b$

B) $a \times b = b \div a$

C) $\sqrt{a^2} = a$

D) $a \times \dfrac{1}{a} = 1$

Answer: B

B is always false. A, C, and D illustrate various properties of inverse relations.

what

46. **Solve for v_0 : $d = at(v_t - v_0)$ (Rigorous)(Skill 4D)**

A) $v_0 = atd - v_t$

B) $v_0 = d - atv_t$

C) $v_0 = atv_t - d$

D) $v_0 = (atv_t - d)/at$

Answer: D

Using the Distributive Property and other properties of equality to isolate v_0 gives
$d = atv_t - atv_0$, $\quad atv_0 = atv_t - d$, $\quad v_0 = \dfrac{atv_t - d}{at}$.

47. **Solve for** x: $18 = 4 + |2x|$ **(Average Rigor)(Skill 4D)**

A) $\{-11, 7\}$

B) $\{-7, 0, 7\}$

C) $\{-7, 7\}$

D) $\{-11, 11\}$

Answer: C

Using the definition of absolute value, two equations are possible: $18 = 4 + 2x$ or $18 = 4 - 2x$. Solving for x gives x = 7 or x = –7.

48. **Simplify** $\dfrac{\frac{3}{4}x^2y^{-3}}{\frac{2}{3}xy}$

(Average Rigor)(Skill 4D)

A) $\frac{1}{2}xy^{-4}$

B) $\frac{1}{2}x^{-1}y^{-4}$

C) $\frac{9}{8}xy^{-4}$

D) $\frac{9}{8}xy^{-2}$

Answer: C

Simplify the complex fraction by inverting the denominator and multiplying: 3/4(3/2)=9/8, then subtract exponents of the variables to obtain the correct answer.

49. **Which of the following is incorrect? (Average Rigor)(Skill 4D)**

   A) $(x^2y^3)^2 = x^4y^6$

   B) $m^2(2n)^3 = 8m^2n^3$

   C) $(m^3n^4)/(m^2n^2) = mn^2$

   D) $(x+y^2)^2 = x^2 + y^4$

Answer: D

Using FOIL to do the expansion, we get $(x + y^2)^2 = (x + y^2)(x + y^2) = x^2 + 2xy^2 + y^4$.

50. **What is the solution set for the following equations? (Rigorous)(Skill 5F)**
   $3x + 2y = 12 \quad 12x + 8y = 15$

   A) all real numbers

   B) x = 4, y = 4

   C) x = 2, y = –1

   D) $\varnothing$

Answer: D

Multiplying the top equation by –4 and adding the equations results in 0 = –33. Since this is a false statement, the correct choice is the null set.

51. **Solve for x by factoring** $2x^2 - 3x - 2 = 0$.
   (Average Rigor) (Skill 6A)

   A) x = (-1,2)

   B) x = (0.5,-2)

   C) x=(-0.5,2)

   D) x=(1,-2)

Answer: C

$2x^2 - 3x - 2 = 2x^2 - 4x + x - 2 = 2x(x - 2) + (x - 2) = (2x + 1)(x - 2) = 0.$
Thus x = -0.5 or 2.

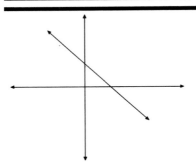

52. Which equation is represented by the above graph? (Average Rigor)(Skill 5D)

A) x − y = 3

B) x − y = −3

C) x + y = 3

D) x + y = −3

Answer: C

By looking at the graph, we can determine the slope to be negative and the y-intercept to be positive. The equation C is the only one that meets both criteria.

53. The length of a picture frame is 2 inches greater than its width. If the area of the frame is 143 square inches, what is its width? (Rigorous) (Skill 6F)

A) 11 inches

B) 13 inches

C) 12 inches

D) 10 inches

Answer: A

First set up the equation for the problem. If the width of the picture frame is w, then w(w+2) = 143. Next, solve the equation to obtain w. Using the method of completing squares we have:

$$w^2 + 2w + 1 = 144; (w + 1)^2 = 144; w + 1 = \pm 12.$$

Thus w = 11 or -13. Since the width cannot be a negative number, the correct answer is 11.

54. What is the slope of any line parallel to the line 2x + 4y = 4?
(Rigorous)(Skill 5A)

    A) -2

    B) -1

    C) $-\dfrac{1}{2}$

    D) 2

Answer: C

The formula for slope is y = mx + b, where m is the slope. Lines that are parallel have the same slope.

$$2x + 4y = 4$$
$$4y = -2x + 4$$
$$y = \frac{-2x}{4} + 1$$
$$y = \frac{-1}{2}x + 1$$

Thus the slope of the line is $-\dfrac{1}{2}$.

55. If cleaning costs are $32 for 4 hours, how much is it for 10.5 hours?
(Average Rigor)(Skill 5E)

    A) $112.50

    B) $87

    C) $84

    D) $76.50

Answer: C

The hourly rate is $8 per hour, so 8 x 10.5 = $84.

56.   **Solve the following equations: 4x + 3y = 24 and 3x + 2y = 20.**
       (Rigorous)(Skill 5F)

   A)   (4/3,3/2)

   B)   (4,5)

   C)   (5,5)

   D)   (12,-8)

Answer: D

Solving the first equation for x we get $x = \dfrac{24 - 3y}{4}$. Placing that value in the second equation we have:

$$\frac{3(24 - 3y)}{4} + 2y = 20$$
$$3(24 - 3y) + 8y = 80$$
$$-y = 8$$
$$y = -8$$

Substituting the value of y in $x = \dfrac{24 - 3y}{4}$, we get x = 12.

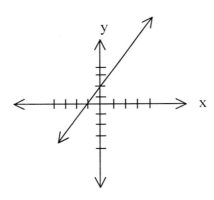

57. What is the equation of the above graph? (Rigorous)(Skill 5D)

A) $2x + y = 2$

B) $2x - y = -2$

C) $2x - y = 2$

D) $2x + y = -2$

Answer: B

By observation, we see that the graph has a y-intercept of 2 and a slope of 2/1 = 2. Therefore its equation is y = mx + b = 2x + 2. Rearranging the terms gives 2x − y = −2.

58. Solve for x and y: x= 3y + 7; 7x + 5y = 23 (Rigorous)(Skill 5F)

A) (−1,4)

B) (4, −1)

C) $(-\dfrac{29}{7}, -\dfrac{26}{7})$

D) (10, 1)

Answer: B

Substituting x in the second equation results in 7(3y + 7) + 5y = 23. Solve by distributing and grouping like terms: 26y+49 = 23, 26y = −26, y = −1. Substitute y into the first equation to obtain x.

59. Solve the system of equations for x, y and z. (Rigorous)(Skill 5F)

$$3x + 2y - z = 0$$
$$2x + 5y = 8z$$
$$x + 3y + 2z = 7$$

A) $(-1,\ 2,\ 1)$

B) $(1,\ 2,\ -1)$

C) $(-3,\ 4,\ -1)$

D) $(0,\ 1,\ 2)$

Answer: A

Multiplying equation 1 by 2, and equation 2 by –3, and then adding together the two resulting equations gives –11y + 22z = 0. Solving for y gives y = 2z. In the meantime, multiplying equation 3 by –2 and adding it to equation 2 gives –y – 12z = –14. Then substituting 2z for y, yields the result z = 1. Subsequently, one can easily find that y = 2, and x = –1.

60. Which set illustrates a function? (Easy)(Skill 6B)

A) { (0,1) (0,2) (0,3) (0,4) }

B) { (3,9) (–3,9) (4,16) (– 4,16)}

C) {(1,2) (2,3) (3,4) (1,4) }

D) { (2,4) (3,6) (4,8) (4,16) }

Answer: B

Each number in the domain can only be matched with one number in the range. A is not a function because 0 is mapped to 4 different numbers in the range. In C, 1 is mapped to two different numbers. In D, 4 is mapped to two different numbers.

61. **Give the domain for the function over the set of real numbers:**

$y = \dfrac{3x+2}{2x^2 - 3}$ (Rigorous)(Skill 6D)

A) all real numbers

B) all real numbers, $x \neq 0$

C) all real numbers, $x \neq -2$ or 3

D) all real numbers, $x \neq \dfrac{\pm\sqrt{6}}{2}$

Answer: D

Solve the denominator for 0. These values will be excluded from the domain.

$$2x^2 - 3 = 0$$
$$2x^2 = 3$$
$$x^2 = 3/2$$
$$x = \sqrt{\frac{3}{2}} = \sqrt{\frac{3}{2}} \bullet \sqrt{\frac{2}{2}} = \frac{\pm\sqrt{6}}{2}$$

62. **If y varies directly as x and x is 2 when y is 6, what is x when y is 18? (Rigorous)(Skill 5B)**

A) 3

B) 6

C) 26

D) 36

Answer: B

The equation for direct variation is y = kx. In this case k = $\dfrac{y}{x}$ = $\dfrac{6}{2} = 3$. Substitute 18 for y and 3 for k and solve: 18 = 3x, x = 6.

63. **State the domain of the function** $f(x) = \dfrac{3x-6}{x^2-25}$ **(Rigorous)(Skill 6D)**

    A) $x \neq 2$

    B) $x \neq 5, -5$

    C) $x \neq 2, -2$

    D) $x \neq 5$

Answer: B

The values of 5 and –5 must be omitted from the domain of all real numbers because if x took on either of those values, the denominator of the fraction would have a value of 0, and therefore the fraction would be undefined.

64. **The volume of water flowing through a pipe varies directly with the square of the radius of the pipe. If the water flows at a rate of 80 liters per minute through a pipe with a radius of 4 cm, at what rate would water flow through a pipe with a radius of 3 cm? (Average Rigor)(Skill 5B)**

    A) 45 liters per minute

    B) 6.67 liters per minute

    C) 60 liters per minute

    D) 4.5 liters per minute

Answer: A

Set up the direct variation: $\dfrac{V_1}{r_1^2} = \dfrac{V_2}{r_2^2}$. Substituting gives $\dfrac{80}{16} = \dfrac{V_2}{9}$. Solving for V_2 gives 45 liters per minute.

65. If y varies inversely as x and x is 4 when y is 6, what is the constant of variation? (Rigorous)(Skill 6D)

    A) 2

    B) 12

    C) $\dfrac{3}{2}$

    D) 24

Answer: D

Since y varies inversely as x, y = k/x (where k is the constant of variation) and k = xy.

66. Find the zeroes of $f(x) = x^3 + x^2 - 14x - 24$ (Rigorous)(Skill 6H)

    A) 4, 3, 2

    B) 3, –8

    C) 7, –2, –1

    D) 4, –3, –2

Answer: D

Possible rational roots of the equation 0 = x³ + x² – 14x –24 are all the positive and negative factors of 24. By substituting into the equation, we find that –2 is a root, and therefore that x+2 is a factor. By performing the long division (x³ + x² – 14x – 24)/(x+2), we can find that another factor of the original equation is x² – x – 12 or (x–4)(x+3). Therefore the zeros of the original function are –2, –3, and 4.

67. **The discriminant of a quadratic equation is evaluated and determined to be –3. The equation has (Rigorous)(Skill 6A)**

    A) one real root

    B) one complex root

    C) two roots, both real

    D) two roots, both complex

Answer: D

The discriminant is the number under the radical sign. Since it is negative, the two roots of the equation are complex.

68. **Evaluate $x^2 - 3x + 7$ when x = 2. (Easy Rigor) (Skill 6A)**

    A) 7

    B) 5

    C) 3

    D) 9

Answer: B

Substitute x=2 in the expression to get $2^2 - 3 \times 2 + 7 = 4 - 6 + 7 = 5$.

69. **Which of the following is a factor of $6 + 48m^3$ (Average Rigor)(Skill 6F)**

    A) (1 + 2m)

    B) (1 – 8m)

    C) (1 + m – 2m)

    D) (1 – m + 2m)

Answer: A

Removing the common factor of 6 and then factoring the sum of two cubes gives
$6 + 48m^3 = 6(1 + 8m^3) = 6(1 + 2m)(1^2 – 2m + (2m)^2)$.

70. **Factor completely:** $8(x - y) + a(y - x)$ (Average Rigor)(Skill 6F)

   A) $(8 + a)(y - x)$

   B) $(8 - a)(y - x)$

   C) $(a - 8)(y - x)$

   D) $(a - 8)(y + x)$

Answer: C

Glancing first at the solution choices, factor $(y - x)$ from each term. This leaves -8 from the first term and 'a' from the second term. Thus $8(x - y) + a(y - x) = (a - 8)(y - x)$.

71. **Which of the following is a factor of $k^3 - m^3$? (Average Rigor)(Skill 6F)**

   A) $k^2 + m^2$

   B) $k + m$

   C) $k^2 - m^2$

   D) $k - m$

Answer: D

The complete factorization for a difference of cubes $k^3 - m^3$ is $(k - m)(k^2 + mk + m^2)$.

72. Which graph represents the solution set for $x^2 - 5x > -6$?
(Rigorous)(Skill 6B)

A)
   $-2 \quad 0 \quad 2$

B)
   $-3 \quad 0 \quad 3$

C)
   $-2 \quad 0 \quad 2$

D)
   $-3 \quad 0 \quad 2 \; 3$

Answer: D

Rewriting the inequality gives $x^2 - 5x + 6 > 0$. Factoring gives $(x - 2)(x - 3) > 0$. The two cut-off points on the number line are now at $x = 2$ and $x = 3$. Choosing a random number in each of the three parts of the number line, we test them to see if they produce a true statement. If $x = 0$ or $x = 4$, $(x-2)(x-3)>0$ is true. If $x = 2.5$, $(x-2)(x-3)>0$ is false. Therefore the solution set is all numbers smaller than 2 or greater than 3.

73. Which of the following is a factor of the expression: $9x^2 + 6x - 35$?
(Average Rigor)(Skill 6A)

A) 3x-5

B) 3x-7

C) x+3

D) x-2

Answer: A

Recognize that the given expression can be written as the sum of two squares and utilize the formula $a^2 - b^2 = (a+b)(a-b)$.

$9x^2 + 6x - 35 = (3x + 1)^2 - 36 = (3x + 1 + 6)(3x + 1 - 6) = (3x + 7)(3x - 5)$

74. $f(x) = 3x - 2; \; f^{-1}(x) =$ **(Rigorous) (Skill 6E)**

A) $3x + 2$

B) $\dfrac{x}{6}$

C) $2x - 3$

D) $\dfrac{x + 2}{3}$

Answer: D

To find the inverse, $f^{-1}(x)$, of the given function, reverse the variables in the given equation, y = 3x – 2, to get x = 3y – 2. Then solve for y as follows:

x+2 = 3y, and y = $\dfrac{x + 2}{3}$.

75. Which graph represents the equation of $y = x^2 + 3x$ **? (Rigorous)(Skill 6A)**

A)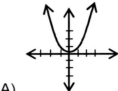

B)

C)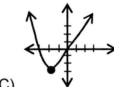

D)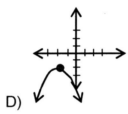

Answer: C

B is not the graph of a function. D is the graph of a parabola where the coefficient of x^2 is negative. A appears to be the graph of $y = x^2$. To find the x-intercepts of $y = x^2 + 3x$, set $y = 0$ and solve for x: $0 = x^2 + 3x = x(x + 3)$ to get x = 0 or x = –3. Therefore, the graph of the function intersects the x-axis at x=0 and x=–3.

76. **Solve for x.** $3x^2 - 2 + 4(x^2 - 3) = 0$ **(Rigorous)(Skill 6A)**

   A) $\{-\sqrt{2}, \sqrt{2}\}$

   B) $\{2, -2\}$

   C) $\{0, \sqrt{3}, -\sqrt{3}\}$

   D) $\{7, -7\}$

Answer: A

Distribute and combine like terms to obtain $7x^2 - 14 = 0$.
Add 14 to both sides, then divide by 7. Since $x^2 = 2$, $x = \pm\sqrt{2}$.

77. **For an acute angle x, sin x = 3/5. What is cot x? (Rigorous) (Skill 8E)**

   A) $\dfrac{5}{3}$

   B) $\dfrac{3}{4}$

   C) 1.33

   D) 1

Answer: C

Using the Pythagorean Identity, we know $\sin^2 x + \cos^2 x = 1$. Thus
$$\cos x = \sqrt{1 - \frac{9}{25}} = \frac{4}{5}; \cot x = \frac{\cos x}{\sin x} = \frac{4}{3}.$$

78. **Which expression is not equal to sin x? (Average Rigor)(Skill 8E)**

A) $\sqrt{1 - \cos^2 x}$

B) $\tan x \cos x$

C) $\dfrac{1}{\csc x}$

D) $\dfrac{1}{\sec x}$

Answer: D

Using the basic definitions of the trigonometric functions and the Pythagorean identity, we see that the first three options are all identical to sin x.
sec x= 1/cosx is not the same as sin x.

79. **The formula for solving a quadratic equation is (Rigorous)(Skill 6A)**

A) $x = \dfrac{-b \pm \sqrt{b^2 - 4ac}}{2a}$

B) $x = \dfrac{-b \pm \sqrt{b^2 - 4a}}{2a}$

C) $x = \dfrac{b \pm \sqrt{b^2 - 4ac}}{2a}$

D) $x = \dfrac{b \pm \sqrt{b^3 - 4ac}}{2a}$

Answer: A

Option B is missing the factor c from the term 4ac within the square root symbol. Option C does not have the minus sign with the term b in the numerator. Option D has b cubed instead of squared within the square root symbol. A is the correct choice.

80. **If you have a triangle with these dimensions, solve for x if angle b is 27 degrees. (Rigorous)(Skill 8E)**

   A) 8.45

   B) 7.26

   C) 7.78

   D) 6.89

Answer: B

$$\text{Sin } b = \frac{\text{opposite}}{\text{hypotenuse}} = .454 = \frac{x}{16} \quad \text{or } x = 7.26$$

81. **Find the missing side c: (Average Rigor)(Skill 8E)**

   A) 11.65

   B) 19.5

32

   C) 23

Angle 35

   D) 26.2

c

Answer: D

$\cos 35 = .8192 = c/32$ or $c = 26.21$

82. Find side c in the following right-angled triangle. (Average rigor) (Skill 8E)

A) 15.56

B) 14.42

C) 16.94

D) 14.60

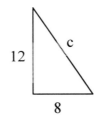

Answer: B

Since $a^2 + b^2 = c^2$ then $c^2 = 12^2 + 8^2 = 208$. $C = \sqrt{208} = 14.42$

83. A car is driving north at 74 miles per hour from point A. Another car is driving due east at 65 miles per hour. How far are the cars away from each other after 2 hours? (Rigorous)(Skill 8E)

A) 175.87

B) 232.66

C) 196.99

D) 202.43

Answer: C

The routes the cars take form a right triangle with edges 74 x 2 and 65 x 2. This gives two sides of a right triangle of 148 and 130. Using the Pythagorean Theorem, we get 148^2 and 130^2 = distance^2. Distance = $\sqrt{21904 + 16900}$ = 196.99.

84. **If three cups of concentrate are needed to make 2 gallons of fruit punch, how many cups are needed to make 5 gallons? (Easy)(Skill 8A)**

    A) 6 cups

    B) 7 cups

    C) 7.5 cups

    D) 10 cups

Answer: C

Set up the proportion 3/2 = x/5, cross multiply to obtain 15=2x, and solve for x to get x = 15/2=7.5.

85. **The mass of a cookie is closest to (Average Rigor)(Skill 8A)**

    A) 0.5 kg

    B) 0.5 grams

    C) 15 grams

    D) 1.5 grams

Answer: C

In terms of commonly used U.S. units, 15 grams is about half an ounce and 0.5 Kg is about a pound.

86. **A man's waist, measured using a tape with the smallest unit of 1 cm, measures 90 cm. What is the greatest possible error for the measurement? (Average)(Skill 8D)**

    A) ± 1 m

    B) ±8 cm

    C) ±1 cm

    D) ±5 mm

Answer: D

The greatest possible error of measurement is ± 1/2 unit, in this case 0.5 cm or 5 mm.

87. **3 km is equivalent to (Easy)(Skill 8D)**

    A) 300 cm

    B) 300 m

    C) 3000 cm

    D) 3000 m

Answer: D

1 kilometer = 1000 meters.

88. **4 square yards is equivalent to (Average Rigor)(Skill 8B)**

    A) 12 square feet

    B) 48 square feet

    C) 36 square feet

    D) 108 square feet

Answer: C

Since 1 yard = 3 feet, there are 9 square feet in a square yard.

89. **2.25 teaspoons equals to how many milliliters? (Easy Rigor)(Skill 8B)**

    A) 11,25 ml

    B) 13.25 ml

    C) 13 ml

    D) 10 ml

Answer: A

2.25 tsp at 5 ml per tsp =5 x 2.25=11.25

90. You have a gallon of water and remove a total of 30 ounces. How many milliliters do you have left? (Rigorous)(Skill 8B)

A) 2900 ml

B) 1100 ml

C) 980 ml

D) 1000 ml

Answer: A

1 gallon = 128 fluid ouces. If 30 ounces are removed, you have 98 ounces left. Since 1 fluid ounce = 29.6 ml, 98 ounces = 2900 ml.

91.

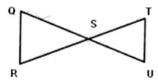

Given QS ≅ TS and RS ≅US,
prove ∆QRS ≅ ∆TUS.

l) QS ≅ TS   1) Given
2) RS ≅ US   2) Given
3) ∠TSU ≅ ∠QSR   3) ?
4) ∆TSU ≅ ∆QSR 4) SAS

(Average Rigor) (Skill 9C)

A) Congruent parts of congruent triangles are congruent

B) Reflexive axiom of equality

C) Alternate interior angle theorem

D) Vertical angle theorem

Answer: D

Non-adjacent angles formed by intersecting lines are called vertical angles and are congruent.

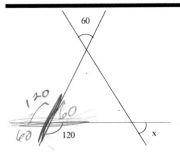

Note: Figure not drawn to scale.

92. In the figure above, what is the value of x? (Rigorous)(Skill 9A)

A) 50

B) 60

C) 75

D) 80

Answer: B

The angles within the triangle make up 180°. Vertical angles are equal, therefore, the angle vertically opposite the 60° angle is also 60°. Adjacent angles add to 180° (straight line). Therefore, the angle inside the triangle adjacent to the 120° angle is 60°. The third angle in the triangle would then be 60° (180 – 60 – 60). Since x is vertically opposite this third angle, it would also be 60°.

93. **Choose the diagram which illustrates the construction of a perpendicular to the line at a given point on the line. (Average Rigor)(Skill 9D)**

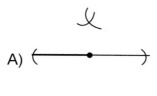

A)

B)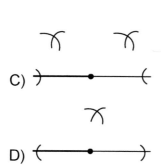

C)

D)

Answer: D

Given a point on a line, place the compass point there and draw two arcs intersecting the line in two points, one on either side of the given point. Then using any radius larger than half the new segment produced, and with the pointer at each end of the new segment, draw arcs which intersect above the line. Connect this new point with the given point.

94. **Which of the following can be defined? (Easy)(Skill 9A)**

   A) point

   B) ray

   C) line

   D) plane

Answer: B

The point, line, and plane are the three undefined concepts on which plane geometry is based.

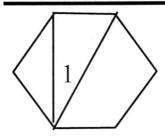

95. **Given the regular hexagon above, determine the measure of angle 1. (Rigorous)(Skill 9E)**

    A) 30°

    B) 60°

    C) 120°

    D) 45°

Answer: A

Each interior angle of the hexagon measures 120°. The isosceles triangle on the left has angles which measure 120, 30, and 30. By alternate interior angle theorem, ∠1 is also 30.

96. Line p has a negative slope and passes through the point (0, 0). If line q is perpendicular to line p, which of the following must be true? (Rigorous)(Skill 11E)

   A) Line q has a negative y-intercept.

   B) Line q passes through the point (0,0)

   C) Line q has a positive slope.

   D) Line q has a positive y-intercept.

Answer: C

Draw a picture to help you visualize the problem.

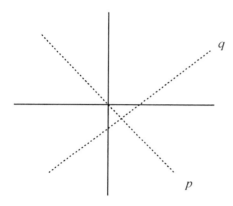

Choices (A) and (D) are not correct because line q could have a positive or a negative y-intercept. Choice (B) is incorrect because line q does not necessarily pass through (0, 0). Since line q is perpendicular to line p. which has a negative slope, it must have a positive slope.

97. What happens to the volume of a square pyramid when the sides of the base are tripled? (Rigorous)(Skill 10B)

   A) The volume is increased by a factor of 9

   B) The volume is increased by a factor of 8

   C) The volume is increased by a factor of 27

   D) The volume is increased by a factor of 16

Answer: A

The area of the base is increased by a factor of 9 while the height remains unchanged.

98. **What is the length of a fourth of a circle with a diameter of 24 cm? (Average Rigor)(Skill 10A)**

    A) 18.85

    B) 75.4

    C) 32.45

    D) 20.75

Answer: A

The circumference of the circle is πd where d is 24. π(24)= 75.4. One fourth of that is 18.85.

99. **If the radius of a right circular cylinder is doubled, how does its volume change? (Rigorous)(Skill 10B)**

    A) no change

    B) also is doubled

    C) four times the original

    D) pi times the original

Answer: C

If the radius r of a right circular cylinder is doubled, the volume is multiplied by four because in the formula $V = \pi r^2 h$, the radius is squared. Therefore the new volume is four times the original.

100. **Determine the volume of a sphere to the nearest cm if the surface area is 113 cm^2. (Rigorous)(Skill 10A)**

    A) 113 cm^3

    B) 339 cm^3

    C) 37.7 cm^3

    D) 226 cm3

Answer: A

Solve for the radius of the sphere using $A = 4\pi r^2$. The radius is 3. Then, find the volume using 4/3 πr^3.

101. Determine the area of the shaded region of the trapezoid in terms of x and y (the height of $\triangle ABC$). $\overline{DE}$ = 2x & $\overline{DC}$ = 3x. **(Rigorous)(Skill 10C)**

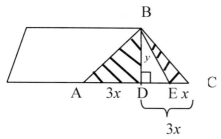

A) $4xy$

B) $2xy$

C) $3x^2y$

D) There is not enough information given.

Answer: B

To find the area of the shaded region, find the area of triangle ABC and then subtract the area of triangle DBE. The area of triangle ABC is .5(6x)(y) = 3xy. The area of triangle DBE is .5(2x)(y) = xy. The difference is 2xy.

102. Compute the surface area of the prism. (Rigorous)(Skill 10A)

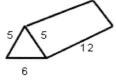

A) 204

B) 216

C) 360

D) 180

$25 * 5 = 35$

$5^2 + X = 6^2$

$\frac{1}{2} \cdot 5 \cdot 6 = \frac{1}{2} \cdot 30 = 15$

$5^2 + 5^2 = 6^2 x$

$25 + 25 = 36 x$

$50 = 36 x$

Answer: B

There are five surfaces which make up the prism. The bottom rectangle has area 6 x 12 = 72. The sloping sides are two rectangles each with an area of 5 x 12 = 60. The height of the end triangles is determined to be 4 using the Pythagorean theorem. Therefore each triangle has area 1/2bh = 1/2(6)(4) =12. Thus, the surface area is 72 + 60 + 60 + 12 + 12 = 216.

103. If the area of the base of a regular square pyramid is tripled, how does its volume change? (Rigorous)(Skill 10B)

A) double the original

B) triple the original

C) nine times the original

D) no change

Answer: B

The volume of a pyramid V = 1/3 bh, where b is the area of the base and h is the height.

104. How does lateral area differ from total surface area in prisms, pyramids and cones? (Easy)(Skill 10A)

A) For the lateral area, only use surfaces perpendicular to the base.

B) They are both the same.

C) The lateral area does not include the base.

D) The lateral area is always a factor of pi.

Answer: C

The lateral area is the surface area without the base.

105. **If the area of the base of a cone is tripled, the volume will be (Average Rigor)(Skill 10B)**

    A) the same as the original

    B) 9 times the original

    C) 3 times the original

    D) 3 π times the original

Answer: C

The formula for the volume of a cone is V = $\frac{1}{3}Bh$, where B is the area of the circular base and h is the height. If the area of the base is tripled, the volume becomes V = $\frac{1}{3}(3B)h = Bh$, or three times the original area.

106. **Find the length of a box with surface area of 94 sq. ft. with a width of 3 feet and a depth of 4 feet. (Rigorous)(Skill 10C)**

    A) 3 ft.

    B) 4 ft.

    C) 5 ft

    D) 6 ft.

Answer: C

94 = 2(3l) + 2(4l) + 2(12)
94 = 6l + 8l + 24
94 = 14l + 24
70 = 14l
5 = l

107. What is the volume of a cylinder of height 8 cm and diameter 4 cm? (Average Rigor)(Skill 10A)

A) 95.45

B) 100.5

C) 110.3

D) 105.4

Answer: B

The volume = $\pi r^2 h$ or $8\pi 2^2 = 100.5$ cm^3.

108. What is the surface area of a sphere with a circumference of 46 cm? (Rigorous)(Skill 10A)

A) 475.6

B) 546.7

C) 673.3

D) 643.5

Answer: C

If the circumference is 46, the radius is 7.32. The surface area is $4\pi r^2 = 673.3$ cm^2

109. Given similar polygons with corresponding sides 6 and 8, what is the area of the smaller if the area of the larger is 64? (Average Rigor)(Skill 10B)

A) 48

B) 36

C) 144

D) 78

Answer: B

In similar polygons, the areas are proportional to the squares of the sides.
$$\frac{36}{64} = \frac{x}{64}$$

110. **In similar polygons, if the perimeters are in a ratio of x : y, the sides are in a ratio of   (Average Rigor)(Skill 10B)**

    A) x : y

    B) $x^2 : y^2$

    C) 2x : y

    D) $\frac{1}{2}$ x : y

Answer: A

The sides are in the same ratio.

111. **If a circle has an area of 25 cm², what is its circumference to the nearest tenth of a centimeter? (Rigorous)(Skill 10A)**

    A) 78.5 cm

    B) 17.7 cm

    C) 8.9 cm

    D) 15.7 cm

Answer: B

Find the radius by solving $\pi r^2 = 25$. Then substitute r=2.82 into C = $2\pi r$ to obtain the circumference.

112. **Compute the area of the shaded region, given a radius of 5 meters. O is the center. (Rigorous)(Skill 10C)**

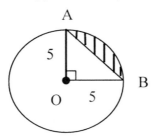

A) 7.13 cm²

B) 7.13 m²

C) 78.5 m²

D) 19.63 m²

Answer: B

Area of triangle AOB is .5(5)(5) = 12.5 square meters. Since $\dfrac{90}{360} = .25$, the area of sector AOB (pie-shaped piece) is approximately $.25(\pi)5^2 = 19.63$. Subtracting the triangle area from the sector area to get the area of segment AB, we get approximately 19.63–12.5 = 7.13 square meters.

113. The above diagram is most likely used in deriving a formula for which of the following? (Easy)(Skill 10A)

A) the area of a rectangle

B) the area of a triangle

C) the perimeter of a triangle

D) the surface area of a prism

Answer: B

The rectangle in the diagram is divided by a diagonal line segment into two congruent triangles. Since the triangles are congruent, the area of each triangle is equal to half the area of the rectangle. As a result, using the rectangle (or, more generally, the parallelogram) formed by the two congruent triangles, a formula for the area of a triangle can be derived. Thus, answer B is most likely to be the correct answer.

114. Find the area of the figure pictured below. (Rigorous)(Skill 10C)

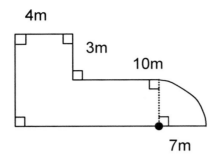

A) 136.47 m²

B) 148.48 m²

C) 293.86 m²

D) 178.47 m²

Answer: B

Divide the figure into 2 rectangles and one quarter circle. The tall rectangle on the left will have dimensions 10 by 4 and area 40. The rectangle in the center will have dimensions 7 by 10 and area 70. The quarter circle will have area .25(π)7² = 38.48. The total area is therefore approximately 148.48.

115. Given a 30 meter x 60 meter garden with a circular fountain with a 5 meter radius, calculate the area of the portion of the garden not occupied by the fountain. (Rigorous)(Skill 10C)

A) 1721 m²

B) 1879 m²

C) 2585 m²

D) 1015 m²

Answer: A

Find the area of the garden and then subtract the area of the fountain: 30(60)– $\pi(5)^2$ or approximately 1721 square meters.

116. Find the area of the shaded region given square ABCD with side AB=10m and circle E. (Rigorous)(Skill 10C)

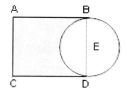

A) 178.5 m^2

B) 139.25 m^2

C) 71 m^2

D) 60.75 m^2

Answer: D

Find the area of the square 10^2 = 100, then subtract 1/2 the area of the circle. The area of the circle is πr^2 = (3.14)(5)(5)=78.5. Therefore the area of the shaded region is 100 – 39.25 – 60.75.

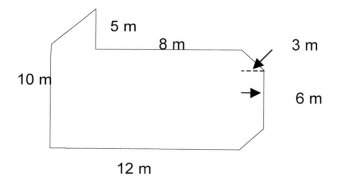

117. Compute the area of the polygon shown above. (Rigorous) (Skill 10C)

A) 178 m^2

B) 154 m^2

C) 43 m^2

D) 188 m^2

Answer: B

Divide the figure into a triangle, a rectangle and a trapezoid. The area of the triangle is 1/2 bh = 1/2 (4)(5) = 10. The area of the rectangle is bh = 12(10)= 120. The area of the trapezoid is 1/2(b + B)h = 1/2(6 + 10)(3) = 1/2 (16)(3) = 24. Thus, the area of the figure is 10 + 120 + 24 =154.

118. Find the area of the figure below. (Rigorous)(Skill 10C)

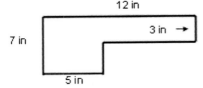

A) 56 in^2

B) 27 in^2

C) 71 in^2

D) 170 in^2

Answer: A

Divide the figure into two rectangles, 7in x 5 in and 7 in x 3 in. The combined area = 35 in^2 + 21 in^2 = 56 in^2

119. Which one is not one of the transformations that occur in a tessellation? (Easy Rigor)(Skill 11B)

A) translation

B) rotation

C) reflection

D) stellar reflection

Answer: D

All but answer D are transformations that can occur during a tessellation.

120. Find the slope of the line (11, 25) and (4, 4)(Rigorous) (Skill 11E)

 A) 3

 B) 4

 C) 4.5

 D) 1.7

Answer: A

Slope of the line is $\dfrac{25-4}{11-4} = \dfrac{21}{7} = 3$

121. Find the center of a circle with a diameter whose endpoints are (4,5) and (-4, -6). (Average Rigor) (Skill 11E)

 A) $(-2, \dfrac{1}{2})$

 B) $(0, -\dfrac{1}{2})$

 C) $(-1, 0)$

 D) $(0, 1)$

Answer: B

$\dfrac{(4+\text{-}4,}{2}\ \dfrac{5+\text{-}6)}{2} = (0, -\dfrac{1}{2})$

122. Find the midpoint of (2,5) and (7,–4). (Average Rigor)(Skill 11E)

 A) (9,–1)

 B) (5, 9)

 C) $(\dfrac{9}{2}, -\dfrac{1}{2})$

 D) $(\dfrac{9}{2}, \dfrac{1}{2})$

Answer: D

Using the midpoint formula

x = (2 + 7)/2   y = (5 + –4)/2

123. What is the first, second and third quartile for the following? (Average Rigor) (Skill 12D)
5, 5, 5, 6, 7, 9, 9, 10, 11, 12, 13, 13, 14, 15, 16, 17,17

A) 5, 10, 15

B) 6, 11, 16

C) 6, 11, 14

D) 6.5, 11, 14.5

Answer: D

The second quartile is the median of the whole while the first and third quartiles are the medians of the first half and the second half respectively. Since the median was part of the first calculation with an odd number of data points, it isn't included in determining the quartiles. There is no consensus on how the median should be calculated for an odd number of data points. If using a TI86 calculator, the answer will be D. However, the correct answer could also be 7, 11, 14 which is obtained by including the median in determining the quartiles.

124. Find the percentile of the score 98. (Average Rigor)(Skill 12F)
33, 35, 38, 49, 59, 70, 89, 93, 98, 99, 104, 108

A) 59 percentile

B) 98 percentile

C) 75 percentile

D) 95 percentile

Answer: C

A total of 9/12ths of the scores are on or below 98. This translates to the 75th percentile.

125. The tenth percentile is in what stanine? (Easy Rigor)(Skill 12F)

A) First

B) Second

C) Third

D) Fourth

Answer: B

The tenth percentile is in the second stanine. Stanines represent a 9-point scale with 9 being the highest. To relate stanine scores to other scores by use the "Rule of Four." Start with either end of the stanine scale, 1 or 9, 4% of the cases in a normal distribution fall into the end of the stanines. Stanine 5 falls in the middle and has 20%, 6 has 17%, 7 has 12%, 8 has 7%, and 9 has 4%. To find the stanine corresponding to any percentile, start from stanine 1 and add up the percents included in consecutive stanines until you find the stanine that includes the percentile you are interested in. 4% stanine 1 +7% stanine 2 = 11%.10% is between 5% and 11%, the 2nd stanine.

126. What is the range of the following numbers? (Average Rigor)(Skill 12D).

34, 14, 43, 35, 45, 18, 33, 42

A) 31

B) 32

C) 26

D) 19

Answer: A

The range is the difference between the highest and lowest number or is 45-14=31.

127. Find the median of the following set of data:

14 3   7   6   11   20

(Average Rigor)(Skill 12D)

A) 9

B) 8.5

C) 7

D) 11

Answer: A

Place the numbers is ascending order: 3 6 7 11 14 20. Find the average of the middle two numbers (7+11)/2 =9.

**128.   Compute the median for the following data set: {12, 19, 13, 16, 17, 14}
(Average Rigor)(Skill 12D)**

A) 14.5

B) 15.17

C) 15

D) 16

Answer: C

Arrange the data in ascending order: 12,13,14,16,17,19. The median is the middle value in a list with an odd number of entries. When there is an even number of entries, the median is the mean of the two center entries. Here the average of 14 and 16 is 15.

129. **Corporate salaries are listed for several employees. Which would be the best measure of central tendency? (Average Rigor)(Skill 12D)**

$24,000 $24,000 $26,000 $28,000 $30,000 $120,000

A) mean

B.) median

C) mode

D) no difference

Answer: B

The median provides the best measure of central tendency in this case where the mode is the lowest number and the mean would be disproportionately skewed by the outlier $120,000.

130. **Half the students in a class scored 80% on an exam, most of the rest scored 85% except for one student who scored 10%. Which would be the best measure of central tendency for the test scores? (Average Rigor)(Skill 12D)**

A) mean

B) median

C) mode

D) either the median or the mode because they are equal

Answer: B

In this set of data, the median (see #14) would be the most representative measure of central tendency since the median is independent of extreme values. Because of the 10% outlier, the mean (average) would be disproportionately skewed.

131. A student scored in the 87th percentile on a standardized test. Which would be the best interpretation of his score? (Average Rigor)(Skill 12F)

A) Only 13% of the students who took the test scored higher.

B) This student should be getting mostly Bs on his report card.

C) This student performed below average on the test.

D) This is the equivalent of missing 13 questions on a 100 question exam.

Answer: A

Percentile ranking tells how the student compared to the norm or the other students taking the test. It does not correspond to the percentage answered correctly, but can indicate how the student compared to the average student tested.

132. Which statement is true about George's budget? (Easy)(Skill 12A)

A) George spends the greatest portion of his income on food.

B) George spends twice as much on utilities as he does on his mortgage.

C) George spends twice as much on utilities as he does on food.

D) George spends the same amount on food and utilities as he does on mortgage.

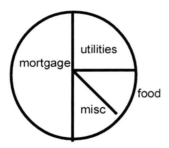

Answer: C

George spends twice as much on utilities than on food.

133. Given a drawer with 5 black socks, 3 blue socks, and 2 red socks, what is the probability that you will draw two black socks in two draws in a dark room? (Average Rigor)(Skill 13B)

A) $\dfrac{2}{9}$

B) $\dfrac{1}{4}$

C) $\dfrac{17}{18}$

D) $\dfrac{1}{18}$

Answer: A

In this example of conditional probability, the probability of drawing a black sock on the first draw is 5/10. It is implied in the problem that there is no replacement, therefore the probability of obtaining a black sock in the second draw is 4/9. Multiply the two probabilities and reduce to lowest terms.

134. A sack of candy has 3 peppermints, 2 butterscotch drops and 3 cinnamon drops. One candy is drawn and replaced, then another candy is drawn; what is the probability that both will be butterscotch? (Average Rigor)(Skill 13B)

A) $\dfrac{1}{2}$

B) $\dfrac{1}{28}$

C) $\dfrac{1}{4}$

D) $\dfrac{1}{16}$

Answer: D

With replacement, the probability of obtaining a butterscotch on the first draw is 2/8 and the probability of drawing a butterscotch on the second draw is also 2/8. Multiply and reduce to lowest terms.

135. Given a spinner with the numbers one through eight, what is the probability that you will spin an even number or a number greater than four? (Easy)(Skill 13B)

A) $\dfrac{1}{4}$

B) $\dfrac{1}{2}$

C) $\dfrac{3}{4}$

D) 1

Answer: C

There are 8 favorable outcomes: 2,4,5,6,7,8 and 8 possibilities. Reduce 6/8 to 3/4.

136. If a horse will probably win three races out of ten, what are the odds that he will win? (Rigorous)(Skill 13B)

A) 3:10

B) 7:10

C) 3:7

D) 7:3

Answer: C

The odds are that he will win 3 and lose 7.

137. A jar contains 3 red marbles, 5 white marbles, 1 green marble and 15 blue marbles. If one marble is picked at random from the jar, what is the probability that it will be red? (Easy)(Skill 13B)

A) $\dfrac{1}{3}$

B) $\dfrac{1}{8}$

C) $\dfrac{3}{8}$

D) $\dfrac{1}{24}$

Answer: B

The total number of marbles is 24 and the number of red marbles is 3. Thus the probability of picking a red marble from the jar is 3/24=1/8.

138. How many ways are there to choose a potato and two green vegetables from a choice of three potatoes and seven green vegetables? (Rigorous)(Skill 13B)

A) 126

B) 63

C) 21

D) 252

Answer: A

There are 3 slots to fill. There are 3 choices for the first, 7 for the second, and 6 for the third. Therefore, the total number of choices is 3(7)(6) = 126.

139. A measure of association between two variables is called: (Easy) (Skill 14E)

A) Associate

B) Correlation

C) Confidence interval

D) Variation

Answer: B

The correlation is a measure of the association between two variables.

140. A boat travels 30 miles upstream in three hours. It makes the return trip in one and a half hours. What is the speed of the boat in still water? (Rigorous)(Skill 15F)

A) 10 mph

B) 15 mph

C) 20 mph

D) 30 mph

Answer: B

Let x = the speed of the boat in still water and c = the speed of the current.

	rate	time	distance
upstream	$x - c$	3	30
downstream	$x + c$	1.5	30

Solve the system:
$$3x - 3c = 30$$
$$1.5x + 1.5c = 30$$

Multiply the 2nd equation by 2, add the two equations and solve for x.

141. Estimate the sum of 1498 + 1309. (Average   Rigor)(Skill 15H)

   A) 2900

   B) 2850

   C) 2800

   D) 2600

Answer: C

As this is an estimate, you add 1500 and 1300 to get 2800.

142. Ginny and Nick head back to their respective colleges after being home for the weekend. They leave their house at the same time and drive for 4 hours. Ginny drives due south at the average rate of 60 miles per hour and Nick drives due east at the average rate of 60 miles per hour. What is the straight-line distance between them, in miles, at the end of the 4 hours? (Rigorous)(Skill 15G)

   A) $120\sqrt{2}$

   B) 240

   C) $240\sqrt{2}$

   D) 288

Answer: C

Draw a picture.

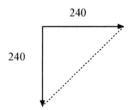

We have a right triangle, so we can use the Pythagorean Theorem to find the distance between the two points.

$$240^2 + 240^2 = c^2$$
$$2(240)^2 = c^2$$
$$240\sqrt{2} = c$$

143. Choose the least appropriate set of manipulatives for a six grade class. (Easy)(Skill 18A)

A) graphing calculators, compasses, rulers, conic section models

B) two color counters, origami paper, markers, yarn, balance, meter stick, colored pencils, beads

C) balance, meter stick, colored pencils, beads

D) paper cups, beans, tangrams, geoboards

Answer: A

The manipulatives in answer A include tools that are most appropriate for students studying more advanced topics in algebra, such as functions and conic sections, as well as more advanced topics in geometry. As a result, these manipulatives may not be appropriate for sixth grade material. The other answers include manipulatives that may be more appropriate for a sixth grade class.

144. Which is not an acceptable way of getting at student performance in math: (Easy Rigor)(Skill 19A)

A) Student Portfolios

B) Formal tests

C) Student Projects

D) Term Paper

Answer: D.

A term paper would not be a good way of assessing performance in mathematics.

145. If 80 students are in sports and 100 students are in band with 20 students in both band and sports, identify that pictorially. (Average Rigor)(Skill 16D)

A)

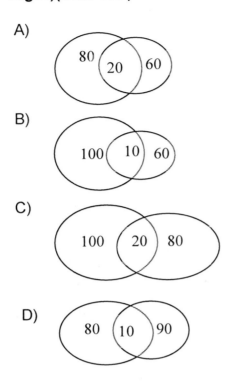

B)

C)

D)

Answer: A

If 20 students are in both band and sports, you need to subtract twenty from those in just band and those in just sports, leaving the answer as A.

XAMonline, INC. 21 Orient Ave. Melrose, MA 02176

Toll Free number 800-509-4128

TO ORDER Fax 781-662-9268 OR www.XAMonline.com

TEXAS EXAMINATION OF EDUCATOR STANDARD-EXAMINATION FOR THE CERTIFICATION OF EDUCATORS   - TEXES/EXCET - 2008

PO#   Store/School:

Address 1:

Address 2 (Ship to other):

City, State Zip

Credit card number_____-_____-_____-_____   expiration_____

EMAIL _____

PHONE   **FAX**

ISBN	TITLE	Qty	Retail	Total
978-1-58197-925-1	ExCET ART SAMPLE TEST (ALL-LEVEL-SECONDARY) 005 006			
978-1-58197-926-8	ExCET FRENCH SAMPLE TEST (SECONDARY) 048			
978-1-58197-927-5	ExCET SPANISH (SECONDARY) 047			
978-1-58197-928-2	TExES PRINCIPAL 068			
978-1-58197-929-9	TExES PEDAGOGY AND PROFESSIONAL RESPONSIBILITIES 4-8 110			
978-1-58197-899-5	TExES PEDAGOGY AND PROFESSIONAL RESPONSIBILITIES EC-4 100			
978-1-58197-271-9	TExES GENERALIST 4-8 111			
978-1-58197-945-9	TExES GENERALIST EC-4 101			
978-1-58197-948-0	TExES MATHEMATICS-SCIENCE 4-8 114			
978-1-58197-295-5	TExES MATHEMATICS 4-8 114-115			
978-1-58197-297-9	TExES SCIENCE 4-8 116			
978-1-58197-931-2	TExES SCIENCE 8-12 136			
978-1-58197-933-6	TExES ENGLISH LANG-ARTS AND READING 4-8 117			
978-1-58197-935-0	TExES ENGLISH LANG-ARTS AND READING 8-12 131			
978-1-58197-661-8	TExES SOCIAL STUDIES 4-8 118			
978-1-58197-621-2	TExES SOCIAL STUDIES 8-12 132			
978-1-58197-339-6	TExES MATHEMATICS 8-12 135			
978-1-58197-618-2	TExES LIFE SCIENCE 8-12 138			
978-1-58197-949-7	TExES CHEMISTRY 8-12 140			
978-1-58197-939-8	TExES MATHEMATICS-PHYSICS 8-12 143			
978-1-58197-940-4	TExES SCHOOL LIBRARIAN 150			
978-1-58197-941-1	TExES READING SPECIALIST 151			
978-1-58197-942-8	TExES SCHOOL COUNSELOR 152			
978-1-58197-620-5	TExES PHYSICAL EDUCATION EC-12 158			
978-1-58197-262-7	TExES SPECIAL EDUCATION EC-12 161			
978-1-58197-606-9	THEA TEXAS HIGHER EDUCATOR ASSESSMENT			
			SUBTOTAL	
			Ship	$8.25
			TOTAL	

LaVergne, TN USA
11 February 2011
216151LV00001B/5/P